Edited by Ann Dale and Jenny Onyx

A Dynamic Balance:
Social Capital and Sustainable
Community Development

UBCPress · Vancouver · Toronto

15 14 13 12 11 10 09 08 07 06 05   5 4 3 2 1

Printed in Canada on acid-free paper that is 100% post-consumer recycled, processed chlorine-free, and printed with vegetable-based, low-VOC inks.

Library and Archives Canada Cataloguing in Publication

A dynamic balance : social capital and sustainable community development / edited by Ann Dale and Jenny Onyx.

(Sustainability and the environment)
Includes bibliographical references and index.
ISBN 0-7748-1143-9 (bound); ISBN 0-7748-1144-7 (pbk.)

1. Rural development – Canada. 2. Sustainable development – Canada. 3. Social capital (Sociology) – Canada. 4. Rural development – Australia. 5. Sustainable development – Australia. 6. Social capital (Sociology) – Australia. I. Dale, Ann, 1948- II. Onyx, Jenny, 1941- III. Series.

HN49.C6D95 2005   307.1'2'0971   C2005-902175-6

Canadä

UBC Press gratefully acknowledges the financial support for our publishing program of the Government of Canada through the Book Publishing Industry Development Program (BPIDP), and of the Canada Council for the Arts, and the British Columbia Arts Council.

The financial support of the Social Sciences and Humanities Research Council of Canada for a standard research grant for the project entitled *Social Capital and Sustainable Development* is also gratefully acknowledged.

UBC Press
The University of British Columbia
2029 West Mall
Vancouver, BC V6T 1Z2
604-822-5959 / Fax: 604-822-6083
www.ubcpress.ca

To our boys who became such fine men,
Danny, Daman, Juston, and Kynan

Contents

Foreword
Richard A. Skinner ·

Nostalgia can tempt one to recall wistfully a "simpler" time when neighbours knew each other, when people organized themselves in a seemingly automatic and undirected fashion to rebuild a family's storm- or fire-damaged home, and when contractual relationships were forged with a handshake. Reminiscence can conjure up bucolic images of face-to-face interaction and a Lockean society in which institutions really did consist of people, many of whom a citizen might actually know by name.

Frustrated by the zero-sum quality of adversarial litigation and its sometime destructive capacity, scholars can ask questions such as whether it is indeed possible to achieve "justice without law." Having accumulated vast amounts of material possessions and huge sums of money, wealthy individuals faced with the emotional poverty of isolated lives may ask the plaintive question of the old ballad, "Is that all there is?"

Social capital – what Robert Putnam defines as "the collective value of all 'social networks' [who people know] and the inclinations that arise from these networks to do things for each other [norms of reciprocity]" (Putnam 2000) – has become something more than the organic evolution of human relationships. Increasingly, it seems, social capital must be planned and constructed, in spite of (in fact, perhaps, because of) the worldwide phenomenon of governments contracting and reducing services. Habits and traditions alone may no longer suffice as means for building up the social capital necessary to sustain communities and societies.

The reduced role of government in and of itself presents the challenge of identifying which institutions within society have the capacity to plan for and create social capital. What the church, synagogue, or mosque was at one point in time – source of material aid to the poor, arbiter of familial and communal disputes – government became, and now governmental institutions are themselves withdrawing or restricting their scope of activity and responsibility. Analysis and action to create anew the stores of social capital lost to the twin forces of globalization and fragmentation must start at ground zero with the question of who or what will be the means or vehicles by which the task begins.

Mastering (and often destroying) the physical world now presents us with the challenge of fashioning something new and vital out of the stuff of human and social interaction, lest we consume the very lifeboat on which we float. As the readings in this book attest, the challenge is a formidable one and answers are not likely to be readily forthcoming. But, in a sense, this is as it ought to be, as Lewis Lapham (1988, 13) wrote some years back:

> The task that confronts the men who would be leaders is a task of the imagi-
> nation. It has less to do with politics than it does with metaphor, less to do
> with the making of laws than with the making of words that allow men to
> see their immortality, not in their monuments or their weapons, but in
> their children. Maybe it is an impossible task, like the juggler's dream of the
> balls standing still in the air, but certainly it is of heroic enough proportion
> to summon leaders capable of drawing swords from stones.

Richard A. Skinner
President and Vice Chancellor, Royal Roads University

References
Lapham, L.H. 1988. "The Sword in the Stone." *Harper's Magazine* 276 (1655): 13.
Putnam, R.D. 2000. Bowling Alone: The Collapse and Revival of American Community.
<http://www.bowlingalone.com/socialcapital.php3> (12 May 2003).

Introduction
Jenny Onyx

In this book we have brought together researchers from Canada and Australia and from diverse disciplines to explore some of the sustainable development challenges facing local (small) communities. Some authors are "experts" in sustainable development, others in social capital research. Together, we look at the links between these two fields, both of which hold tremendous promise for our future, if we can understand their potential synergy for mobilizing social change for humanity's future sustainable development.

The link between social capital and sustainable development, however, is elusive, as both concepts are in themselves highly contested. They cannot be defined precisely, but we argue that both are critical to humanity. Many of the things that are important to our civilization, such as integrity, truth, love, and beauty, cannot be precisely defined, and yet, each of us has clear meanings for these constructs. Those of us who are "expert" in issues of sustainability and sustainable development are inclined to focus on the implications of the different positions taken. Those of us who are "expert" in matters of social capital are inclined to accept a simplified view of sustainable development but contest the finer details of the different positions taken on social capital. Both concepts are fuzzy but nonetheless important starting points for meaningful dialogue about the future of our planet. Many of the perspectives arise from the different disciplinary approaches taken, as well as from the different political/value positions adopted, and the scale at which a particular researcher is interested. Nonetheless, it is this kind of cross-disciplinary and cross-national discussion that may prove useful in advancing our knowledge, particularly as we are all united by a conviction that the two concepts are somehow related.

In this book, we begin with a definition of sustainable development – rather than sustainability – that we all accept as a starting point for discussion. We have chosen to use the former over the latter because it brings a constructive ambiguity to the debate, with its tension between sustainable and development, which of course, is the heart of the problem that many single-resource communities are facing. In addition, many Canadian experts in this field have converged on the following definition (Canadian Consortium for Sustainable Development Research 1998).

Sustainable development is defined as a process of reconciliation of three imperatives: (1) the ecological imperative to live within global biophysical carrying capacity and maintain biodiversity; (2) the social imperative to ensure the development of democratic systems of governance to effectively propagate and sustain the values that people wish to live by; and (3) the economic imperative to ensure that basic needs are met worldwide. And equitable access to these three resources – ecological, social, and economic – is fundamental to its realization (Dale 2001; Robinson and Tinker 1998).

We take sustainable development to refer to a fundamental reconciliation of the three imperatives, of which the ecological imperative is the most primordial, as it is the foundation for all life. Much has been written about the economic imperative, and in most analyses, it is regarded as dominant. While we acknowledge its importance, and we cannot escape its pervasiveness in all case analyses, this book does not focus directly on that imperative, as we believe the failure to implement sustainable development is fundamentally a social problem (Dale forthcoming). Thus, our focus is on the second imperative, the social, referring primarily to "democratic systems of governance." Perhaps this is one answer to the question, what is the link? It lies in the definition; the social must be reconciled with the other imperatives or there is no sustainable development.

Yet that is a very limited response. The "social," as Dale uses it, incorporates both social and human capital. Human capital refers to the sum of human capacity, including the knowledge and skills that can be used in the production of wealth and that form the basis of any collective and purposive human endeavour. Social capital encompasses much more than "democratic systems of governance." The latter is one fortunate outcome of the appropriate use of social capital, and reflects a public policy focus. There are other equally important outcomes of the appropriate use of social capital, for example, good health (Putnam 2000), good education (Coleman 1988), and economic well-being (Woolcock and Narayan 2001).

So what is social capital? There are many definitions, and some scholars are critical of the concept for this reason (see, for example, Portes 1998; Woolcock 1998). However, we take the position that this diversity of definitions simply reflects the relatively new state of social capital research and its discourses. While there is much agreement about some of the constituent elements of social capital, we are not sure about which of these is essential, or core to the concept, and which are associated or peripheral phenomena. Indeed, several of the chapters in this book will help clarify some of these relationships further. Two of the most frequently used definitions of social capital reflect a fundamental theoretical difference. Bourdieu (1985, 248; 1980) defines the concept as "the aggregate of the actual or potential resources which are linked to possession of a durable network of more of less institutionalized relationships of mutual acquaintance or recognition." Further, he argues that social networks are not a natural given and must be constructed through investment strategies oriented to the institutionalization of group relations, usable as a reliable source of benefits (Portes 1998). This approach locates the social capital possessed in any given network for the use and strategic advantage of the individual. Other definitions are more explicitly social in orientation. Social capital is located within the social structures, the space between people, and not within the individual. Coleman (1988) defines social capital by its function with two elements in common: with some aspect of social structures that facilitate certain action by actors – whether persons or corporate actors – within the structure. Putnam provides the most commonly used definition, one that clearly locates social capital within social structures. Putnam, Leonardi, and Nanetti (1993, 167) define social capital as "those features of social organization, such as trust, norms and networks[,] that can improve the efficiency of society by facilitating coordinated actions." Nevertheless, consensus is growing in the literature that social capital stands for the ability of actors (both group and individual) to secure benefits by virtue of membership in social networks or other social structures (Portes 1998).

One point of discussion concerns the centrality of trust. For some it is critical (Fukuyama 1995; Misztal 1996; Putnam, Leonardi, and Nanetti 1993), for others simply a fortunate side effect (Portes 1998; Woolcock 2001; Schuller 2001). Other scholars have emphasized different core elements of social capital, elements such as reciprocity (Putnam, Leonardi, and Nanetti 1993) and social agency (Leonard and Onyx 2004). Agency refers to the capacity to take the initiative, to be proactive. One of the early attempts to define social capital by empirical, statistical means identified several group factors, all of which contributed to an underlying common factor (Onyx and Bullen 2000). Those group factors included "community participation," "trust," and "social agency," as well as other aspects such as "neighbourhood connections" and "tolerance of diversity."

The point is not that some of these definitions or components are correct and others incorrect. Social capital, we are coming to understand, is a complex and multi-layered concept. Within the broad scope of social capital there are probably some elements that are core and others that are effects of the core. We are not yet in a position to clearly delineate the boundaries of the concept (any more than we can do so for concepts such as "beauty" or "governance" or "intelligence"). The contributors to this book each emphasize a slightly different aspect of social capital. However, we can all agree that the core to social capital includes "the networks that facilitate collective action" (Woolcock 2001). These networks are not value neutral, but are held together by a set of implicit rules and underlying values (hence, "norms"). Social capital, we agree, does not refer to the collective action itself but to the potential for such collective action to occur. The outcome of social capital always concerns the "common good," as its members define it. However, that common good may in fact be quite destructive to individual members or to outsiders (Portes 1998). Social capital itself, like money, is neither good nor evil. It is always essential, but whether used for good or ill depends on those who shape it.

A related issue of considerable current debate is the relationship between social capital and social structure, or structural bases of power. It is important to recognize from the outset that social capital is not presented as a kind of spray-on solution to economic, environmental, and social problems. A political economy must be included in any analysis (Fine 2001). We know, for instance, that social capital is most likely to work effectively among equals; inequality, exploitation, and power tactics are highly destructive of working social capital. Several chapters in this book take a cautionary look at the negative impacts of such conflict. It is also clearly the case that the operation of social capital at the local level will be shaped and constrained by wider structural, economic, and political forces operating at the state (provincial), national, and global levels, and which impact on the local. Several chapters specifically acknowledge and examine these wider structural forces, including the chapters by Black and Hughes, and Barraket. However, we reject the structural determinism of authors such as Harriss (2001), who portray the ordinary citizen as victim and who see the only possibility of social change residing in the mobilization of political action along traditional (class) interests. The primary focus of the book is a positive one. If given the opportunity, what can be achieved at the local level through people's combined and cooperative actions?

This book focuses on small communities, particularly small rural communities. That of course raises the question of what a community is. Like the other concepts, this one is also ambiguous and contested. We take it to refer to all regularly interacting collectivities of people, or locally integrated institutional and social networks (Day and Murdoch 1993). A community is almost always self-defined as such. In most cases communities are geographically bounded, and characterized by multiple and overlapping networks of engagement. Place is important to them. However, communities do not have to be geographically focused. Communities of practice (Lesser and Prusak 2000) refer to networks of people with a common learning or action focus, as discussed by Kilpatrick and Vanclay in this book. Communities of interest are also bound by a common interest, or a common self-identifying feature such as ethnic origin, and may well be geographically dispersed. Virtual communities may exist in space rather than place. Nonetheless, to maintain the label "community" requires that they form a regularly interacting system of networks.

Most of the cases in this book refer to rural communities. This should not be taken to mean that urban environments are not relevant to the arguments, simply that, being more complex, they require a separate analysis, one beyond the immediate scope of this book. We believe that smaller, rural communities are more vulnerable for two reasons. One is that small rural communities are experiencing high levels of stress within the current globalizing context. Many of them are single-resource economies and therefore more vulnerable to global market forces, and they are struggling to diversify their economies reactively. In both Canada and Australia, small rural communities are experiencing the highest levels of population loss and economic decline of all types of communities. On the other hand, they have the advantage of potentially high levels of bonding social capital. This creates the possibility for effective collective action. From an analytic point of view, this means that they make ideal natural laboratories in terms of identifying the dynamics operating within a clearly delineated system of social networks. Their achieving diversification, many of the authors in this book argue, is dependent on their access to resources, and particularly on their bridging and linking social capital and using it to draw on outside resources of expertise and financial capital, which urban centres because of their scale have in much greater abundance. Thus, we need to reconcile and reconnect small and urban communities in new, dynamic ways, in order to avoid large islands of haves and have-nots. Sustainable development is critical to this dynamic balance, as both are inversely affected by questions of scale.

This book is organized into four parts, similar to other titles in UBC Press's Sustainability and the Environment series. The first part, "Vision," contains chapters describing significant Canadian initiatives in some aspect of creating a sustainable society for Canada. The second part, "Connections," tries to reach beyond the field of sustainable development as conventionally defined. In this section we include authors and address topics from other fields, having in each case asked the author to draw connections to the field of sustainable development. In this way, we hope to increase interdisciplinary linkages between disciplines. The third part, "Action," is the heart of the book. It contains chapters and includes case studies making critical linkages between social capital and sustainable development, some more tenuous than others. The fourth part, "Assessing Progress," analyzes the contributions that sustainable development has made and can make to the social capital conversation. Authors were encouraged to make concrete proposals for action wherever possible, based on the premise that we know enough and, indeed, we must act now (Dale and Robinson 1995).

A number of themes guide the work of this book. Two in particular are worth mentioning at the outset. The first is the focus on collective action, or at least its potential. In this we follow Melucci's (1996) analysis. Collective action is socially constructed, complex, and highly context-dependent within the system of relationships within which such action occurs. To quote Melucci,

> It [collective action] is a purposive orientation built on social relations within a field of opportunities and constraints. It therefore cannot be considered as either the simple effect of structural preconditions or the expression of values and beliefs. Individuals and groups acting collectively construct their action by means of organized investments: in other words, they define in cognitive and affective terms the field of possibilities and limits which they perceive, and they simultaneously activate their relationships to create meaning out of their joint behaviour, so as to give sense to their "being together" and to the goals they pursue. (Melucci 1996, 39)

We would argue, beyond this definition, that social capital is essential to sustainable development because reconciliation of the three imperatives can occur only through collective action, and collective action will not occur unless there is an adequate stock of social capital to provide the potential for this. Of course, that raises many questions, some of which will be pursued in the following chapters. How is social capital formed and mobilized? What prevents or inhibits its formation? Is it possible to have an adequate stock of social capital that nonetheless is not mobilized, and if so, what prevents its mobilization? More specifically, what are the mechanisms by which social capital is activated? How are decisions for action made and by whom? Is a democratic form of governance essential at this grounded level? What does that involve? What kind of leadership is effective? Are external resources required before collective action is productive, and if so, how are these resources accessed? Of recurring concern is the role of government in the mobilization of social capital for the implementation of sustainable development.

A second theme of the book starts to identify what goes wrong in the mobilization of collective action. We argue that, just as reconciliation of the three imperatives is essential for sustainability, so too a disconnection between these imperatives prevents effective collective action. There are many potential sources of disconnect. There is the obvious disconnection between the ecological, the social, and the economic. That occurs when one is pursued relentlessly at the expense of the others. It occurs when one of the capitals, usually the economic, dominates and swamps the other capitals (the ecological, the social, the human). However, our main focus in this book is the potential disconnection between levels of operation, that is, between the local or micro-level and the global or macro-level of operation. We have found a recurring tension between the interests and needs of the small community and national agendas, between the discourse of the parochial and the discourse of big science. We are not arguing that one be privileged over the other, only that the validity of each be recognized. We are beginning to identify the complex set of interdependencies between all levels of action in which the total (or the global) is much more than the sum of its individual parts. But if those individual parts are ignored, or invalidated, or dominated, then the local disconnects from the larger level, and collective action at the local level is diminished. As you will discover in the following chapters, the outcomes of such disconnects are not only that the local is swamped by global forces, but that the integrity of the local community and its constituent groups is destroyed (see especially the chapters by Boydell and by Benn and Onyx). In those circumstances the small, local community simply is not viable. Two chapters in particular examine ecological and social capital in the context of Indigenous communities (Memmott and Meltzer, Moody and Cordua-von Specht). Although drawn from different regions of the world and seen through the eyes of different disciplines, the message of these two chapters is the same. The wisdom of traditional Indigenous practices provided far more sustainable ecological practices than is now the case. At the same time, the social capital that has always been generated from traditional Indigenous ways of organizing is regularly discounted by the requirements of the modern Anglo state. The disconnect is almost total. In the longer run, trust in government, and in science, is eroded, and the national agenda is not achieved either (see the chapter by Sheng).

As Schuurman (2003, 1008) argues, social capital has the potential to help understand the link between the social and the political: "Explicit attention should be awarded to the extent that power differentials within the social as well as between the social domain and the political domain are related to the absence of social capital and trust." If we are to understand the connections between social capital and sustainable development at the local level, we must understand power and conflict and how these are played out in the subpolitics of the local (Beck 1992). We go beyond the warm and fuzzies of social capital to identify the factionalism of vested interests and how these may create a kind of disconnect within the local. Collective action will not be effective if the collective is characterized by ongoing conflict. Yet conflict is surely inevitable. Several chapters explore the genesis and outcomes of such factionalism and vested interests, including those by Barraket, by Onyx and Osburn, by Boydell, and by Sheng. The issue then becomes how such conflict is managed. Silence and avoidance is unlikely to resolve the issues. Nor is dominance by a small elite, particularly one that draws its advantage from national or global economic interests. Yet on the positive side, there are examples of communities that are able to bridge their own divides and mobilize themselves for collective action, thus creating the "power to" of people power. A collective determination can overcome external obstacles. We need to understand more about what makes this collective capacity possible in the face of conflict. We will explore the complexity and chaos of new forms of decision making. Democratic forms of governance require the active participation of many stakeholders at all levels of decision making. Several chapters argue for new ways of engaging citizen participation in decision making, and the potentially positive role government agencies can play (see chapters by Sparkes, Tansey, and Sheng in particular). New ideas are likely to emerge from new and diverse actors. One side of this positive positioning almost certainly entails the mobilization of new forms of collective learning, as described by Kilpatrick and Vanclay, and the constructive mobilization of diversity.

Of course, all these developments depend on the capacity for measurement. We are in the very early stages of realizing our capacity to measure either ecological integrity or social capital at the local level, let alone the impact of either on current practices. The chapters that follow provide an exploration of a variety of forms of measurement, from the use of community surveys (see chapters by Black and Hughes, and by Sheng) to in-depth case studies (Onyx and Osburn, Memmott and Meltzer) to the creative use of simulations (Tansey) and various applications of action research techniques (Sparkes, Kirkpatrick and Vanclay). Several chapters argue that the measurement itself must be located and contextualized within the specific communities in question. Again, the failure to do so is most graphically evident in the case of Indigenous communities (Moody and Cordua-von Specht, Memmott and Meltzer)

The first two chapters provide interesting new theoretical perspectives on the potential relationships between social and ecological capital. Dale provides a vision of how the relationship between social capital and sustainable development may be conceptualized. Wilson explores the uncanny parallels between the essential system conditions of both ecological and social systems. Then follows the core of the book: ten chapters, which explore "Actions." We each grapple with some of the complexities of the themes outlined above, within and through the empirical specificity of real situations, communities, dilemmas. Notice that we draw on the knowledge of different disciplines and different literatures, yet come back to the same or very similar conclusions.

These are but some of the themes that will emerge in the following chapters. They have transpired from a deliberative dialogue between the authors, at a research conference where most papers were presented for scrutiny, not only by each other but also by an audience of other academics, government policy makers, and practitioners. Thus, we were able to explore the meaning of diversity within social capital but also within our own research. We, the writers of this book, are also diverse. We come from diverse disciplines and background expertise. We carry different values and assumptions. We use diverse methodologies and theoretical paradigms. The project of this book represents a deliberative dialogue between Canadian and Australian research, culture, contexts, and policies. We share much in common, being large, resource-rich, English-speaking countries with a shared British tradition and common dilemmas within the global context. We share similar colonial histories, a similar disregard for Indigenous people's rights, a similar struggle to settle and exploit vast empty spaces, and similar development of single-industry towns, many of which are now struggling as resources are exhausted. *The Wellbeing of Nations* (Prescott-Allen 2001) identifies both countries as having relatively good human well-being indicators but an ecosystem deficit, meaning that they have high standards of living but excessive impacts on the global environment. Australia's performance is worse on this measure of ecosystem well-being.

We also share a common passion that should be apparent in these chapters: a shared commitment to sustainable development and the search for knowledge to allow us to realize its implementation in this decade. Our epistemological base is also consistent. We hold neither a functionalist nor a structuralist position, as these both imply the kind of social determinism that makes deliberative collective action impossible. We fundamentally hold that it is both necessary and possible for deliberative human action to create a more sustainable world.

References

Beck, U. 1992. *Risk Society: Towards a New Modernity.* London: Sage.

Bourdieu, P. 1980. *The Logic of Practice.* Cambridge: Polity Press.

–. 1985. "The Forms of Capital." In J.G. Richardson, ed., *Handbook of Theory and Research for the Sociology of Education.* New York: Greenwood Press.

Canadian Consortium for Sustainable Development Research (CCSDR). 1998. Mandate Statement.

Coleman, J. 1988. "Social Capital in the Creation of Human Capital." *American Journal of Sociology* 94: 95-120.

Dale, A. Forthcoming. *Integrated Resource Management.* Toronto: Oxford Press.

–. 2001. *At the Edge: Sustainable Development in the 21st Century.* Vancouver: UBC Press.

Dale, A., and J.B. Robinson. 1995. *Achieving Sustainable Development.* Vancouver: UBC Press.

Day, G., and J. Murdoch. 1993. "Locality and Community: Coming to Terms with Place." *Sociological Review* 41(1): 82-111.

Fine, B. 2001. *Social Capital versus Social Theory: Political Economy and Social Science at the Turn of the Millennium.* London: Routledge.

Fukuyama, F. 1995. *Trust: The Social Virtues and the Creation of Prosperity.* London: Penguin.

Harriss, J. 2002. *Depoliticizing Development: The World Bank and Social Capital.* London: Anthem Press.

Leonard, R., and J. Onyx. 2004. *Social Capital and Community Building: Spinning Straw into Gold.* London: Janus.

Lesser, E., and L. Prusak. 2000. "Communities of Practice, Social Capital and Organisational Knowledge." In E.L. Lesser, M.A. Fontaine, and J.A. Slusher, eds., *Knowledge and Communities.* Boston: Butterworth-Heinemann.

Melucci, A. 1996. *Challenging Codes: Collective Action in the Information Age.* Cambridge: University of Cambridge Press.

Misztal, B. 1996. *Trust in Modern Societies.* Cambridge, MA: Polity Press.

Onyx, J., and P. Bullen. 2000. "Measuring Social Capital in Five Communities." *Journal of Applied Behavioural Science* 36(1): 23-42.

Portes, A. 1998. "Social Capital: Its Origins and Applications in Modern Sociology." *Annual Review of Sociology* 24(1): 1-24.

Prescott-Allen, R. 2001. *The Wellbeing of Nations.* Washington, DC: Island Press.

Putnam, R. 2000. *Bowling Alone.* New York: Simon and Schuster.

Putnam, R., R. Leonardi, and R. Nanetti. 1993. *Making Democracy Work: Civic Traditions in Modern Italy.* Princeton, NJ: Princeton University Press.

Robinson, J., and J. Tinker. 1998. "Reconciling Ecological, Economic, and Social Imperatives." In J. Schnurr and S. Holtz, eds., *The Cornerstone of Development: Integrating Environmental, Social and Economic Policies.* Ottawa: International Development Research Centre; New York: Lewis Publishers.

Schuller, T. 2001. "The Complementary Roles of Human and Social Capital." *Canadian Journal of Policy Research* 2(1): 18-24.

Schuurman, F. 2003. "Social Capital: The Politico-Emancipatory Potential of a Disputed Concept." *Third World Quarterly* 24(6): 991-1010.

Woolcock, M. 1998. "Social Capital and Economic Development: Toward a Theoretical Synthesis and Policy Framework." *Theory and Society,* 27: 151-208.

–. 2001. "The Place of Social Capital in Understanding Social and Economic Outcomes." *Canadian Journal of Policy Research* 2(1): 11-17.

Woolcock, M., and D. Narayan. 2001. "Implications for Development Theory, Research and Policy." *World Bank Research Observer* 15: 225-49.

Part 1
Vision

1

Social Capital and Sustainable Community Development: Is There a Relationship?

Ann Dale

> It is true that metalogues are fuzzy in the sense that one cannot
> determine a priori with any precision when the process will be
> completed, which values will prevail, or which new public policies
> will be endorsed. In effect, one can predict only that the process
> often will be disjointed, emotive, repetitive, and meandering. But
> these are all earmarks of processes that truly engage a mass of
> people in examining, redefining, and redirecting their values and
> moral commitments – earmarks of moral dialogues, essential for
> truly endorsed social change.
> – Amitai Etzioni (2000a)

Communities worldwide are facing formidable challenges: significant demographic urban growth, with associated problems of urban sprawl and development; economic and population losses in many rural and resource dependent communities, with associated job loss and community decline; difficulties in meeting the basic necessities for clean air, clean water, energy, transportation, land use, housing, jobs, health, and waste disposal. Such problems are dynamically interconnected and cannot be dealt with in isolation by any one community alone, as many of them span traditional jurisdictions and local capacity. Thus new approaches, frameworks, partnerships, and tools to address them in an integrative fashion are required. It is not sufficient merely to improve current modes of operation (Gunderson, Holling, and Light 1995). Fundamental transformations are required in all sectors of society, including changes to our social, economic, and governance structures and shifts in cultures and practices.

Canadian communities are also attempting to redefine themselves in the twenty-first-century context of increased innovation, diversity, and knowledge management to meet the rapidly accelerating pace of change affecting communities at multiple scales, involving multiple sectors, and many levels of decision makers. Since these challenges are beyond the capacity of any single organization, community, or discipline to meet (Trist 1983), new transdisciplinary networks are critical to responding to these challenges. Possibly the greatest challenge is not necessarily one of scientific or managed origin, rather, "it is about dealing with people and their diverse cultures, interests, visions, priorities and needs" (Norgaard 1994). But communities differ tremendously in their engagement in those issues, their capacity, their resources, and their understanding of sustainable development.

As well, the meaning of "sustainable community" in a world of increasing globalization and ecological interdependence is changing constantly as many communities struggle with outside forces beyond their immediate control. In particular, many single-resource-economy communities are especially vulnerable because of their lack of diversity in the face of global markets where mobilization of capitals – human and natural – has never been greater. For example, in Canada some 600 communities are dependent on the natural resource sector (Canada 2002) and of these, 128 rely directly on the mining industry (Veiga, Scoble, and McAllister 2001). Many communities, particularly communities dependent on a single resource sector such as mining, are facing collapse. Globally, some estimates place the number of large-scale mine closures over the next decade at twenty-five (Sheldon, Strongman, and Weber-Fahr 2002).

In addition, many kinds of civic engagement critical to community have declined, including participation in voluntary associations, public life, and religious activities (Putnam 2001). This disengagement and resulting anomie has diverse effects on individuals, and one of the most portent indicators may be the prevalent rate of male youth suicide in North America and the rising increase of homeless youth in large urban centres. Without meaning or purpose, individually and collectively, through a core of shared values, individuals and their communities are unable to respond to the dynamic centrifugal forces of this era. For twenty-first-century issues are similar to the complexities inherent in the meaning and purpose of relationships: we need to become fully conscious of the relationships critical to our well-being. And one of the relationships we least appreciate may be critical to our very survival – the importance of our relationships with natural systems and with other species. We are now at a stage in human evolution where we can deliberately choose and design our potentiality, and indeed, our very survival may be linked to our capacity for deliberative social design, given our dominance as a species on the planet (Dale 2001). If indeed healthy communities are communities that engage in moral dialogues on the meaning of community, we need to actively re-engage in those dialogues that will result in the affirmation of new directions (Etzioni 2000b) leading to more sustainable societies. Thus, we are entering an age when communities need to define "new shared moral cultures" through deliberative dialogue on the meaning of place, limits, and scale in the twenty-first century context of sustainable development.

This chapter is based on a three-year research project funded by the Canadian Social Sciences and Humanities Research Council (SSHRC). Although the research project is in its infancy compared with some of the Australian chapters, I wanted to share both our conceptual thinking and some of our preliminary observations based on five case studies in the interests of intellectual collaboration in a timely and proactive fashion.

Since most Canadians are members of multiple and overlapping communities, communities are defined broadly in this research not only by place but also communities of practice (Lesser and Prusak 2000), professional affiliation, shared interests, and networks (Canadian Policy Research Networks 2003), and space, that is, virtual communities. "Deliberative dialogue" is defined as deliberately designed safe-to-fail learning environments that allow diverse groups of people to engage in informed discussion with their peers and experts, to explore their implications, and to examine alternative social responses. E-dialogues are a means of making deliberative discourse and dialogue accessible to a wider audience of engaged citizens and policy makers alike, who through shared dialogue and learning on-line form novel electronic communities.

Social capital can be defined as the set of norms, networks, and organizations through which people gain access to power and resources, and through which decision making and policy formulation occur (Grootaert 1998). In this chapter, I also refer to four capitals – natural (ecological), social (collective), human (individual), and economic. More than 1,200 definitions of sustainable development now exist, and there are equally as many definitions for social capital (Bourdieu 1985; Coleman 1988; Fukuyama 1995; Portes 1998; Putnam, Leonardi, and Nanetti 1993; Woolcock 2000), as well as increasingly finer discriminations between the various "capitals." But finer discriminations can lead to losing the integrity and essence of a concept in our attempts to define, measure, and quantify the undefinable, the immeasurable, and the very things that may be the most critical for life. Reconciliation implies equally valuing the quantitative and qualitative, a dynamic balance of knowing when and what to measure, and what is immeasurable.

As I have argued earlier, reconciliation is key to the realization of sustainable development; natural, social, human, and economic capital all have limited value if not reconciled with one another. Similarly, as ecological imperatives are the most primordial of the three imperatives (Dale 2001), social capital is the most critical capital for human reconciliation of the three imperatives. Why? Because changes of the magnitude necessary for sustainable development require collective mobilization of people in communities worldwide.

Although sustainable development has been criticized as being an oxymoron, some analysts have argued that it brings a constructive ambiguity to the negotiation table by bringing a diversity of expertise, sectors, and experience to these tables engaged in meaningful dialogue (ibid.). And meaningful dialogue and socially constructed scenarios (Tansey et al. 2001) may be crucial in building more sustainable community development and, in many cases, community redevelopment. Why? It is clear that human societies are now at a stage in their evolution when communities need to define "new shared moral cultures" (Etzioni 2000b) through deliberatively designed dialogues.

But how to affect such dialogues, at a realizable scale, when human societies are so plural, incredibly complex, and diverse in their structures, values, and behaviours? I have argued that the reconciliation of ecological, social, and economic imperatives is the fundamental human imperative of this century, needed before we reach irreversible thresholds. And reconciliation needs to take place at all scales, as diverse communities search for practical answers to real problems with broad-ranging, long-term economic, social, and ecological consequences that transcend political boundaries. For it is becoming increasingly clear that as we approach critical sustainable development thresholds, we are bound by the same limits and scale phenomena as natural systems.

Why are place, scale, limits, and diversity so important? Because each community is located in a specific geographic, historical, and ecological landscape, and as such, each possesses particular and unique socioeconomic and cultural characteristics. Place is important in that it determines access to particular types of resources, not the least of which are natural resources, the backbone of the Canadian economy. Scale is as equally important to sustainable community development – is there an optimum scale for urban and rural development? Cities are becoming larger and larger (see e-Dialogues 2002b) and yet there is evidence showing that their ecological footprint far exceeds their local carrying capacity (Rees 1996). What is the relationship between rural and urban populations, and what are the most effective ways for communities to collectively formulate shared values (Etzioni 1997)? And what are the limits to growth, development, and consumption? Coming to understand the diversity of place – physical and nonphysical; the diversity of space – mental, emotional, and spiritual; and the diversity of life – human and nonhuman – may be one of the most important social imperatives facing communities in this century. As more and more places, species, and cultures become endangered, a range of moral decisions will have to be made about when or whether to intervene based on considerations that will include governments' limited financial resources. The meaning of diversity to the capacity of a community to move from a single-resource industry to other economic opportunities may be key to competing in an interconnected global marketplace.

Community decisions on the meaning of place, scale, limits, and diversity are highly pluralistic and normative, and therefore can be decided only by sharing and learning strategies in the community. These inevitably rely on sustained dialogue and enhanced civic literacy on critical social and political – as well as ecological – questions of limits. There is no one clear, simple measure; it is entirely dependent on what a particular community values and defines as its needs. But of all the imperatives, the social dimension of sustainable development is the most complex. In addition to problems of measurement, it is further complicated because, "since we are natural as well as social beings, the emergent aspect of our social and technical systems will always be the tip of an iceberg, of which the greater part is ordinarily complex" (Funtowicz and Ravetz 1994, 570).

Moreover, many analysts have stated that the most serious impediments to the implementation of sustainable development are structural (Dale 2001; Folke et al. 1998; Robinson and Tinker 1997). I have argued that, in Canada, we have serious structural impediments because of the solitudes, silos, and stovepipes that so characterize the relationships (or lack thereof) between sectors in this country (Dale 2001). As well, communities vary greatly in terms of their ecological, social, and economical access to resources, but an emerging feature of twenty-first-century society is knowledge management and building a knowledge-sharing culture. Ingenuity gaps have been identified (Homer-Dixon 2001); such a gap exists between the requirement for and the supply of ingenuity in periods of rapid change, including technological change. Ornstein and Ehrlich (1989) have argued that we have a gap between old mind and new world; that is, that we are still working with a mind that doesn't perceive danger or threat unless we taste, smell, or see it.

And this is the key intersection between social capital and sustainable development. Social capital is about relationships – relationships within communities, and between communities nationally and internationally through our global interconnectedness. We need to re-examine our relationships with the natural world (our environment) and with other species. One can "have" a relationship or one can be "in relationship" with another – a subtle but nonetheless critical difference. Our relationships are often based on dominance, seeing ourselves as "apart" rather than being "a part" of natural systems. And this perceived separation eliminates the personal from the professional, and means we have relationships rather than being in relationship. As Stuart Hill discusses in Chapter 3, we will not realize sustainable development unless we understand the personal imperative, as well as its dynamics. Sustainable development is ultimately "an issue of human behaviour, and negotiation over preferred futures, under conditions of deep contingency and uncertainty" (Robinson 2004). Complex, turbulent environmental contexts (Emery and Emery 1976) in conditions of deep contingency and uncertainty demand unprecedented levels of collaboration in societal dialogues on the meaning of community. What is important to sustain them?

Just as social capital is the key linkage to mobilizing sustainable community development, dialogue is critical to re-examining our relationships with natural systems. Dialogue has the ability to bridge asymmetries within and between communities by building collective norms, values, and governance among diverse sectors (or "stakeholders," in the modern parlance of government). In this way, dialogue differs from consensus building or consultation, since it provides a more permanent, open-ended, and inclusive modality of shared decision making with the public (Dale and Naylor, in press). These dialogues will not happen spontaneously; they need to be deliberatively designed, and the importance of emergent properties of reflection and contradiction valued (Funtowicz and Ravetz 1993).

How do we measure the benefits of dialogue, multi-stakeholder processes, and their complex issues of power and control, as Benn and Onyx discuss in their chapter? Quantitative measurement is not well suited to measuring the quality of relationships, though it can measure the quantity of relationships and networks. Quantitative measurements, in particular economic measures, are a human construct, and they have now achieved a perceived objective reality independent of their social construction. Yet it is often the undefinable things in life, the operationally immeasurable, such as beauty and trust, that provide meaning and purpose to humanity (Frankel 1959).

Moreover, many researchers continue to occupy themselves with criticisms about the lack of definition of sustainable development. One has to ask whether these definitional discourses are simply a means to avoiding change and, as Hill refers to, the need for personal transformation through the personal imperative. Even though we cannot precisely define beauty, we still realize how important it is to human civilization – as is the realization of sustainable development. How important are these disconnections – between the quantitative and the qualitative, the large versus the small, the personal and the professional – to the mobilization of social capital for sustainable community development?

Besides these disconnections or separations, another major problem with unsustainable development globally is that we often can't see, taste, or feel the problem until approaching crisis points (Ornstein and Ehrlich 1989). Thus, it is only through the mobilization of social capital, through deliberative dialogues, that we will be able to collectively "see" the problems, and the critical actions necessary in human behaviours and values locally, nationally, and globally. Social capital can be massively organized as a mobilizing force, as evidenced by our responses in the Second World War and

Figure 1.1

Why is social capital important?

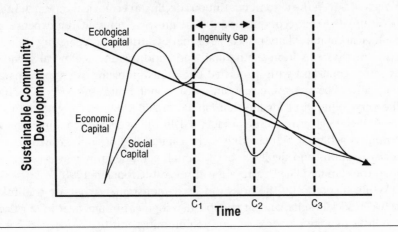

more recently with the collapse of the Soviet Union. The necessary will and engagement, individually and collectively, has to be mobilized, and this is why social capital is the most critical capital for the more rapid diffusion of sustainable development principles and practices, as illustrated in the above heuristic model. In this model and subsequent models in this chapter, the y-axis represents varying degrees of reconciliation or separation of the three imperatives, and the x-axis represents the evolution of human society over time (see Figure 1.1).

The model assumes continuing ecological decline consistent with the most recent statistics (United Nations Environment Programme 2000; The Guardian 2002; Intergovernmental Panel on Climate Change 2003; White and Vanasselt 2003; Worldwatch Institute 2003), and as evidenced by the many single-resource-economy communities around the world that are facing collapse. A number of crisis points are represented by C_1, C_2, and C_3. C_1 is the first crisis point, when social capital begins to decline along the same trajectory as ecological capital. These points represent progressively more serious states of imbalance and disintegration of the capitals. C_2 represents another crisis point: when all three capitals are beginning to trend down. The economic capital curve lags behind the other two capitals simply because of the system preconditions that provide incentives to continue beyond natural threshold limits. C_3 represents a point where all three capitals are declining toward system collapse. Clearly, the mobilization of one form of capital may multiply the effects of another in a positive, or a vicious, cycle. Equally, the misuse or overuse of one may reduce or destroy another.

What is critical for strategic government interventions is to develop policies and incentives to bridge the ingenuity gap between C_1 and C_2 and ideally, before C_1.

As well, given the current continuous decline in ecological capital, it may be postulated that economic capital is "growing" only at the expense of ecological capital. Many now believe that by artificially separating human economic systems from the natural world and treating ecological services as a free good and with associated commons problems, we appear, paradoxically, to be increasing economic wealth, but only at the cost of eroding the very foundation for life (Ehrlich 1982; Hill 1980; Holling 1986; Rees 1996). Just as gross domestic product (GDP) will overstate economic gain if output is achieved by depleting social capital, if economic growth severs social relations and depletes social capital, genuine growth will be lower than the standard GDP aggregate will suggest (Grootaert 1998).

While theoretically the links can be demonstrated, what are the links between social capital and sustainable development in practice? In practice, the links may be paradoxical, and require much further research. For example, the Canadian province of Newfoundland, and its communities, has incredibly high social capital, evidenced by its strong sense of community, and yet is facing ecological and economic decline because of severely depleted fish stocks. However, Newfoundland has the lowest per capita income and the highest level of charitable giving. Meanwhile, British Columbia, one of Canada's richest resource economies, and in particular the island on which I live, Vancouver Island, has the highest per capita income and one of the lowest levels of charitable donation, illuminating the complexities of social capital. There can be strong social capital in some communities with few ties to others, and with segmentation along spatial or ethnic lines (ibid.). Clearly, social capital can be both inclusive and exclusive, and equally, social cohesion can be both positive and negative (Onyx and Bullen 2000), if it acts as a barrier to diversity of human capital.

Similarly, exclusivity can be an outcome of one of the defining elements of social capital: bonding. Bonding can be both positive and negative, depending on how tight or loose the connections are (Onyx and Leonard 2000). Paradoxically, however, a society that seeks to eliminate exclusivity completely will grossly neglect the profound human need for social bonds (Etzioni 2000b). Balancing the forces of light and the forces of dark is indeed delicate, as communities that have high levels of bonding, particularly island cultures, may not be as open to "others." Diversity, so critical to natural systems, may also be equally critical to moving beyond bonding to bridging and linking social capital. And the capacity to move from bonding to bridging and linking, and openness to new ideas, new people, new ways of doing things, may be critical to increasing access to resources. In addition to its role in information sharing and creating mutual knowledge of how

Figure 1.2

Building social capital

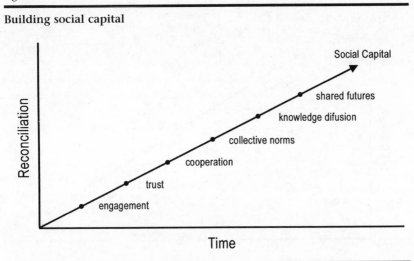

others may or may not respond, social capital may also play a critical role in knowledge diffusion (Grootaert 1998), which is again key to diversification and the implementation of sustainable development.

To better understand the nature of social capital and its relationship to sustainable development, key elements of social capital have been identified that collectively illustrate the power of this capital to positively redirect the other capitals toward greater sustainable community development. Various researchers have identified the elements of engagement, trust, cooperation, collective norms, knowledge diffusion, and a sense of shared futures as key to building social capital (Bohm and Nichol 1996; Dale 2001; Etzioni 2000a; Robinson 2004). Although these diagrams are linear, in reality, the movement from one point to another is far more complex. However, for simplicity, in Figure 1.2 it has been drawn linearly to highlight the complexity of the relationship between the elements that build social capital.

To understand how to build and mobilize social capital, it is necessary to understand what destroys it. Figure 1.3 depicts this. Again, the y-axis represents increasing separation of the three imperatives of sustainable development. Given that many are now reaching consensus that we may be approaching critical thresholds or, in fact, may already have reached them (Dale, Robinson, and Massey 1995), all these models assume a finite and absolute limit to human activities. Factors that seem to be prevalent as separation increases on the human and social capital side are vested interests, expertise, alienation, distrust, disconnection, finally moving to anomie, and disintegration of the self. At the individual level, this last point represents

Figure 1.3

Destroying social capital

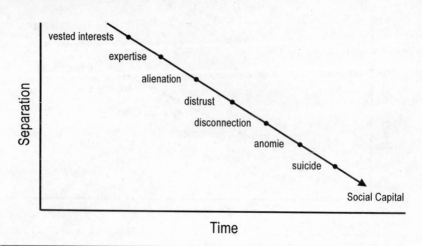

suicide, a deliberate process that can perhaps be viewed as a polar opposite of deliberate dialogue, the latter requiring engagement and agency. This may help illuminate the high suicide rates among youth that so pervades North America, which we are massively denying as a major social phenomenon. For example, in Canada, suicide was the leading cause of death of men between the ages of twenty-five and twenty-nine, and for women aged thirty to thirty-four; Aboriginal communities lost three times as many potential years of life to suicide as did Canadians overall in 1999 (Canadian Institutes of Health Research 2003). Moreover, suicide is the single greatest cause of violent death around the globe, according to the World Health Organization. While it is highly contestable that the factors listed above are the cause of the decline in social capital, they do serve as the beginnings of a theoretical framework with which to illustrate some key indicators for its disintegration.

What, then, builds social capital, and what is the relationship between social capital and sustainable community development? Figure 1.4 attempts to illustrate how certain elements contribute to sustainable community development.

Hopefully I have provided a compelling argument that restoring and rebuilding communities depends on reconciling the ecological, social, and economic imperatives, as well as their social capital formation. Sustainable communities depend on the formation and maintenance of networks, particularly at the bridging and linking levels, in order to build any of the imperatives and capitals. The world we inhabit is highly interconnected;

Figure 1.4

Sustainable community development

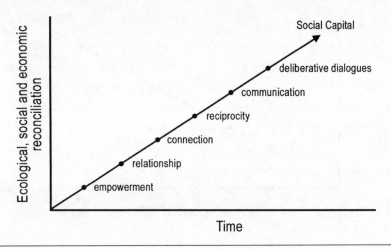

one way to counterbalance global interconnectedness may be through greater network formation within and between communities. Networks are sets of interconnected nodes of people, characterized by open structures that are able to expand without limits, and can integrate new nodes as long as these nodes share the same communication codes (Castells 1996). And these networks may play a pivotal role in sustaining common values that in turn lead to community-wide shared decisions and policies, for "autonomy does not exist in a vacuum but is developed, enunciated, and ultimately exercised in our common life together" (Etzioni 1996, 161).

Again, I will use a figure to illustrate the relationship between social capital and network formation. The integration of six steps – empowerment, relationship, connection, reciprocity, communication, and deliberative dialogue, as shown in Figure 1.5 – is essential to sustainable community development, and particularly redevelopment. These six steps can be seen as deliberate building blocks toward this goal, though they are not necessarily linear; communities, depending on their ability to increase access to resources and power, may be able to build on some of the six elements simultaneously. However, it is crucial to realize both the constructive and destructive properties of the model: each of the six factors of "light" along the x-axis have an opposing "force of dark" (engagement/alienation, trust/mistrust, cooperation/disjointedness, collective norms/vested interests, knowledge diffusion/disciplinary expertise, and shared futures/anomie).

For people to be able to act, they must be engaged, either intellectually or emotionally, or, even better, intellectually *and* emotionally. Before anything

Figure 1.5

Network formation

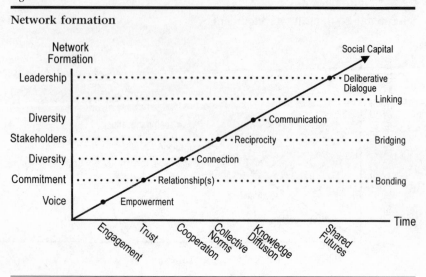

else, humans need the capacity – the freedom and power – to act; that is, they must be empowered to be able to help themselves, and others. Thus, empowerment is a crucial first step for the building of human and social capital and for the restoration and maintenance of ecological capital. This is dependent, of course, on the infrastructures in place that allow individuals and their communities to make informed choices, not the least of which is regarding governance.

Following engagement, trust is critical to the building of relationships, be they intellectual, social, economic, or relational, virtual or real. Trusting relationships are equally important for social cohesion and for economic success (Leadbeater 1999). In most cases, of course, time is crucial to the building of trust, but while it is essential at the bonding level, perhaps it is less so at the bridging and linking levels, or perhaps it simply has different dynamics. For example, trust may have a greater role to play in turbulent, complex environments than in more benign, stable environments (Emery and Emery 1976). Mistrust, on the other hand, leads to the breakdown of relationships and increases the degree of separation people feel from one another and from their various communities, including the natural. Trust/ mistrust may also influence our perceptions of the world as one of plenty or one of scarcity (Holling 1994).

Cooperation is essential to social capital, as well as shared values (Dobell 1995). Cooperation is the glue that holds together connection, the lubricant between our joints, involving the joining and working together for a common objective or objectives. Cooperation may be a necessary first condition for network formation. Without cooperation, people become disjointed, disconnected from their communities, their relationships, and ultimately, their reality. Perhaps more important, without connection, and connection to something outside of "self," one cannot comprehend one's meaning nor realize one's spirituality. In a recent student-led e-Dialogue (2002a) on spirituality and sustainable development, two key elements emerged: openness and connection – connection to each other and to natural systems. Perhaps with an erosion of connection, without a sense of purpose, a sense of meaning that has the capacity to transcend, it is easier to succumb to the "forces of dark," to take one's own life. Both connection and openness appear to be precursors to spirituality, and spirituality may be one way to transcend self and isolation, and potentially to provide greater meaning and purpose to life.

Norms can be defined as the standards of conduct that should or must be followed (Agnes 1999). They can also be defined as "patterns of expectations, regulations, laws and so on [depending on the degree of formalization] by which concrete patterns of social life are actually regulated" (Mayhew 1982, 18). The solidarity that norms provide is important in societies because "without some degree of shared orientation to something greater than a particular interest, mutual interference among individuals and groups oriented exclusively to their own ends would greatly increase the likelihood of a breakdown in the pattern of social relations that are the cement of any society" (Lewis 1994, 13). This highlights that group adherence to norms, and the values from which norms are derived, is the foundation for individuals coming together as a society (ibid.). Collective norms are dependent on shared values. However, if vested interests dominate collective norms, there is a decreased level of reciprocity, leading to a downward spiral of disconnection, mistrust, alienation, and anomie. Reconciliation of sustainable development imperatives can be realized only through unprecedented levels of cooperation, shared values, and collective norms about the meaning of sustainable societies and their physical space, that is, community.

Since by definition sustainable development crosses disciplines, jurisdictions, and sectors of society, its achievement requires the engagement of a diverse variety of community actors, including the full spectrum of civil society, in "conversations for the future" through deliberate dialogue. Dialogue and engagement between the business, research, and community nongovernmental organizations, and with all levels of government, are urgently needed in order to build on successful practices and innovative business strategies that are cropping up in pockets across the country. The Canadian context has clearly shown that dialogue – at the same time, in the same place, and with a continuity of stakeholders – leads to a deeper understanding of sustainable development issues than do traditional forms of expertise (Dale 2001).

Deliberate dialogue designed to lead to new shared futures is equally dependent on an informed and engaged citizenry. Therefore, increasing literacy, particularly ecological literacy, is critical. Increasing literacy on an individual level must be complemented by knowledge diffusion at the societal level, as sustainable community development must address not just one but a whole system of problems beyond the capacity of a single organization or community to meet (Dale 2001). Because it deals with the interaction of human and natural systems, sustainable development solutions must be grounded in rigorous attempts to develop some theoretical understanding of the interrelationships among human and natural systems. This implies an attempt to combine integrated understanding of human activities (itself based on a wide range of social scientific and humanistic understandings) with an equivalently integrated approach to biophysical phenomena, and the manifold forms of interaction among them. As humans are integral components of ecosystems, their survival will also depend on the maintenance of the functions and services of the local ecosystems in which communities are based. There is therefore a need to link human activities, their impacts, and the strategies at an integrated ecosystem level. The changes in behaviour, actions, or technology will have impacts on more than one other component of the ecosystem.

There is considerable evidence that high levels of social capital may well be a prerequisite for the process of reconciliation between the ecological, social, and economic imperatives (Putnam, Leonardi, and Nanetti 1993; World Bank 2003). Sustainable development will likely require modification of governance structures, cultures, processes, and tools, as it is becoming increasingly clear that the task of postmodern governments now extends from regulating the present to creating the enabling conditions for the future (Emery and Trist 1972). If this is indeed true, it is critical that governments determine at what levels, if any, they can intervene to enhance social capital development. A key feature of social capital for institutions might lie in their capacity to restore agency and trust to citizens concerning formal structures and processes (Dobell 1995). Through the development of transnational social movements, partly enabled through the emergence of information communications technologies, networks are now proliferating in all areas of social and economic life (Wellman 1999), offering new ways of working together and new methods of logic. Networks are an important way to build empowerment, trust, cooperation, and collective norms. They are also critical to transferring and holding knowledge in both the informal and formal sectors, often leading to a reconciliation of previously competing information, interests, and agendas. They can also contribute to more rapid knowledge diffusion and are a means by which shared futures are developed, built, and enacted. By developing a better understanding of the precise mechanisms and properties through which networks contribute to

Figure 1.6

Research model

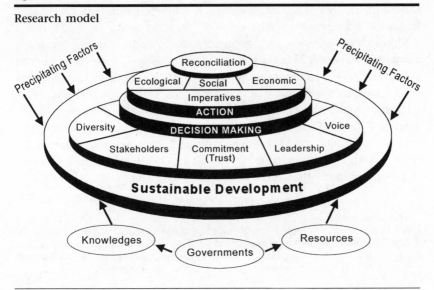

increased social capital, communities may develop greater capacity to determine the best use of resources to achieve that end. It is my assumption that in some cases, unless they are strategic in their interventions, governments can actually destroy existing social capital, particularly at the community level and particularly with "emerging" network associations. As well, networks, given the above model, must have a degree of autonomy and empowerment at the bonding level for long-term sustainability, and it may well be that government interventions are effective only at the bridging and linking levels.

Gray (1999) summarizes four indicators of social capital formation important for collaboration: (1) an increase in the number of ties among stakeholders, (2) bounded solidarity among similar stakeholders, (3) enforceable trust, and (4) development of intra- and inter-group norms to regulate stakeholder interaction. The particular aspects of network formation that our research will be examining through the model shown in Figure 1.6, are diversity, stakeholder engagement, commitment, leadership, and voice in terms of their relationship to engagement, trust, cooperation, collective norms, knowledge diffusion, and shared futures. Also important is what role these attributes play in facilitating access to greater resources, at both the vertical and horizontal levels, and the relevance of weak versus strong ties through diversity. Granovetter (1973) has demonstrated that weak ties can be more effective because they facilitate access to a wider and more heterogeneous set of connections through bridging, whereas bonding ties link more or less homogeneous members. Diversity, therefore, may be the critical network feature that allows a local network to access different and critical capitals – human and financial.

Although this research focuses on network formation, sustainable development is the outer boundary and the ultimate goal. That is, remaining within our ecological limits is the ultimate goal of human societies everywhere, since we are equally bound by place, scale, time, and diversity, as are natural systems. And consensus about the meaning and nature of these limits will be achieved only through "the patient construction of communities of belief that provide legitimacy through inclusion rather than exclusion, through participation rather than mystification, and through transparency rather than black boxing" (Jasanoff and Wynne 1998, 77).

Acknowledgments
Funds in support of this project were provided by SSHRC, Ottawa, and the Office of Research, Royal Roads University. I am indebted to Dr. Mary Bernard for her support and to my research assistant, Leanna Braid, for her research and collaboration. As always, I am privileged to work with so many fine younger scholars and colleagues.

References
Agnes, M., ed. 1999. *Webster's New World College Dictionary*, 4th ed. New York: Macmillan.
Bohm, D., and L. Nichol. 1996. *On Dialogue*. London: Routledge Press.
Bourdieu, P. 1985. "The Forms of Capital." In J.G. Richardson, ed., *Handbook of Theory of Research for the Sociology of Education*. New York: Greenwood Press.
Canada, Natural Resources Canada. 2002. *Canada's Natural Resource Sectors and Allied Industries: Background on Performance and Potential*. Ottawa: Government of Canada.
Canadian Institutes of Health Research. 2003. "Canadian Suicide Experts Focus on Finding Solutions." Press Release, Montreal, 9 February.
Canadian Policy Research Networks. 2003. *A Citizen's Dialogue on Canada's Future*. Ottawa: Canadian Policy Research Networks.
Castells, M. 1996. *The Information Age, Volume 1: The Rise of the Network Society*. Oxford: Basil Blackwell.
Coleman, J. 1988. "Social Capital in the Creation of Human Capital." *American Journal of Sociology* 94: S95-S120.
Dale, A. 2001. *At the Edge: Sustainable Development in the 21st Century*. Vancouver: UBC Press.
Dale, A., and T. Naylor. In press. "Dialogue and Public Space: An Exploration of Radio and Information Communication Technologies." *Journal of Political Science*.
Dale, A., J.B. Robinson, and C. Massey, eds. 1995. *Reconciling Human Welfare and Ecological Carrying Capacity*. Vancouver: Sustainable Development Research Institute.
Dobell, R. 1995. "The 'Dance of the Deficit' and the Real World of Wealth: Re-Thinking Economic Management for Social Purpose." Paper prepared for the National Forum on Family Security, March.
e-Dialogues. 2002a. "Spirituality and Sustainable Development: Who Cares?" Online at <http://www.e-dialogues.ca>, 17, 19, 21 June 2002.
–. 2002b. "Sustainable Communities in Canada: Does One Exist?" Online at <http://www.e-dialogues.ca>, 2-4 December 2002.
Ehrlich, P.R. 1982. "Human Carrying Capacity, Extinctions and Nature Reserves." *BioScience* 32(5): 331.
Emery, F., and M. Emery. 1976. *A Choice of Futures: To Enlighten or Inform*. Leiden, The Netherlands: Martinus Nijhoff.

Emery, F.E., and E.L. Trist. 1972. *Towards a Social Ecology: Contextual Appreciation of the Future in the Present.* London: Plenum Press.

Etzioni, A. 1996. "A Moderate Communitarian Proposal." *Political Theory* 24(2): 155-71.

–. 1997. *The New Golden Rule: Community and Morality in a Democratic Society.* New York: Basic Books.

–. 2000a. "Creating Good Communities and Good Societies." *Contemporary Sociology* 29(1): 188-95.

–. 2000b. "Moral Dialogues in Public Debates." *The Public Perspective* 11(2): 27-30.

Folke, C., L. Pritchard Jr., F. Berkes, J. Colding, and U. Svedin. 1998. "The Problem of Fit between Ecosystems and Institutions." IHDP Working Paper, Rep. No. 2, International Human Dimensions Programme on Global Environmental Change.

Frankel, V. 1959. *Man's Search for Meaning.* New York: Washington Square Press.

Fukuyama, F. 1995. *Trust: The Social Virtues and the Creation of Prosperity.* London: Penguin Press.

Funtowicz, S., and J. Ravetz. 1993. "Science for the Post Normal Age." *Futures* 25(7): 739-55.

–. 1994. "Emergent Complex Systems." *Futures* 26(6): 568-82.

Granovetter, M. 1973. "The Strength of Weak Ties." *American Journal of Sociology* 78(6): 1360-80.

Gray, B. 1999. "Theoretical Perspectives on Collaboration over the Last Decade: Looking Back and Looking Forward." Paper presented at the Collaboration Research Workshop, Collaboration Research Group, May, University of Technology, Sydney.

Grootaert, C. 1998. *Social Capital: The Missing Link?* Social Capital Initiative Working Paper No. 3. Washington, DC: World Bank.

The Guardian. 2002. "Ecological Decline 'Far Worse' Than Official Estimates: Leaked Paper – OECD's Grim Warning on Climate Change" (26 August). <http://www.guardian.co.uk/worldsummit2002/story/0,12264,780730,00.html> (accessed 20 September 2003).

Gunderson, L., C.S. Holling, and S.S. Light. 1995. *Barriers and Bridges to the Renewal of Ecosystems and Institutions.* New York: Columbia University Press.

Hill, S.B. 1980. "Observing Stressed and Unstressed Ecosystems and Human Systems: Means for Recovery and Identification." In *Absolute Values and the Search for the Peace of Mankind.* Vol. 2. *Proceedings of the Ninth International Conference on the Unity of the Sciences,* 22-30 November, Miami Beach, Florida.

Holling, C.S. 1986. "Resilience of Ecosystems: Local Surprise and Global Change." In W.C. Clark and R.E. Munn, eds., *Sustainable Development of the Biosphere.* Cambridge, UK: Cambridge University Press.

–. 1994. "Simplifying the Complex: The New Paradigms of Ecological Function and Structures." *Futures* 26(6): 598-609.

Homer-Dixon, T. 2001. *Environment, Scarcity and Violence.* Princeton, NJ: Princeton University Press.

Intergovernmental Panel on Climate Change (IPCC). 2003. "Climate Change and Biodiversity." IPCC Technical Paper No. 5 (April 2002). <http://www.ipcc.ch/pub/tpbiodiv.pdf> (20 September 2003).

Jasanoff, S., and B. Wynne. 1998. "Science and Decisionmaking." In S. Rayner and E. Malone, eds., *Human Choice and Climate Change.* Vol. 1. Columbus, OH: Battelle Press.

Leadbeater, C. 1999. *Living on Thin Air: The New Economy.* Harmondsworth: Penguin Books

Lesser, E., and L. Prusak. 2000. "Communities of Practice, Social Capital and Organizational Knowledge." In E. Lesser, M. Fonaine, and J. Slusher, eds., *Knowledge and Communities.* Boston: Butterworth Heinemann.

Lewis, B. 1994. *Problem Analysis: The Social Dimension of Ecosystem Management.* Social and Economic Dimensions of Ecosystem Management Project, USDA Forest Service, North Central Forest Experiment Station.

Mayhew, L.H., ed. 1982. *Talcott Parsons on Institutions and Social Evolution.* Chicago: University of Chicago Press.

Norgaard, R.B. 1994. *Development Betrayed: The End of Progress and a Co-Evolutionary Revisioning of the Future.* London: Routledge.

Onyx, J., and P. Bullen. 2000. "Measuring Social Capital in Five Communities." *Journal of Applied Behavioral Science* 36(1): 23-42.

Onyx, J., and R. Leonard. 2000. *Rural Renewal and Social Capital: The Case of Sweden and Australia*. Working Paper Series No. 46. Sidney Centre for Australian Community Organisations and Management.

Ornstein, R., and P. Ehrlich. 1989. *New World, New Mind: Moving Toward Conscious Evolution*. New York: Doubleday.

Portes, A. 1998. "Social Capital: Its Origins and Applications in Modern Sociology." *Annual Review of Sociology* 24(1): 1-24.

Putnam, R. 1993. *Making Democracy Work: Civic Traditions in Modern Italy*. Princeton, NJ: Princeton University Press.

–. 2001. "Social Capital Measurement and Consequences." *Isuma* 2(1): 41-52.

Putnam, R., R. Leonardi, and R. Nanetti. 1993. *Making Democracy Work: Civic Traditions in Modern Italy*. Princeton, NJ: Princeton University Press.

Rees, W.E. 1996. "Revisiting Carrying Capacity: Area-Based Indicators of Sustainability." *Population and Environment: A Journal of Interdisciplinary Studies* 17(3): 195-201.

Robinson, J.B. Forthcoming. 2004. "Squaring the Circle? Some Thoughts on the Idea of Sustainable Development." *Ecological Economics* 48: 369-84.

Robinson, J.B., and J. Tinker. 1997. "Reconciling Ecological, Economic and Social Imperatives: A New Conceptual Framework." In T. Schrecker, ed., *Surviving Globalism: Social and Environmental Dimensions*. London: Macmillan.

Sheldon, C.G., J.E. Strongman, and M. Weber-Fahr. 2002. "It's Not Over When It's Over: Mine Closure around the World." Washington, DC: World Bank's Mining Department, 2002. <http://www.natural-resources.org/minerals/CD/docs/twb/mine_closure.pdf> (19 September 2003).

Tansey, J., J. Carmichael, R. VanWynsberghe, and J. Robinson. 2001. *The Future Is Not What It Used To Be: Participatory Integrated Assessment in the Georgia Basin*. Submitted to Global Environmental Change.

Trist, E.L. 1983. "Referent Organizations and the Development of Inter-Organizational Domains." *Human Relations* 36(3): 269-84.

United Nations Environment Programme. 2000. *Global Environment Outlook*. UNEP: Earthscan.

Veiga, M.M., M. Scoble, and M.L. McAllister. 2001. *Mining with Communities*. Natural Resources Forum 25: 191-202.

Wellman, B., ed. 1999. *Networks in the Global Village: Life in Contemporary Communities*. Boulder, CO: Westview.

White, R.P., and W. Vanasselt. 2003. "Still and Silent Ecosystems: Declining Grassland Biodiversity." In *Pilot Analysis of Global Ecosystems: Grassland Ecosystems*. <http://earthtrends. wri.org/> (20 September 2003).

Williamson, G.S., and I.H. Pearse. 1980. *Science, Synthesis and Sanity: An Inquiry into the Nature of Living*. Edinburgh: Scottish Academic Press.

Woolcock, M. 2000. "Why Should We Care about Social Capital?" *Canberra Bulletin of Public Administration* 98: 17-19.

World Bank. 2003. "Social Capital for Development." <http://www.worldbank.org/poverty/ scapital/index.htm> (19 September 2003).

Worldwatch Institute. 2003. *Vital Signs 2000: The Environmental Trends That Are Shaping Our Future*. New York: W.W. Norton.

Part 2
Connections

2
Ecological and Social Systems: Essential System Conditions
Vivienne Wilson

As a child, I was fuelled by the intricate imaginings of science-fiction writers such as Isaac Asimov. I believed that the destiny of humankind was to make good a promise to the world, the universe, to future observers of planet Earth, to strive for excellence in the efficiency and technology of our society. Two decades later, I see that we have worked on that promise at great cost to the ecosystems in which we live – systems far more intricate and efficient than any human imaginings. For this chapter I have been asked to step back from such intricacies and describe the essential elements that bind together the function of ecosystems and the function of social systems. This step back requires distinguishing not only the trees from the wood and the forest from the trees, but also the world from the forest. Luckily, the frame of reference for understanding these systems is the same – our experience of acting as part of the Earth's ecosystems.

Defining the Systems

It is appropriate that this chapter is placed in the "Connections" section of this book, given the definition of ecological and social systems that I would like to use. All environmental sciences involve an interdisciplinary study of connections and interactions that occur between living organisms and their environment. Within this broad framework, ecology can be defined as a bioscience that "measures and analyzes the flows of energy, material and information between organisms and their ecosystems" (Miller and Rees 2000, 7). Long-time criticisms of ecology as a science have included the difficulties in interpreting collected data on these energy, material, and information flows in terms of ecosystem dynamics (a situation that has been recognized and partially rectified), as well as ecologists' tendency to focus almost exclusively on other species. This has been called a "perceptual impediment" – a dualism that describes a disjunct between humans and the rest of nature (ibid., 6). Implicit in the use of the word "organism" in the definition I use above is the understanding that a human is not an organism

for the purposes of ecological study. The irony here is the paradox identified by Schrödinger and his cat – that the act of observing a system causes
an intrinsic change. Schrödinger would doubtless be puzzled that most ecological studies carried out by humans do not recognize humans as part of
the system, nor do they consider the impact of measurement by humans on
the system. That the system response may be governed by the method or
character of human observation is not often taken into account, and when
it is, there are few ways to analyze the impact. Notwithstanding this failure
to recognize and integrate the activities of humans as a connected species
and component of a web of ecological interactions, the essential system
dynamics described by ecological studies give us a way to understand the
root of social system conditions.

The definition of "social system" is somewhat more involved. Jennie
Sparkes goes into more detail in her chapter in this book, where she refers
to a model of the human ecosystem developed by Machlis, Force, and Burch
(1997). The human ecosystem is supplied by and functions using three types
of critical resources: natural resources (the product of natural ecosystems),
socioeconomic resources (the product of human labour and economy), and
cultural resources. The human social system is the mechanism by which
these three resource types are distributed. It can be broken down into three
subsystems: social institutions, social cycles, and social order (ibid.). These
subsystems essentially describe mechanisms by which humans structure and
perpetuate the social system. Almost all organisms with some form of social
structure can be described using these subsystems; the predominance of
each will change depending on the intricacy of social structure. Already it is
possible to see the links between ecological and social systems by recognizing that the way we identify and categorize levels of interaction is the same
in both kinds of systems.

The way we measure how well our ecological and social systems are functioning is the same way we measure how well our economic system is functioning – by calculating the amount of capital generated and flowing
through the system. Economists see that capital is wealth used to sustain
and generate more wealth (Miller 2002). Natural capital is maintained and
generated by the environment and ecosystems within it. Energy from the
sun can be regarded as "solar capital," and resources such as air, water, soil,
wildlife, minerals, and recycling systems such as purification and pest control can be considered natural capital. Social capital is generated by social
systems and can be defined as "networks, norms and trust, and the way
these allow agents and institutions to be more effective in achieving common objectives" (Schuller 2000, 2). The theme running through all discourses on the topic of social capital is that it is based on relationships, and
is a property of groups rather than individuals. It is at this point that I
worry about using economic nomenclature to describe the value of eco-

logical and social systems. Our economic and social system appears to confuse capital with income – it has created a pricing system that effectively discounts or ignores the amount of future capital and is quickly depleting stored natural capital without considering that supplies are finite. The phrase so often accompanying income-generating advertisements – "For a limited time" – is perhaps more accurate than we think; that is, consumers' desire for hamburgers or laundry soap will long outlast the availability of the commodity.

How then can we reconcile the essential system conditions for ecological and social systems? In her book *At The Edge: Sustainable Development in the 21st Century* (2001), Ann Dale lists principles for human decision making that have been derived from ecological systems. These principles are a distillation of information from a series of e-dialogues between 1996 and 1998 and include the following concepts: cyclical processes; diversity; self-organizing, holartic systems; enlarged decision-making contexts; equity; information; feedback loops; integrity; humility; limits; multiple perspectives; resilience; scale; systems approach; and values. In this chapter I consider the information at a lower magnification level and look for the essential concepts to which these principles belong.

The challenge lies in our struggle to reconcile the taxonomy used to describe the two systems. This chapter makes a step toward a reconciliation by linking the essential system conditions described for ecology to the conditions required for our social system, especially the underlying structure required to support the growth of social capital. Three key areas, I believe, describe essential conditions for ecological and social systems:

- the physics of the laws of thermodynamics
- the nature of the closed-loop system inherent in being part of the Earth's ecosystem
- the variable levels of complexity and diversity that characterize healthy ecological and social systems.

Below, I provide an example of ecological principles being used in a way that intrinsically links the processes of ecological and social consensus and literacy, and demonstrates the synergy created by knitting these processes together.

An Energetic Start
Three laws of thermodynamics govern all ecological systems:

1 The first law of thermodynamics states that energy cannot be created or destroyed. Energy can be converted in form, but the quantity of energy is conserved.

2 The second law of thermodynamics states that in all processes, some of the energy involved degrades to a quality where it cannot do further work. There is a net decrease in the amount of usable energy.

3 The third law of thermodynamics states that all processes tend to slow down as they reach a level of thermodynamic equilibrium, which makes it difficult to reach an equilibrium level in anything but theory.

How do these laws affect the processes of ecological systems? Energy flow through ecological systems is governed by the first law; energy may change in form as it passes through the various stages of a food chain or chemical reaction, but no more energy can be derived in this flow than was originally contributed by the sun, or the bonds in inorganic chemicals. No matter how efficient human technology may become, we cannot get something for nothing in terms of energy quantity. This is a concept that has proven misleading in public discussions about technologies such as cold fusion. We can make energy transformations as efficient as possible, but we are limited by the tenets of the first law.

The second law of thermodynamics is key to the way energy passes through ecological systems and explains the pyramidal form of energy flow diagrams. In any energy conversion, the end result is less usable-energy than we started with. Some of the energy in the conversion will be irreversibly converted to heat, or to another form that is unavailable for producing work (Krippendorf 1986). This is known as thermodynamic entropy. If energy is unavailable for producing work, it is said to be of low quality (ibid.). The construction of energy-flow pyramids in ecological studies has shown that the efficiency of energy flow from one level to the next varies from 5 to 20 percent, with 10 percent being the most common (Miller 2002). That means that in a pyramid with a 10 percent efficiency, 90 percent of the energy is lost in the transition (mostly as heat) between one level and another, for example from phytoplankton to zooplankton, and this loss is realized at each pyramid level until the top carnivore level is reached. It is not possible to recycle or reuse high-quality energy to perform work. Trying to upgrade low-quality heat energy to, for example, high-quality chemical energy requires a massive input of some other high-quality energy form and ends up with a net energy deficit. The irreversibility of the direction of energy flow is key to understanding the mechanism and components of every ecological system on Earth.

The third law of thermodynamics is sometimes called the asymptotic law for the way in which its effects can be graphically presented (a slow approach but an infinite time to reach a zero or equilibrium level). Processes occur more slowly as they reach a thermodynamic equilibrium. In relation to the infinitesimal speed with which solar and planetary processes occur (on a human time scale), the processes occurring within organization of living organisms occur at a powerful and fast rate. Krippendorf (1986) comments that the type of fast processes typical of living organisms, and even more so of the technology efficiency for which humans strive, must occur at levels far from thermodynamic equilibrium. Humans will therefore always foster a fast throughput of energy in technological systems because of the nature of our position at the top of many energy flow pyramids, and our ability to utilize energy from multiple sources.

How do the laws of thermodynamics impact social systems? At the most basic level it could be said that economic and social systems are necessarily harnessed to ecological processes because they are part of the world ecosystem, and therefore the impact of laws at the ecological level impact social systems. I believe that the analogy reaches farther.

The concept and use of language used to describe the laws of thermodynamics applies also to concepts used in considering the sustainability of social systems. The idea of entropy and of low-quality energy dispersion is particularly abstract, and difficult to present. And yet social and ecological scientists consider it intuitively when they refer to states such as disorder, waste, and loss of time or information. In a recent e-dialogue facilitated by Ann Dale of Royal Roads University, entitled "Sustainable Communities in Canada: Does One Exist?" Liette Vasseur (2003) commented that "waste is an inherent part of any system ... entropy." In the same e-dialogue Nik Luka commented, "I'd like to start by saying that 'sustainability' should be understood as a state that cannot really ever be achieved; we can only approach it. It's a kind of meta-goal, if you like, not unlike the graph of a function that approaches zero, but never actually touches the axis. So while we can get close, we'll never actually achieve this state of being. This is especially true for settlement patterns, since strictly speaking, towns and cities are not sustainable – having people living at such high concentrations is far more than any local ecosystem can handle." Nik Luka (2003) has identified one of the areas in which social systems obey the third law of thermodynamics. According to the second and third laws, we could predict that it will be possible for communities to become sustainable, but the rate at which it happens will slow the nearer a community gets to sustainable state, and complete sustainability will never be reached because of the law of entropic energy conversion.

I have given a lot of consideration to whether the interconnection between economic, social, and ecological capitals obeys the first and second laws of thermodynamics. The quantity of any of these capitals is bound by the idea that there is a fixed amount of ecological capital on Earth, the form of which can be "renewably" changed by the one-way flow of energy from the sun. The matter on Earth that can be changed in this manner must be cycled through energy states. Apart from the occasional asteroid strike, we do not receive continual input of matter from space. Does a change in the quantity of capital in one area cause a change in the quantities of the two others? A decrease in ecological capital could increase economic capital and have a negative or positive effect on social capital depending on the nature of the change. But ecosystems are *not* self-contained, self-sustaining systems, nor do they have distinct boundaries. The same can be said for social and economic systems. Judging patterns of change between the three capital types requires a delineation of the boundaries on these systems, even before we are able to trace the flow of change within the three types of capital. It also seems that social capital has a synergistic quality to it – the work of 1 + 1 + 1 = 3. A small social capital change can have momentous results and catalyze further change. If we consider how the synergistic quality of social capital is supported, we can argue that bringing together a group of individuals and converting their individual energy and time to form a collective resource necessarily entails a considerable loss of individual energy (Onyx 2003). This change from individual to group energy appears to obey the laws of thermodynamics in terms of energy conversion and state.

However, the one point that is obvious from examining the laws of thermodynamics is that ignorance of how the rules of energy flow in ecological systems work has led to the malaise of undervaluing ecological capital. It is not well understood that energy conversion of any sort results in an entropic lowering of energy quality overall, nor that no amount of technological advance can circumvent this irreversible physical change. James Karr (2000, 215) comments that "society ... has chronically undervalued biological components. We have behaved as if we could repair or replace any lost or broken parts of living systems ... we are rapidly converting the world to corn, cows, cars, cancer, carbon dioxide and computers." In this respect I would argue that changes in social capital are and will be founded on fundamentally unsustainable concepts until the laws of energy conversion are understood and taken into account in designing how humans interact within the world ecosystem.

Closing the Loop

Allied to the concepts of the laws of thermodynamics is the nature of the closed loop system characteristic of every ecological system on Earth – closed loop not only because of the cycling of energy within the system but because sustaining life on Earth requires cycling of resources at all levels of organization. At the most basic level, three interconnected factors provide the supporting structure for closed loops in ecosystem function:

- the renewable flow of energy from the sun (considered renewable on the human time scale though it is in fact a finite and limited process)
- the cycling of matter (as mentioned above, there is little input of new matter from space and therefore all accessible matter is present already)

- the force of gravity, which retains matter on the surface of Earth and causes downward movement of molecules in ecological cycles.

The process of boiling down information winnowed from ecological studies to these three factors has mainly been one of observing ecological systems of great diversity and ecosystems under stress. In the same way that we can cross-reference literature to work down to common themes, we can cross-reference between ecological and social systems to find the analogues of these factors.

Responses within an ecological system to intensifying stress or interruption of the influence of these basic factors include reaching a state of increased species mortality, rates of community biomass export and consumption that exceed net production, and replacement of sensitive species with tolerant ones (Freedman 1989). Chronically stressed ecosystems reach a relatively stable state of reduced species and structural complexity, and small rates of biomass production, productivity, decomposition, and nutrient cycling (Freedman 1992). We can see these states in ecosystems today as they respond to the chronic stress of higher human population numbers than can be sustainably supported. This population stress has been described by the concept of carrying capacity, first introduced by Garrett Hardin in 1968. Carrying capacity is defined as "the maximum population of a given species that can be supported indefinitely in a habitat without destroying that habitat" (Hardin 2002, 252). The conventional view of human carrying capacity is that it is made ever expandable by virtue of humans' ability to eliminate competing species, create greater efficiency through the use of technology, and move scarce resources to areas of need (Wollard and Rees 1999). Hardin's view of carrying capacity is that humans' economic and social systems are an intrinsic component of the Earth's ecosystem and therefore there are real ecological limits. The ultimate limits are met when the three essential factors listed above can no longer provide the structure required to support any ecosystems.

Accountability for the function of ecological and social systems rests in meeting a basic set of factors that describe a closed-loop process. How do we recognize closed-loop factors in social systems? Von Glaserfeld (2003) defines closed loop systems as "the circular arrangement of feedback mechanisms that maintain a given value within certain limits. They work toward an invariant, but the invariant is achieved not by a steady resistance, the way a rock stands unmoved in the wind, but by compensation over time."

For social systems, the essential factors for closing the loop are complex - it is difficult to define them in terms of single "invariants" because they reside in the quality of relationships between people. The social system is made up of three subsystems (Machlis, Force, and Dalton 1995), described in more detail in Jennie Sparkes's chapter in this book: (1) a set of social institutions that are collective solutions to universal social challenges or needs, (2) a series of social cycles that are temporal patterns for allocating human activity, and (3) social order, a set of cultural patterns for organizing interaction among people and groups. These subsystems act as the essential factors for maintenance of the social system. Social institutions act as a renewable source of energy for the building of social capital. Social cycles allocate human activity as the activity of matter is governed by ecological cycles. And the social order defines the direction of processes occurring in social cycles – it is the grounding and constant directional pattern for organizing human interaction.

The three subsystems of the social system can be regarded as a closed loop in that they work toward the building of social capital through a series of compensatory feedback mechanisms. Social systems must have feedback loops to act as a monitoring and judging process. As Dale (2001) quotes from Brown in *At the Edge,* "since complex systems have both changing and largely unknown natural boundaries, it is conceivable that human activity systems could badly misjudge which components and parameters to consider in their decision-making process." Inconsistencies and biases – based on the scope of the relatively limited information social systems can incorporate into decision making – can be tracked in a feedback model, and the direction of social institutions and social cycles adjusted accordingly.

Complexity and Diversity
An ecological system functioning under the three integral closed-loop factors described in the previous section is said to display ecological integrity. The indicators of ecological integrity, as outlined by Freedman (1989), are:

- resistance and resilience toward stress
- high levels of biodiversity
- structural and functional complexity
- large species and higher-order predators present
- controlled nutrient cycling with no leakage of natural capital from the system
- an intrinsic capability of maintaining its own ecological values.

Measures of ecological integrity must take place at the metabolic, organismal, population, community, and landscape levels, and must consider complexes of these levels. Half of these ecological integrity indicators make reference to the biodiversity and complexity of species and environmental complexes within the ecosystem. Lister (in Dale 2001, 123-24) comments that "[diversity] is an essential feature of all self-organizing systems, whether socioeconomic, political, or ecological. To homogenize diversity and foster uniformity is to rob any complex system of future evolution."

The processes of system evolution and development of complexity and diversity are intrinsically linked. Krippendorf (1986) notes that, on a systems level, "blind variation and selective retention tend to produce increases in both the structural and functional complexity of evolving systems." Why is this the case? Ashby's law of requisite variety states that in order for a control system to achieve complete control, the variety of actions it should be able to perform must be at least as great as the variety of environmental perturbations that need to be compensated. This is true of any control system; in ecosystems, it is manifested as an increase in the complexity and diversity of component organisms. Although there will always be more variety in the environment as a whole, the more complex and diverse the ecosystem, the more likely it is that it will be able to control its immediate environment. To consider a social system example, as individuals and organizations tend to gather more knowledge and more resources, increasing the range of actions they can take, they become more able to cope with the widest possible range of problems appearing in their environment. As individuals and organizations become more knowledgeable and resourceful, other individuals and organizations will have to become more knowledgeable and resourceful in order to respond to the challenge. The result is an accelerating race toward more knowledge and more creative and efficient tools, creating the "information explosion" we are currently living in.

Not only do ecosystems contain many niches that will eventually be filled by new species but there is a self-reinforcing tendency to create new niches (Wilson 1994). A niche is defined as a range of conditions and resource qualities in which an individual or species can survive (Ricklefs 2001). A new species occupying a formerly empty niche creates a set of new niches just because of its presence – new niches providing a different set of resources and conditions. This self-reinforcing niche formation results in a cascade of biodiversity in any ecological system and also in any social system.

In any ecosystem there will be a few species that are abundant and many that are rare. Membership in local communities within that ecosystem is restricted to species that can coexist in the same habitat (ibid.). The number of member species in a community reflects the variety and abundance of available resources and the influence of competing predators and disease. In social systems there is also a range of conditions and resource qualities that effectively define niches for social capital-building opportunities. Social capital can be defined in terms of networks, norms, and trust, and the way these allow agents and institutions to be more effective in achieving common objectives (Schuller 2000). The most common measures of social capital look at participation in various forms of civic engagement, such as membership of voluntary associations, churches, or political parties, or at levels of expressed trust in other people (Dale 2001). These categories of participation could also be expressed as niches occupied by social groups working with many different types of resources. The concept of niches can be turned around to provide information about the structural organization of an ecosystem or social system – such as how many social groups are supported in the various types of civic engagement for a particular community or region.

Ecologically, as the size of a regional area increases, species are added to local communities, though there tends to be greater turnover of species in particular niches (Ricklefs 2001). This means that membership in a local community becomes more difficult as the total number of species increases. Invasion of particular niche types in a community becomes more likely as the total number of species in a region increases. In social systems, the development of community-level social capital may be more difficult as the number of people, groups, and organizations in an area increases, but it could also be argued that the number of people who can take advantage of a specific opportunity (or niche) also increases. Where does the balance lie? A resolution of this problem may lie in identifying small community areas with a specific and immediate interest (a niche). This is outlined in the next section.

Finally, species diversity in ecological systems has an intrinsic value in stabilizing ecosystem function. So a diverse system is better able to maintain high productivity in the face of environmental variation – the concept described by the law of requisite variety. An essential system requirement for social systems would therefore appear to be the maintenance of diversity and variety in the opportunities and people who are able to fill them. This not only supports the work of all social capital-building exercises but insulates the system against sudden change that may alter or remove opportunities. Lister (in Dale 2001) comments that dynamic, self-organizing, holartic systems "are diverse and flexible, and, therefore, resilient; that is, they actively respond to learned experience." The resilience of social systems is going to be tested as we face increased stress from environmental degradation and scarcity of resources.

An Example that Reinforces the Connection between Ecological and Social Systems

One of the difficulties in examining essential system conditions for ecological and social systems is that there are relatively few examples that address both at the same time in a manner that has been shown to be effective in a range of situations.

One example that does include evidence of meeting all three essential system conditions described in this chapter is the Municipal Fresh Water Planning Process (MFWPP) put in place to address the mandate of achieving collaborative and community stewardship of riparian areas and wetlands.[1] The core of the MFWPP is the use of the proper functioning condition

(PFC) assessment – an assessment of the health and function of riparian and wetland areas that (a) temporarily sets aside values and concentrates on the function of the ecosystem as a whole and (b) uses a multidisciplinary team to carry out the assessment (Malmkvist 2002). The approach of PFC is to determine the current ability of a system to withstand stress events, and it can then be used to target and prescribe a set of restoration measures to return function to the ecosystem. With the return of that function come many of the values traditionally appreciated by communities, such as fish habitat, and recreational and aesthetic areas.

A letter from the United States Department of Interior Bureau of Land Management and United States Department of Agriculture Forest Service in 1996 stated that "[restoration] will not happen by regulation, changes in the law, more money, or any of the normal bureaucratic approaches. It will only occur through the integration of ecological, economic, and social factors, and participation of affected interests." In other words, it was necessary to create an effective and resourceful social network that would be interested in restoring riparian areas, and would oversee their maintenance and pass the word on. This network currently comprise two groups:

- a national riparian service team (NRST) and state training cadres in the US, and a cross-border team in Canada
- an assessment and restoration coordination network from government, university, industry, conservation, and community organizations.

The emphasis of the NRST and training teams in Canada is on education of community groups with a direct interest in the health of a riparian ecosystem, and collaboration with financial and support partners to see the restoration work implemented in a planned and system-oriented manner. A planned series of educational seminars and field workshops have been designed to provide a common language of riparian restoration for all community participants and the restoration coordination network. The presentation of these seminars and workshops is itself a cooperative effort, with the NRST and Canadian teams providing time and knowledge resources, and the community providing a venue and support.

The MWFPP, PFC assessment, and the educational infrastructure that supports them are good examples of a closed-loop process that encourages input from a diverse range of social groups. The MWFPP consists of five steps: (1) development of a strategic management plan, (2) assessment of ecosystem health (function), (3) development of prescriptions, (4) development of treatments, and, (5) an ongoing and organized auditing and monitoring process that reiterates steps 2, 3, and 4 (a feedback loop) to ensure the prescriptions, diagnoses, and treatments were correct in identifying the problems and effective in restoring ecological function (Malmkvist 2002).

To compare with the three essential system conditions identified in this chapter, the focus of the MFWPP is on the function of ecosystems and the cycling of materials in them. The structure of the MFWPP is a closed-loop system and requires the diversity of a multidisciplinary assessment team. Most importantly, it brings together a diverse and complex collaboration of community partners to complete the restoration work. As riparian areas and wetlands are among the first landscape features to reflect impact from management activities and urbanization, their condition can be a good measure of the strength of social capital operating within communities. Karr (2000, 214) comments that "using the condition of living systems as a guide – something to steady or direct what we do – is vital when it comes to protecting the biosphere." The proper functioning condition assessment recognizes that the values society wants and needs can be supplied sustainably only by systems in a "proper" or ecologically functioning system.

Reinforcing Ecological and Social System Function
The reality is that human population and current economic and social systems are no longer supported by the land they occupy. The mechanism of population control is going to involve (and already does involve in many regions) food shortages, poverty, disease, and social and political strife (Ricklefs 2001). These are symptomatic of ecological and social systems that are not functioning and are not in balance.

In this chapter I have identified and described three essential system conditions for the health and longevity of both ecological and social systems:

1 the dynamics of energy conversion and entropy embodied in the laws of thermodynamics;
2 the nature of the closed-loop system that describes the flow of energy and resources within any system on Earth;
3 the dynamics of species diversity and complexity that determine the flexibility and resilience of an ecological or social system.

How can these essential system conditions be achieved and supported? The two main themes that appear when attempting to answer this question are those of social consensus building through education and environmental literacy (Dale 2001; Freedman 1989), and the reinforcement of feedback loops by encouraging research and monitoring programs in ecological and social systems.

Environmental literacy has a pervasive influence on public attitudes toward ecosystem function. It influences aspects of social interaction at every level, from lifestyle choices to implementation of appropriate social and environmental programs by decision makers. Providing and supporting access to research and monitoring programs is one of the major ways to improve environmental literacy levels in social systems.

Environmental monitoring measures change in dynamic systems and gives us some mechanism to assess the success or failure of restoration efforts. Brown et al. (2000, 388) comment that "ecosystems comprise thousands of species interacting in dynamic relationships ... yet [they] have structure, pattern and predictability despite the radically contingent forces that have created them." Although the methods by which social systems can be monitored are fewer in number and more difficult to achieve meaningful answers in (and that is really saying something, given the frequent quality issues surrounding environmental monitoring), they may allow some degree of comfort to people involved in significant social system change. Increasing comfort level can be helpful in working toward consensus – a state that is usually tacit in ecosystems (Ricklefs 2001) – but that will require education in the ecological principles that form the foundation of self-sustaining social systems.

I recently read a book by Thomas Davis (2000) that describes how the Menominee Indian Tribe of Wisconsin has honoured its tribal teachings in the way it has preserved and used forest land on its reservation, and how it has continued the education process by setting up the Sustainable Development Institute, which many scholars and environmentalists visit. The basic message of the Menominee is described as this: "If humankind decides to take a long-range view towards managing earth's resources, then neither scientific, technological nor economic development has to stop. Short-term sacrifices might be necessary, but in the long term human ingenuity combined with stewardship can avoid the worst pitfalls" (ibid., 255). Humans need to evolve and maintain a set of institutions, grounded by the essential conditions of social and ecological systems, that are able to adapt over time, and that ensure that some rules of behaviour are maintained. A small part of me hopes that Isaac Asimov's far-sighted dreams were not in vain.

Acknowledgments
My thanks to Dr. Jenny Onyx, Neil Reimer, and Lehna Malmkvist for their helpful comments on this chapter.

Note
1 This mandate was developed by the United States Department of Interior Bureau of Land Management (USDI BLM) and United States Department of Agriculture Forest Service (USDA FS) in conjunction with the USDA Natural Resources Conservation Service for rural areas (USDI/USDA letter, 1996; USDI/BLM manual 1737-15, 1998), and has been modified and updated to address the specific issues of urban areas by Aqua-Tex Scientific Consulting in British Columbia, Canada (Lucey et al. 2001; Edmonds 2002; Malmkvist 2002).

46 *Vivienne Wilson*

References

Brown, D.A., J.P. Manno, L. Westra, D. Pimentel, and P. Crabbé. 2000. "Implementing Global Ecological Integrity: A Synthesis." In D. Pimentel, L. Westra, and R.F. Noss, eds., *Ecological Integrity: Integrating Environment, Conservation and Health*, 385-406. Washington, DC: Island Press.

Dale, A. 2001. *At the Edge: Sustainable Development in the 21st Century.* Vancouver: UBC Press.

Davis, T. 2000. *Sustaining the Forest, the People, and the Spirit.* Albany, NY : State University of New York Press.

Edmonds, P.D. 2002. "Urban Stream Reconstruction Design Criteria: Case Study Applying Proper Functioning Condition Principles to Leeds Creek, Victoria." MSc thesis, University of Victoria, BC.

Freedman, B. 1989. *Environmental Ecology: The Ecological Effects of Pollution, Disturbance, and Other Stresses.* 2nd ed. Toronto: Academic Press.

–. 1992. "Environmental Stress and the Management of Ecological Reserves." In J.H.M. Willison, S. Bondrup-Nielsen, C. Drysdale, T.B. Herman, N.W.P. Munro, and T.L. Pollock, eds., *International Conference on Science and the Management of Protected Area*, 383-88. Amsterdam: Elsevier.

Hardin, G. 2002. "Moral Implications of Cultural Carrying Capacity." In G.T. Miller, ed., *Living in the Environment*, 252-53. Belmont, CA: Wadsworth Group.

Karr, J. 2000. "Health, Integrity and Biological Assessment: The Importance of Measuring Whole Things." In D. Pimentel, L. Westra, and R.F. Noss, eds., *Ecological Integrity: Integrating Environment, Conservation and Health*, 209-26. Washington, DC: Island Press.

Krippendorf, K. 1986. Web Dictionary of Cybernetics and Systems. <http://pespmc1.vub.ac.be/ASC/THERMODYNAM.html> (15 January 2003).

Lucey, W.P., C.L. Barraclough, L.K. Malmkvist, P.D. Edmonds, B. LaCas, R. Lloyd, A. Pollard, T. Kraft, G. Mott, and C. Donaldson. 2001. "Re-Establishing the Proper Functioning Condition of Municipal Watersheds: Ecological and Economic Stability in Urban Freshwater Ecosystems." Paper presented by L.K. Malmkvist at the Society for Ecological Restoration 13th annual International Conference, 4-6 October, Niagara Falls, ON.

Luka, N. 2003. E-dialogue. "Sustainable Communities in Canada: Does One Exist?" <www.e-dialogues.com> (2 December). Facilitated by A. Dale.

Machlis, G.E., J.E. Force, and S.E. Dalton. 1995. "Monitoring Social Indicators for Ecosystem Management." Paper prepared for the Eastside Management Project, Walla Walla, WA.

Machlis, G.E., J.E. Force, and W.R. Burch Jr. 1997. "The Human Ecosystem, Part I: The Human Ecosystem as an Organizing Concept in Ecosystem Management." *Society and Natural Resources* 10: 347-67.

Malmkvist, L.K. 2002. "Smart Municipal Development: Urban Stream Restoration and Stormwater Management in Residential and Agricultural Development Areas in Saanich, B.C." MSc thesis, University of Victoria, BC.

Miller, G.T. 2002. *Living in the Environment.* Belmont, CA: Wadsworth Group.

Miller, P., and W.E. Rees. 2000. "Introduction." In D. Pimental, L. Westra, and R.F. Noss, eds., *Ecological Integrity: Integrating Environment, Conservation and Health*, 3-18. Washington, DC: Island Press.

Onyx, Jenny. 2003. Personal communication, 31 January.

Ricklefs, R.E. 2001. *The Economy of Nature.* 5th ed. New York: W.H. Freeman.

Schuller, Tom. 2000. "Thinking About Social Capital." <http://www.open.ac.uk/lifelong-learning/papers/393B8E05-0008-65B9-0000015700000157.html> (15 January 2003).

United States, Department of Interior Bureau of Land Management. 1998. Technical Reference 1737-15. "Riparian Area Management: A User Guide to Assessing Proper Functioning Condition and the Supporting Science for Lotic Areas."

–, Department of Interior Bureau of Land Management and United States Department of Agriculture Forest Service letter. Dated 20 March 1996. Reference #6740(BLM-WO330)/2520(FS).

Vasseur, L. 2003. E-dialogue. "Sustainable Communities in Canada: Does One Exist?" <www.e-dialogues.com> (2 December). Facilitated by A. Dale.

Von Glaserfeld, E. 2003. "Cybernetics, Experience and the Concept of Self." <http://www.oikos.org/vonen.html> (15 January 2003).

Wilson, E.O. 1994. *The Diversity of Life*. London: Penguin.

Wollard R., and W. Rees. 1999. "Social Evolution and Urban Systems: Directions for Sustainability." In J.T. Pierce and A. Dale, eds., *Communities, Development, and Sustainability across Canada*, 27-45. Vancouver: UBC Press.

3

Social Ecology as a Framework for Understanding and Working with Social Capital and Sustainability within Rural Communities

Stuart B. Hill

My aim in this chapter is to use my approach to social ecology (Hill 1999b) to support the ongoing co-evolution of the theories and practices associated with sustainability and social capital. Although this has relevance to the well-being of all communities, the focus here will be on agricultural and rural communities in Australia, particularly because so many are suffering from so many interrelated expressions of increasing degradation and decline (Hill 1998, 2001b). I will introduce some of the core concepts of social ecology; illustrate how they may be used to broaden, deepen, redesign, and improve our conceptions of sustainability and social capital; reflect on the progressive development of such concepts; make a case for the much more extensive application of our ecological understandings to lifestyle design (including its sustainability and social capital aspects), using "maintenance and limiting factors within ecosystems" as exemplars; and briefly describe how I have effectively used this approach when working with farmers, both in Canada and Australia, to build social capital and improve their sustainability. Because my aim here is to challenge what I regard as naive thinking about social capital and sustainability – and to expand our thinking about these concepts – some of the descriptions and lists of factors to consider may seem tedious. I encourage you to critically engage with every statement by checking each one against your own field experience, and particularly to ask to what extent are you taking into account each of the factors and phenomena that I claim are important (and, in the process, also identify those that I may have neglected).

Social Ecology as a Framework for Broadening, Deepening, Redesigning, and Improving Our Conceptions of Sustainability and Social Capital

Social ecology has multiple origins, all around the middle of the last century, although it is most commonly associated with the extensive writings of the Vermont-based ecoanarchist and ecolibertarian Murray Bookchin, who is better known for what he has critiqued – hierarchical systems, mysticism, primitivism, postmodernism, and deep ecology – than for what he stands for, including unity in diversity and complexity, spontaneity, complementary and mutualistic relationships, active and informed participatory democracy and decision making (e.g., through town meetings), and bioregionalism (Bookchin 1995). After accepting the Chair of Social Ecology in 1996 at the University of Western Sydney's Hawkesbury Campus, I was under considerable pressure – by the university, not the staff and students at the school – to define social ecology. One of the things that contributes to the richness of our teaching and research programs in social ecology is our openness to a wide diversity of emphasis within this developing field. Consequently, I offer the following definition as provisional, knowing that it reflects my particular approach to understanding, my historical biases, and current interests: social ecology is the study and practice of personal, social, and ecological sustainability and progressive change based on the critical application and integration of ecological, humanistic, relational, community, and spiritual values.

In unpacking this definition, I hope to illustrate how it may help deepen our understanding of sustainability and social capital. For me, the most important point is the explicit inclusion of the personal, emphasizing our relational self (Josselson 1996; Shem and Surrey 1998). Most comparable so-called holistic frameworks for sustainability and change use three main categories for reconciliation (e.g., Dale 2001): economics, society, and the environment. I believe that this privileging of economic imperatives as being more important than all our other social constructions – more important than politics, religion, the arts, science and technology, education, and all other systems of values and ethics – is both a major part of our problem and the predictable consequence of our psychosocial history of adaptation to the imposition of others' agendas (goals, rules, frameworks, languages, and ways of understanding, being, and acting) on social beings in the process of forming their own agendas (deMause 1982). Privileging economic imperatives and neglecting our other social constructions is, I believe, helping to perpetuate a narrow monetary system of decision making and concentrating power in the hands of those with the most money. A broader and more diverse base for decision making would be more compatible with and supportive of a participatory democracy. Also, the common neglect of the personal (ourselves) supports the widespread perception that our problems can be solved only by heroes (mythologized to a status beyond real people), particularly politicians and scientists, rather than by problem solving (and, more importantly, prevention), which is a collaborative project that requires all of our contributions. Money, along with our other institutional structures, instruments, and processes, is better regarded as a tool that needs to be designed or redesigned and used wisely to help us implement

our life-affirming values. Such tools need to be subservient to and supportive of such values, not the other way round. Taking such an approach would
cause us to pay much more attention to the development and clarification
of our values and to their centrality in our day-to-day discourse, decision
making, and action. So many of the crises reported in the news each day
provide clear feedback that most of our institutional structures, instruments,
and processes are in urgent need of such redesign. There is an understandable resistance to acknowledging this, however, and to embarking on the
necessary task of transformation. This calls to mind R.D. Laing's (1971) in-
sightful observation that many behave as if they have been hypnotised twice,
firstly into accepting pseudoreality as reality, and secondly to believing that
we have not been hypnotised.

My own tentative vision of a preferable society, based on the above argument, might have the following features. A right to meaningful work and
access to the ingredients needed to construct healthy and creative lives would
gradually replace our current economics-dominated view of labour as a cost
to be minimized and even eliminated. This might help us recognize this
current dominant attitude as just one expression of our enslavement to a
manipulated, deceptively simple economic bottom line (when the absolute
bottom line is, in fact, ecological). With a more widespread recognition of
the importance of ecological limits and opportunities, solar and appropriate technologies could be emphasized, and nonrenewable resources conserved for higher priorities than running cars and heating houses. And the
value of conserving the rich biodiversity with which we share this amazing
planet would be much easier to understand. This contrasts with our current
oversimplified division of nature into resources to be managed and sold for
profit, and pests to be eliminated with the vast chemical arsenal we have
assembled to – tragically, usually nonspecifically – eliminate life. What is
most amazing about this situation is that many people seem to assume that
they are somehow immune to these nonspecific attacks – perhaps a predictable outcome of our common view of ourselves as being somehow separate
from the rest of nature. We should expect, rather than be surprised by, the
common increases in degenerative diseases, immune system breakdown,
and associated behavioural problems. Indeed, these should be regarded as
indicators to be responded to at the causal level, rather than as new en-
emies to be subjected to the same faulty thinking and overkill technologies
that got us into this mess in the first place. Most new biotechnology "solutions" are sadly being conceived within this same deceptively simple construction of nature. This time, however, the ability of naively reconstructed
organisms to multiply themselves and conduct their own "experiments"
could lead to much greater crises than our naive physical and chemical
experiments. Thus, the difference between highlighting the personal or economic is, for me, far from trivial. It has important consequences, not least

of which is the heightened imperative for designing structures and processes capable of supporting the development of competencies such as relating, participating, collaborating, creating, taking responsibility, and developing a sense of place, purpose, and meaning, and for understanding the ways in which such abilities interrelate (Hill forthcoming).

Richard Norgaard's (1994) co-evolutionary framework for sustainable development and change similarly stresses the importance of values. It also highlights the tendency of our overemphasis on powerful institutional structures, such as global economies and the transnational corporations they serve, together with certain powerful technologies, to colonize and compromise our values, diverse knowledge systems, and the health of our environment, our communities, our relationships, and ourselves. He argues that genuine sustainable development requires a tick in each of these areas without such compromise.

The highlighting of sustainability and progressive change in social ecology emphasizes the dominant features of all living systems: maintenance, into which most resources and energy are naturally channelled, and development, transformation, adaptation, and co-evolution. These also relate to two interrelated ways of being in the world that are essential for well-being: knowing (necessary for action) and unknowing (necessary for learning). The key is to be able to move flexibly and appropriately between these two in an emergent spiral, not getting stuck for too long on one or the other. If we become stuck on knowing, we are in danger of becoming boring, oppressive, and controlling know-it-alls with well-developed defences against further learning. People stuck on unknowing, on the other hand, often present themselves as perpetually apathetic, lost, searching, postponing, or hypercritical unknow-it-alls. Learning to work flexibly and spontaneously with knowing and unknowing; the rational and the mystical; science and spirituality; the modern and postmodern; order and chaos; goals and plans, visions, and dreams; and sustainability and change is one important expression of the essential competence of being able to embrace, learn from, and work with paradox, an essential competence that is neglected in most curricula.

In terms of sustainability – the rehabilitation, development, conservation, and maintenance of ecological, cultural, and personal capital, including especially mutually beneficial relationships – it is important to recognize that whereas ecological sustainability is concerned with absolutes, such as the air, water, and nutrients for life, together with a vast range of mutualistic relationships, the requirements for social, cultural, and personal sustainability are relative and much more flexible. Because money has no comparable requirements, economic sustainability, in contrast, is dependent primarily on the wisdom of our decisions and actions (hardly comparable with resources such as air and water). Thus, economic sustainability must serve ecological sustainability first, and sociocultural and personal sustainability second, and not vice-versa.

The absolute nature of ecological sustainability has important legislative, legal, and regulatory implications. Thus, interventions into ecosystems (simplification, harvesting, waste disposal, release of novel chemicals and genetically modified organisms) must be regarded as guilty until proven innocent, with much reliance on the precautionary principle (Harding and Fisher 1999; Raffensperger and Tickner 1999). Similarly, risk studies need to be conducted with reference to ecological absolutes and sociocultural values, and not based simply on economics. Currently, as part of a tendency to preserve the status quo (or extrapolations of it), most risk studies, which should be providing us with valuable feedback for necessary redesign, are concerned only with problem measurement and assessment – what I call "monitoring our extinction" – rather than with risk reduction and avoidance.

In terms of change, it is important to distinguish between deep sustainable change, which usually requires fundamental redesign of the systems involved, and of our relationships with them, and shallow adaptive, substitutive, and compensatory change, which usually unintentionally protects and perpetuates the very structures and processes that are the sources of the problems we are endeavouring to solve. In my work I distinguish between efficiency, substitution (shallow) and redesign (deep) approaches to change (Hill 1998). Although this "E-S-R" model was first developed for reconceptualizing pest control (from inefficient to efficient use of pesticides, to the use of substitutes such as biological controls, to the integrated redesign and design of complex pest-proof agroecosystems – to favour the crops and natural controls and not the pests), I have found it to be more widely applicable (e.g., Hill 1985, forthcoming). Within this model, efficiency and substitution strategies may serve either as stepping stones or as barriers to the ultimately essential redesign approaches. This tendency to suspect that a phenomenon detected in one part of a system might also be operational in other parts of the system – in generically similar but specifically different ways – is one expression of the 'holographic paradigm' and of 'holonomy' (Harman and Sahtouris 1998), which are also central to my approach to social ecology.

I have found when working with social change that it is important to meet people where they are, acknowledge their past and present efforts, support their next small meaningful steps, and, if appropriate, celebrate their progress and completions publicly to facilitate their contagion. This is in contrast to the more common overemphasis on Olympic-scale mega-projects, heroes, experts, and heavy-handed technological and legislative interventions.

Another key to sustainable change is to be imaginative in integrating personal, social (including institutional), and ecological approaches, while also being aware of their limited substitutability. For example, the provision of a benign environment may, even in the absence of personal change initiatives, or the fundamental redesign of institutions, lead to benign behaviour and health. This was achieved most dramatically in the Peckham Experiment in the United Kingdom in which over 1,000 families that had access to a supportive recreational centre in Peckham between 1935 and 1950 experienced no marriage breakdowns, no violence, little interest in competitive games, the widespread formation of mutually beneficial relationships, the building of social capital, high levels of creativity, and dramatic improvements in health and well-being (Stallibráss 1989; Williamson and Pearse 1980). Similarly, there are numerous examples of individuals in deep psychotherapy, or who have been members of a supportive peer counselling or relationship counselling group, in the absence of environmental or institutional changes, significantly transforming their ways of being and relating in the world, and similarly achieving dramatic improvement in their relationships, health, and well-being (Gruen 1988; Hill 2003; Jackins 1992; Janov 1971; Mahrer 1978; Rowan 1993; Shem and Surrey 1998; Stettbacher 1991). The greatest gains are likely to be achieved, however, when mutually supportive and potentially synergistic initiatives are being taken in each of these three areas, and in integrated ways.

Conversely, in a culture that emphasizes growth, greed, individualism, power, hierarchy, compensatory stimulatory consumption (particularly through commodification and manipulative advertising), and other characteristics listed in the left-hand column of Table 3.1, it is not surprising that disempowerment, relationship breakdown, apathy, irresponsibility, addiction, and violence will be common. Clearly, if we are to achieve sustainability and benign change, and build social capital, we will need to pay much more attention to the neglected and blocked expressions of humanity listed in the right-hand column of Table 3.1.

As reference to ecological, humanistic, relational, and community values have been made throughout this chapter, only certain contentious points will be highlighted here. These values need to be considered together to avoid arriving at conflicting imperatives. As indicated above, however, it is essential that at every level our species recognizes the primacy of those ecological values concerned with our survival, health, and well-being. Because these are currently being compromised within our societies by so many political, business, and compensatory personal decisions, this point cannot be overemphasized.

Enlightened humanistic values (Bookchin 1995) ask that we live up to our potential as human beings. There is currently much confusion and polarization in this area. Social ecology has been labelled by some of its critics as being overly anthropocentric and has been contrasted with the supposedly more biocentric deep ecology perspective of Arne Naess and followers

Table 3.1

Dominant pressures and areas of neglect within globalized, industrial societies

Dominant grand narrative of "progress" within globalized societies	Neglected/blocked area within globalized societies
Production (regardless of cost)	Maintenance, caring, love
Growth, no limits	Sustainability, respect of limits (resources, ecological)
Competition	Collaboration, mutualism, synergy
Wealth	Sense of enough
Individualism	Community, mutualistic relationships, anonymous giving
Consumerism (emphasizing compensatory wants)	Conserver society (meeting basic needs)
Homogenization, simplification	Maintenance of mutualistic diversity
"Controlling" science ("understanding" science and arts as a disposable luxury)	"Understanding" science and arts
Powerful technologies (often centralized, imported, inaccessible, unrepairable)	Appropriate technologies (decentralized, locally accessible, repairable)
Market forces (manipulated demand, excessive advertising)	Values based decisions (participatory democracy, cooperacy)
Economic rationalism (monetary system of values)	Meeting the greatest "good" (equitable access, social justice)
Transglobal corporate managerialism	Regional self-reliance and responsibility
Mobile, disposable workforce (disconnected from place)	Sense of place, right to meaningful work
The myths that these are embedded in are inadequate for securing a "good" future for most in present and future generations.	We need to search for new life-promoting myths that can accommodate these characteristics: all can be found deep within ourselves and within nature (and ecology).

(Naess 1989). My version of social ecology is critical of both positions. Because all healthy humans naturally have a survival instinct, we are, in this respect, innately anthropocentric. To value another species above, or exactly equal to, that of one's own might even be indicative of a deeper problem of transference and projection. For example, if as a child one's "animal" nature was not acknowledged, nurtured, and integrated into one's personality, one adaptive compensatory response might be to seek alternative external ways of keeping this alive, perhaps through an excessive concern for other species. My point here is that by raising children to value their "animal" nature (along with their other natures), they are more likely to be proactive in valuing the richness and diversity of nature as a whole, and to be consistent in acting on this knowing in responsible ways. In contrast, compensatory preoccupations tend to be relatively temporary and the energy invested is often more cathartic than constructive. The other extreme adaptive response to such deficient child rearing might be to largely deny one's "animal" nature and, in so doing, also the value of external nature. A parallel argument has been applied to valuing and nurturing the feminine, as well as the masculine, in males, and the masculine, as well as the feminine, in females (Shem and Surrey 1998). Certainly we live in a world dominated by patriarchy, androcentrism, extreme anthropocentrism, technocentrism, racism, ageism, and a range of other uncaring and irresponsible prejudices, and these must be addressed if we are to not disadvantage future generations and further diminish the planet's biodiversity and habitat quality. Trying to resolve these problems by fanatically focusing on a particular type of "otherness" tends to lead to further problems, not least of which is a common lack of respect for and heightened competition between those committed to different "others." The key, I believe, is to develop our understanding and caring for both our selves (our diverse natures) and otherness. Part of the common concern for making these equal (rather than equitable), simply by taking from one and giving to the other, may come from an assumption that there is not enough caring to go around (another common lesson from childhood). The personal task is to respect, value, support, and develop mutualistic relationships with others so that their needs may be satisfied and their creativity and gifts to the world expressed. The social task is to create contexts that are supportive of doing this, and especially of nurturing humanistic values and mutualistic relationships in children. Key child rearing and personal development references that integrate this awareness include Josselson (1996), Sazanna (1999), Shem and Surrey (1998), Solter (1989), and Stallibrass (1989). My argument is that such building of personal capital establishes the foundation on which social and natural capital can be built and maintained.

The importance of relational and community values follows from the above, for children need to be raised in diverse interactive communities in which they feel cared for and can form meaningful relationships. Although the current widespread loss of community, unlike the loss of species, is reversible, it is nevertheless a source of immense pain and diverse compensatory consumptive and impacting behaviours. It is also an example of an externality that is rarely considered in our obsession with short-term economic efficiency and associated economic rationalism. At the personal level, the loss of individuals – for example, through suicide – is a parallel process that is devastating to those in relationship.

One approach used by many social ecologists to help address such problems involves supporting the formation of learning communities (Senge 1992) and collaborative inquiry groups (Heron 1996). These may then provide the ground within which the needed benign structures and processes can co-evolve. Hunter, Bailey, and Taylor (1997) have integrated these and other approaches into what they call cooperacy, which they regard as the next stage after autocracy and democracy. Central principles within a cooperacy might include caring and sharing, transparency and access, inclusiveness and participation, comprehensiveness, responsibility, and proactivity – all qualities that are critical to the building of social capital and the improvement of sustainability. Within such societies, trust, volunteerism, and the establishment of networks (commonly associated with social capital), and conserver lifestyles (necessary for sustainability) are most likely to be found.

The final inclusion in my short definition of social ecology refers to spiritual values. Here I am concerned that spirituality function as a spontaneous and integrated expression of our core nature, and not as compensation or escape. For me, spirituality is concerned with the "rest," the mystery, the unmeasurable wonder and amazingness of it all – from our still largely unknown origins to our unknowable futures. As such, spirituality is related mostly to the unknowing side of the spiral referred to above. It is not something that needs to be explained and organized in great detail. Rather, it is one expression of being human – a source for our creativity and openness to learn. In our distressed state, however, we have subjected spirituality to the same organizing and controlling forces we have applied to our other social constructions – hence the existence of so many religions. Although claiming to cater to our deep spiritual needs, most religions are more obviously designed and managed to meet the superficial compensatory desires of their constructors and followers. I believe that such over-organization of spirituality is robbing so many of us of contexts within which to develop our sense of wonder, so necessary in turn for the development of our values, respect, caring, and responsibility.

Thus, by linking the social (subsuming and not privileging economics) with the ecological, personal, and spiritual, and by emphasizing sustainability (healthy system maintenance) and co-evolutionary "progressive" change (especially through the fundamental redesign of human systems), social ecology can provide an inclusive, broadly informed, yet focused, liberational framework for understanding and working effectively with both sustainability and social capital. This is reflected in Table 3.2, in which the usual measures of these qualities are integrated into a broader social ecology

Table 3.2

A social ecology framework for broadening and contextualizing the concepts of sustainability and social capital by means of applying critical "testing questions" to all initiatives

To what extent does any sustainability or social capital initiative (e.g., policies, programs, plans, regulations, decisions, actions) support or undermine each of the following qualities:

Personal area	1	Empowerment, awareness, creative visioning, values and worldview clarification, acquisition of essential literacies and competencies, responsibility, well-being and health maintenance practices, vitality and *spontaneity* (building and maintaining personal capital – personal sustainability)?
	2	Caring, loving, responsible, mutualistic, *negentropic relationships* with diverse others (valuing equity and social justice), other species, place, and planet (home and ecosystem maintenance)?
	3	Positive total life cycle *personal development* (lifelong learning) and "progressive" change?
Sociopolitical area	4	Trust, accessible, collaborative, responsible, creative, celebrational, *life-promoting community and political structures and processes* (<u>building and maintaining social capital</u> – cultural, including economic, sustainability)?
	5	The valuing of "functional" high *cultural diversity* and mutualistic relationships?
	6	Positive *cultural development* and co-evolutionary change?
Environmental area	7	Effective *ecosystems functioning* (<u>building and maintaining natural capital</u> – ecological sustainability)?
	8	"Functional" high *biodiversity*, and prioritized use and conservation of resources?
	9	Positive *ecosystem development* and co-evolutionary change?
General area	10	*Proactive* (vs. reactive), *design/redesign* (vs. just efficiency and substitution) and *small meaningful collaborative and individual initiatives* that can be achieved (vs. heroic, Olympic-scale, exclusive, high-risk ones) and their *public celebration* at each stage – to facilitate the spread of concern for well-being and environmental responsibility?
	11	Focusing on key opportunities and *windows for change* (pre-existing and contextually unique change "moments" and places)?

▶

◄   *Table 3.2*

12   Effective monitoring and evaluation of progress (broad, long term, as well as specific and short term) by identifying and using *integrator indicators* and *testing questions,* and by being attentive to all feedback and outcomes (and redesigning future actions and initiatives accordingly)?

Note: Note particularly the implied mutualistic relationships between personal, social, and natural capital; between the rich diversity of one's personal relationships and both cultural diversity and biodiversity; and between personal, cultural, and ecological development. Text has been underlined and italicized for the reader to reflect on possible interrelationships.

framework, all being regarded as potential indicators of healthy systems, and all being tested against a single strategic question (Peavey 1994).

Despite the growing interest in both sustainability and social capital, it should be clear from the above that their implications for governance, policies, regulations, decision-making processes, program design, provision of services, education, professional codes of conduct, business, lifestyles, and activities in general have still hardly scratched the surface of their potential. This is partly because of the enormity of the changes that they imply, and the fears associated with these changes, particularly the fears of the haves of losing what they have, and the fears of the have-nots of what they might be deprived of ever having.

Another reason is that these concepts are at an early stage in their development and as a result are still more preoccupied with issues of definition and measurement (the early stages in the development of all ideas) than with relationships, systemic and paradoxical qualities, and proactive radical design and redesign implications. This has been explained by Rachel Lauer (1983), who has argued that all fields of understanding seem to commonly evolve in ways that reflect the following overlapping and inclusive stages, or epistemes:

1 initial recognition of the thing, concept, or phenomenon (in this case sustainability and social capital)
2 its definition, classification, and measurement (the stage to not get stuck in!)
3 understanding its relationships with other things and phenomena (e.g., well-being, peace, love)
4 critical reflection on its meaning (e.g., contexts in which it is emergent)
5 recognizing its unifying and core qualities, while also acknowledging its vast unknown (and even mystical) and paradoxical qualities (the stage most linked to wisdom and progressive cultural change).

This latter stage is also the one most likely to be associated with paradigm shifts (Kuhn 1970) and radical changes in world views, both of which are needed if the benefits of concepts such as sustainability and social capital are to be fully realized. Such a "progressive" view is paralleled by the ideas of Clare W. Graves (popularized by Beck and Cowan [1996] as "spiral dynamics"), Ken Wilber's (1998) levels of being, Ruthellen Josselson's (1996) stages in the development of relational competence (see also Hill 2003), and Lloyd deMause's (1982) psychogenic theory of history, which he argues reflect changes in our approaches to child rearing. I believe that, although all these ideas are themselves very preliminary, because of their developmental (step-wise) and visionary qualities, they have much to contribute to our evolving understanding of sustainability and social capital. They also enable us to recognize the stage we are working with and what might be required to progress to the next stage.

Based on my change work, particularly in agriculture (Hill 2001b), I have found that the following overlapping stages are commonly experienced when working with change:

1 ignorance and denial (primarily in distressed, disempowered, and fearful individuals): because we are alive now, we must already be living sustainably
2 awareness and acknowledgement: we probably do need to look into this a bit
3 understanding and competence: these are some designs, structures, and processes that I believe will enable us to live more sustainably and equitably
4 effective action and project-based initiatives: we are engaged in the implementation of projects that emphasis ecological systems of natural resource management and ecodesign of all human activities
5 ongoing co-evolution of responsible life-affirming practice: it is amazing that it took our species so long to learn how to live sustainably and in harmony and peace.

Because different barriers are associated with progression between each of the above stages, to be effective in working with change it is necessary to ask strategic questions (Peavey 1994) that are fine-tuned to the stage most dominant in the particular context. Such contextual sensitivity and fine-tuning of action is critical to achieving sustainable progressive change in any area. Thus, our engagement with sustainability and social capital ranges from disinterest; ridicule; marginalization; and manipulation to endless measuring; superficial understanding and add-on projects; deeper understanding and radical redesign of personal lifestyles, our institutional structures, and processes; and our caring for ourselves, one another, and nature.

Because most Australians (as in other industrialized countries) have not yet progressed to the later stages, most rural areas in Australia are suffering from many of the major problems (listed below) facing rural areas globally. These may be usefully considered as indicators of breakdown within both nature and human systems.

Planet
- Exhaustion of fossil fuel reserves and other nonrenewables
- Global warming and associated rising sea level
- Thinning of the ozone layer and accumulation of "garbage" in space
- Fluctuating water tables, drought, drying lakes and rivers, and flooding
- Contamination of soil, water, and organisms with pollutants
- Deforestation, desertification, and soil erosion and degradation
- Loss of biodiversity, species extinctions, and loss of varieties

Agrosystems
- Loss of natural capital (soil, water, biodiversity) and declining energy efficiency
- Breakdown of maintenance functions (soil regeneration, natural pest control)
- Increased vulnerability and pest, weed, disease, and livestock stress problems
- Increased dependence on imported resources, curative inputs, and "experts"

Rural Societies and Economies
- War, prejudice, oppression, and maldistribution problems
- Displacement from land and lack of access to basic needs
- Farm bankruptcies, decaying rural communities, and loss of social capital
- Increasing dependencies on subsidies and imported inputs
- Dependence on unstable distant and world markets and other external controls
- Malnourishment, zoonosis, allergies, and stress-related and degenerative conditions
- Illiteracy, learning disabilities, emotional disturbance, and depression
- "Compensatory" addictive, compulsive, and aggressive and self-harming behaviours
- Feelings of isolation, hopelessness, and helplessness

What is particularly disturbing about this list of problems is that none of the outcomes mentioned above is systematically included in the usual cost-benefit analyses that determine most decisions relating to the design and management of natural resource systems and rural communities. Even those that aim to include externalities (most of which cannot be easily measured) neglect most of them. All these areas must be carefully considered and taken into account in our efforts to understand and improve sustainability and social capital, which must involve proactivity, caring for the well-being of the planet, our managed ecosystems, our communities, and ourselves.

Some Key Ecological Concepts and Their Application to Sustainability and Social Capital

In addition to taking a social ecology approach, I also believe that further reflection on many of the core concepts in ecology will open up numerous new, productive ways of thinking about sustainability and social capital (Mulligan and Hill 2001). Ecological concepts that immediately come to mind include limiting factors and their substitutes; microhabitats, niches, and territoriality; guilds, roles, and keystone species; system maintenance and service functions; resilience and ecosystem resistance; succession, developmental, and intergenerational change; feedback loops, co-evolutionary processes, altruism, and group selection; edge effect and boundary phenomena; functional diversity, system stability, and homeostasis; specialists and generalists (eurytypic and stenotypic expressions of lifestyle), and r and K strategists; entropy and negentropy; specific indicators and integrator indicators; time and space specificity; synergy and mutualism; catalysis and amplification; non-linearity and threshold relationships; integrated web-like relationships; homeostatic, self-regulative, and regenerative processes; adaptation, addiction, allergy, and degeneration; numbers, biomass, energy flow, and the specifics of resource partitioning and budgeting; and hierarchical and systems phenomena at every level. Information about these and other related phenomena can be found in most major ecology textbooks (e.g., Andrewartha and Birch 1984; Begon, Harper, and Townsend 1996; Krebs 2001; Odum 1983; Smith 2001), and also in dictionaries of ecology (e.g., Allaby 1998; Lincoln, Boxshall, and Clark 1998).

It may also help to remember that whereas all other species do what they do without thinking about it (at least in the way we do), our thinking so often leads us into inappropriate, unprioritized, or postponed actions. However, it is this very freedom to behave irresponsibly that is also the source of our creativity, genius, and psychosocial evolution.

To illustrate my argument, I will briefly refer to the concepts of maintenance and limiting factors in ecosystems. Much more could be said about each of these concepts, and also about each of the other ecological concepts listed above (plus others not mentioned).

The Importance of Maintenance in Ecosystems and Its Neglect in Human Systems

Whereas most resources in ecosystems are used for system maintenance at all levels, self-regulation, and development, modern human systems tend to overemphasize and reward "production" and neglect maintenance, hence the ongoing decline in capital within most systems. Thus, farmers are rewarded primarily for yield (weight of produce) and not for the maintenance of the ecosystem (e.g., soil) health, habitats for natural control organisms, and for other organisms concerned with ecosystem services or with the geochemical cycles on which all life depends. Indeed, within the context of a global cheap-food policy, farmers are commonly rewarded only for the quantity of their produce and not for its health promoting (e.g., nutritional) quality. The consequence of this is the degradation of ecosystems, communities, families, most enterprises, and individuals (Hill 1998). Nearly all efforts to reverse these trends focus on the back-end of the process, emphasizing problem solving. Such reactive and curative approaches fail to adequately recognize the need to support and reward rehabilitation and maintenance (sustainability and social capital building) processes. In contrast, most attention needs to be focused on redesign and front-end, proactive, elegant design and management initiatives. One glimmer of hope of such a necessary recognition is the common response by purchasers of the generally more expensive organically grown food when asked why they are willing to pay more for it: "I think it is better for both my health and the environment" (the beginnings of taking responsibility for maintenance-sustainability and the building of personal, social, and natural capital). Clearly, we need to go much farther in this direction if we are to rehabilitate and maintain our degraded agroecosystems, decaying rural communities, and threatened farm families and enterprises. Whereas sustainability is concerned with the rehabilitation, development, and maintenance of healthy systems (personal, social, and ecological), social capital is particularly concerned with the rehabilitation, development, and maintenance of institutional structures and processes (as was achieved in the Peckham Experiment, described above), and group and personal competencies, to support resilience and well-being within communities. My key point is that all these developments are limited and enabled by the level of sustainability and capital at the personal level.

The Importance of Limiting Factors in Ecosystems and Their Neglect in Human Systems

Within ecosystems, limiting factors are the key variables that actually limit life in all its expressions, and consequently they are the factors that must be changed to remove such limits. So often when change agents, and the scientists, technologists, and policy people who support them, set out to achieve certain outcomes, they choose initiatives that are characterized by the qualities of convenience, naive simplicity, conspicuous power, and a hoped for quick result (e.g., pesticides, antibiotics, soluble fertilizers, irrigation schemes, bioengineered organisms, commodity specialization, curative subsidies, and social manipulation) or, if there is widespread fear of the needed changes, they tend to choose initiatives that postpone decision making and action (e.g., the endless studying of the problem and the measurement of symptoms, and distraction by attending to peripheral and non-core issues – a classic expression of displacement behaviour [Barnard 1983]).

Displacement behaviour is evident also in our excessive preoccupation with economics. For me, this is evident in the highly problematic definitions in the literature of human capital that link it to economic activity (e.g., Organization for Economic Cooperation and Development 1998, 9). Because of this, I prefer to use the term "personal capital," which relates more to well-being in its broadest sense and to functioning at one's potential and in meaningful and sustainable ways, rather than in relation to one's contribution to some artificially constructed monetary measurement.

Inclusion of the personal in change projects commonly reveals that change leading to genuine improvement – that is life- and well-being-affirming, socially just, ecologically sustainable, and supportive of our psychosocial co-evolution – is more often limited at the causal (root) level not by issues relating to money and economics but by issues relating (both historically and in the present) to personal qualities: empowerment, power, gender, and access; awareness and competence; imagination, vision, and creativity; and values and world views. For example, at a conference on sustainable agriculture in Montreal in the mid-1980s, when I asked the audience of farmers, "What stops you from farming sustainably?" nearly half answered, "lack of money," yet later when I asked them what they needed to enable them to farm sustainably, most answers related to access to more reliable and accurate information, development of new skills, and more encouragement and relevant support; only 15 percent mentioned anything connected with finances or even markets for their value-added sustainable produce. Money is more often used (often not consciously) as an excuse for inaction, rather than being a root cause of lack of engagement (Hill 1985). It is not that money is unimportant, but rather that the focus should be on what it is perceived to be needed for. This permits attention to be placed on the full spectrum of tools (including money) that may be used to reach the desired goals.

Similarly, programs for change often naively start by focusing on identifying the problems and trying to come up with plans to solve them. This results in neglecting the earlier prerequisite (limiting) stages of recognizing and acknowledging the feelings and passions associated with the systems involved (e.g., What do you love about the soil?), and of establishing the supportive contexts for the needed imagination and creativity on which effective redesign plans can only be based (Hill 1991, 1999a, 2001b, forthcoming; cf. Heron 1992, 20).

This opening up to the importance of creativity and imagination also serves to remind us of the important role of the arts in building and using social capital. This has been particularly present for me in my association with the Mildura Palimpsest programs, which were initiated by Ian Hamilton, director of the Mildura Arts Centre in the Australian state of Victoria, in 1998 (the fourth was held in April 2003). These have provided opportunities for local and visiting artists, some in association with scientists, to construct installations highlighting environmental and community issues within the region, and particularly in relation to the Murray-Darling River System and surrounding farmland. So powerful are some of these installations that they have enabled viewers to bypass denial, focus on the essence of the issues, validate the human spirit, facilitate collaboration across difference, and liberate imaginative approaches toward improved futures (Fettling 2000; Hill 2000).

Working with Farmers to Improve Sustainability and Social Capital Using a Social Ecology Framework

When working with farmers I find that once we have agreed on the priority issues, the most effective first step is to acknowledge what each participant (or if it is a group activity, the group) has already done toward addressing them. Then I ask, "What have you wondered about doing next?" and "What (resources and supports) might you need to actually do this?" and "What barriers might get in the way, and what might you need to overcome them?" I encourage participants to refine these intentions, particularly by converting them into what I call "small meaningful initiatives that you can guarantee to carry through to completion." I also ask them how they will know when they have been successful, or when they have made significant progress (Hill 2001a, 2001b). Most change agents, in their effort to achieve adoption of their – usually curative – "solutions," and to bring about quick change, fail to adequately acknowledge the participant's passions, past efforts, present priorities, familiarity with the details of the situation, and ability to come up with creative and effective approaches that match their particular contexts, personality preferences, competencies, and sense of purpose and meaning. Such agents commonly dream up much too grandiose (scale-insensitive), unachievable, and contextually irrelevant goals and plans that ignore local limiting factors and opportunities. It is important to meet people where they are, to support them in taking their next most meaningful steps, particularly in addressing the driving and restraining forces operating within their particular situations (Lewin 1935) and to publicly celebrate their effective processes and successes in order to facilitate their spread (rather like making health contagious [compare with Williamson and Pearse 1980]). In such communities, growing trust, collaboration, caring, and sharing (all expressions of social capital) become the norm.

I have also used paradoxical approaches when working with farmers – asking them to boldly lie about changes they have already brought about – to help liberate them from habitual patterns that limit their imagination, power, and action. I find that this enables people to a broader vision in relation to their core values rather than settling for tinkering with the status quo. I believe that part of the reason why this works so well is because many of us have paradoxically had to protect our values as children by lying (for example, to maintain our perception of ourselves as good people, we may have chosen to lie when accused of engaging in some minor misdemeanour, knowing that if we confessed we would be told, not that this was not a good thing to do, but that we were a bad person). I have used this approach successfully when working with several of the Resource Consulting Services groups Kirkpatrick and Vanclay refer to in Chapter 8.

Australia's Landcare organization (Brown 1996; Campbell 1994) has already played a leading role in advancing the concepts of sustainability and social capital in rural communities, but it has also hardly scratched the surface of its potential and needs to progress to the next stage in its development (Hill 1996, 1999a). A parallel development that I have been associated with in my region is the creation of the highly successful organization Hawkesbury Harvest, which has enabled numerous producers from around Windsor, NSW, to build social capital and improve the sustainability of their enterprises, partly by tapping into the lucrative tourism market through the establishment of the Farm Gate Trail (Hawkesbury Harvest 2003). The Farm Gate Trail is a route, available as a map, showing farms in the particular region that sell produce directly to the public, usually on the weekend. This has been one expression of a social capital building initiative called Community Supported Agriculture (Groh and McFadden 1997), which is much more developed in North America and Europe than in Australia.

Final Comments

The more we reflect on our history and think in transdisciplinary ways, the more we are likely to realize that the "new" concepts of sustainability and social capital have been around for much longer than their recent popularity might suggest. New labels do, however, provide opportunities for accessing funding for important projects, and for creating fora for dialogue, which may lead to broadening and deepening our understanding of such concepts.

Most species devote, both individually and mutualistically, considerable resources and effort to the long-term maintenance of their resource base (sustainability), and the survival of all populations of social species (Wilson 1975) is dependent on their maintenance of social capital (their ability to survive malenities [Andewartha and Birch 1984], which is achieved by the partitioning of key roles and responsibilities within the group). The difference between the situation for humans and other social species is that whereas in the latter such roles are built-in and not based on free choice, humans have the capacity to choose to behave unsustainably and in ways that erode or fail to maintain social capital. Indeed, the reward systems in most human societies encourage such behaviour. With growing globalization, the effects of this situation and the challenges of addressing it are increasing by orders of magnitude. As a consequence, people are increasingly feeling trapped and disempowered as they realize that, though their efforts may slow down local rates of degradation, they are not enough to reverse the overall global trends. Indeed, many global forces sadly work from a distance to undermine existing social capital within communities.

Sustainability and social capital need to be understood in the context of our dominant cultural and institutional structures and processes, and in terms of their negentropic (capital building, progressive) co-evolutionary development. Any attempts to ghettoize such concepts – for example, by linking them exclusively with certain branches of social, political, or economic theory – must be challenged and insights from all areas concerned with living systems, particularly human systems – such as ecology, psychology, philosophy, and spirituality – must be welcomed. Enormous opportunities exist for the further development and implementation of the concepts of sustainability and social capital by expanding the boundaries disciplinary experts commonly apply to them and by approaching them holistically and holographically.

In terms of our present understandings, whereas sustainability is concerned with the rehabilitation, development, and maintenance of healthy living systems in general, social capital is more focused on expressions of mutualism and "we"-relationships (Shem and Surrey 1998) in human populations that support at the species level our psychosocial evolution (Huxley 1952, 134-53; deMause 1982) and, at the group level, our persistent health and well-being, in the broadest sense (Stallibrass 1989), in the face of diverse and changing conditions. The expression and ongoing development of both concepts is dependent on shared human qualities and processes that include effective relating and trust, caring and compassion, commitment and a sense of responsibility, collaboration and networking, informed wise decision making, a sense of place and connectedness, and a passion for learning and life. These, along with one's level of empowerment and freedom from distress, awareness, vision, and clarity of values and world views, and the diverse range of institutional structures and processes within our societies, may also be regarded as the key limiting factors for both sustainability and social capital (Hill 1991, 2001b, 2003).

References

Allaby, M., ed. 1998. *A Dictionary of Ecology*. 2nd ed. Oxford: Oxford University Press.

Andrewartha, H.G., and L.C. Birch. 1984. *The Ecological Web*. Chicago: University of Chicago Press.

Barnard, C.J. 1983. *Animal Behaviour: Ecology and Evolution*. London: Croom Helm.

Beck, D.E., and C.C. Cowan. 1996. *Spiral Dynamics: Mastering Values, Leadership, and Change: Exploring the New Science of Memetics*. Cambridge, MA: Blackwell. See also <http://www.spiraldynamics.com/>.

Begon, M., J.L. Harper, and C.R. Townsend. 1996. *Ecology: Individuals, Populations and Communities*. 3rd ed. Cambridge, MA: Blackwell Scientific.

Bookchin, M. 1995. *Re-Enchanting Humanity: A Defence of the Human Spirit Against Anti-Humanism, Misanthropy, Mysticism and Primitivism*. New York: Cassell.

Brown, V., ed. 1996. *Landcare Languages*. Canberra, ACT: Commonwealth of Australia.

Campbell, A. 1994. *Landcare: Communities Shaping the Land and the Future*. St. Leonards, NSW: Allen and Unwin.

Dale, A. 2001. *At the Edge: Sustainable Development in the 21st Century*. Vancouver: UBC Press.

deMause, L. 1982. *Foundations of Psychohistory*. New York: Creative Roots.

Fettling, N. 2000. "Theorising Regions." *Artlink* 20(3): 57-59. See also <http://www.mediaust.com.au/palimpsest_2001/main_frameset.html>.

Groh, T., and S.S.H. McFadden. 1997. *Farms of Tomorrow Revisited: Community Supported Agriculture, Farm Supported Community*. Kimberton, PA: Biodynamic Farming and Gardening Association.

Gruen, A. 1988. *The Betrayal of the Self: The Fear of Autonomy in Men and Women*. New York: Grove.

Harding, R., and E. Fisher, eds. 1999. *Perspectives on the Precautionary Principle*. Leichhardt, NSW: Federation.

Harman, W.W., and E. Sahtouris. 1998. *Biology Revisioned*. Berkeley, CA: North Atlantic.

Hawkesbury Harvest. 2003. <http://www.hawkesburyharvest.com.au/> (9 September 2003).

Heron, J. 1992. *Feeling and Personhood*. London: Sage.

–. 1996. *Collaborative Inquiry*. London: Sage.

Hill, S.B. 1985. "Redesigning the Food System for Sustainability." *Alternatives* 12(3/4): 32-36.

–. 1991. "Ecological and Psychological Prerequisites for the Establishment of Sustainable Prairie Agricultural Communities." In J. Martin, ed., *Alternative Futures for Prairie Agricultural Communities*, 197-229. Edmonton, AB: Faculty of Extension, University of Alberta.

–. 1996. "Acknowledging the Past and Visioning the Future." In V. Brown, ed., *Landcare Languages*, 136-46. Canberra, ACT: Commonwealth of Australia.

–. 1998. "Redesigning Agroecosystems for Environmental Sustainability: A Deep Systems Approach." *Systems Research* 15: 391-402.

–. 1999a. "Landcare: A Multi-Stakeholder Approach to Agricultural Sustainability in Australia." In A.K. Dragun and C. Tisdell, eds., *Sustainable Agriculture and Environment: Globalisation and the Impact of Trade Liberalisation*, 125-34. Cheltenham, UK: Edward Elgar.

–. 1999b. "Social Ecology as Future Stories." *Social Ecology Journal* 1: 197-208.

–. 2000. "Social Ecology for a Sustainable Future." *Artlink* 20(3): 50-52.

–. 2001a. "Achieving Agricultural Sustainability in Australia by 2020: A Social Ecology Framework." In H. Haidn, ed., *The Best of ... Exploring Sustainable Alternatives: An Introduction to Sustainable Agriculture*, 135-40. Saskatoon, SK: Canadian Centre for Sustainable Agriculture.

–. 2001b. "Working with Processes of Change, Particularly Psychological Processes, When Implementing Sustainable Agriculture." In H. Haidn, ed., *The Best of ... Exploring Sustainable Alternatives: An Introduction to Sustainable Agriculture*, 125-134. Saskatoon, SK: Canadian Centre for Sustainable Agriculture.

–. 2003. "Autonomy, Mutualistic Relationships, Sense of Place, and Conscious Caring: A Hopeful View of the Present and Future." In J.I. Cameron, ed., *Changing Places: Re-Imagining Australia*, 180-96. Sydney: Longueville.

–. Forthcoming. "Redesign as Deep Industrial Ecology: Lessons from Ecological Agriculture and Social Ecology." In R. Cote, J. Tansey, and A. Dale, eds., *Industrial Ecology*. Vancouver: UBC Press.

Hunter, D., A Bailey, and B. Taylor. 1997. *Co-Operacy: A New Way of Being at Work*. Birkenhead, NZ: Tandem.

Huxley, J. 1952. *Evolution in Action*. London: Scientific Book Club.

Jackins, H. 1992. *A Better World*. Seattle, WA: Rational Island.

Janov, A. 1971. *The Anatomy of Mental Illness*. New York: Berkley Windhover Books.

Josselson, R. 1996. *The Space between Us: Exploring the Dimensions of Human Relationships*. Thousand Oaks, CA: Sage.

Krebs, C.J. 2001. *Ecology*. 5th ed. San Francisco: Benjamin Cummings.

Kuhn, T.S. 1970. *The Structure of Scientific Revolutions*, 2nd edition. Chicago: University of Chicago Press.

Laing, R.D. 1971. *The Politics of the Family*. New York: Penguin.

Lauer, R.M. 1983. "An Introduction to a Theory of Adult Development or, After Piaget, What?" In M. Levy, ed., *Research and Theory in Developmental Psychology*, 195-219. Lovington, NY: New York State Psychological Association. See also <www.generalsemantics.org/Education>.

Lewin, K. 1935. *A Dynamic Theory of Personality: Selected Papers by Kurt Lewin*. New York: McGraw Hill.

Lincoln, R., G. Boxshall, and P. Clark. 1998. *A Dictionary of Ecology, Evolution and Systematics*. 2nd ed. New York: Cambridge University Press.

Mahrer, A.R. 1978. *Experiencing: A Humanistic Theory of Psychology and Psychiatry*. New York: Brunner/Mazel.

Mulligan, M., and S.B. Hill. 2001. *Ecological Pioneers: A Social History of Australian Ecological Thought and Action*. Melbourne, VIC: Cambridge University Press.

Naess, A. 1989. *Ecology, Community and Lifestyle: Outline of an Ecosophy*. Cambridge, UK: Cambridge University Press.

Norgaard, R. 1994. *Development Betrayed: The End of Progress and a Coevolutionary Revisioning of the Future*. New York: Routledge.

Odum, E.P. 1983. *Basic Ecology*. New York: Saunders College.

Organization for Economic Cooperation and Development. 1998. *Human Capital Investment: An International Comparison*. Paris: Organization for Economic Cooperation and Development.

Peavey, F. 1994. *By Life's Grace*. Philadelphia: New Society.

Raffensperger, C., and J. Tickner, eds. 1999. *Protecting Public Health and the Environment: Implementing the Precautionary Principle*. Washington, DC: Island Press.

Rowen, J. 1993. *The Transpersonal: Psychotherapy and Counselling*. London: Routledge.

Sazanna, J. 1999. *Understanding and Supporting Young People*. Seattle, WA: Rational Island Press.

Senge, P.M. 1992. *The Fifth Discipline: The Art and Practice of the Learning Organisation*. Sydney: Random House.

Shem, S., and J. Surrey. 1998. *We Have to Talk: Healing Dialogues between Women and Men*. New York: Basic Books.

Smith, R.L. 2001. *Ecology and Field Biology*. 6th ed. San Francisco: Benjamin Cummings.

Solter, A. 1989. *Helping Young Children Flourish*. Goleta, CA: Shining Star.

Stallibrass, A. 1989. *Being Me and Also Us: Lessons from the Peckham Experiment*. Edinburgh: Scottish Academic.

Stettbacher, J.K. 1991. *Making Sense of Suffering*. New York: Dutton.

Wilber, K. 1998. *The Marriage of Sense and Soul*. New York: St. Martin's.

Williamson, G.S., and I.H. Pearse. 1980. *Science, Synthesis and Sanity*. Edinburgh: Scottish Academic.

Wilson, E.O. 1975. *Sociobiology: The New Synthesis*. Cambridge, MA: Harvard University Press.

Part 3
Actions

4
Enabling Structures for Coordinated Action: Community Organizations, Social Capital, and Rural Community Sustainability
Jo Barraket

Throughout Australia, as in other countries, rural communities are responding to the local effects of economic, political, and social restructuring. While federal and state governments have historically taken a "top down" regional economic development approach in this country,[1] there is now a growing emphasis being placed on the role of local actors in achieving effective responses to community challenges across economic, social, and environmental indicators. The concept of social capital – which, drawing on Putnam, Leonardi, and Nanetti's (1993, 167) definitions, constitutes "those features of social organisation, such as trust, norms, and networks, that can improve the efficiency of society by facilitating coordinated actions" – has gained increasing popularity in policy discourses that seek to locate effective responses to global problems within local community.

The social capital approach has gained popularity with development practitioners and theorists who give primacy to individual and collective agency in the development process. The value of introducing social capital to understandings of community development is that this concept illuminates the effects of informal social relations on broader development objectives. At the same time, this approach has drawn criticism from those who view its focus on individual and collective agency as a convenient means of sidestepping the structural inequities that socioeconomically excluded individuals and communities face. A related problem is the extent to which the social capital approach has tended toward locating community as the site of development action, with limited regard for the interdependence of communities and the broader social systems in which they function.

In this chapter, I call for a social capital approach to rural renewal that acknowledges the importance of addressing the structural aspects of development and the relationship between local communities and the broader society in which they function. This includes recognizing the impacts of external structures and institutions on communities of place, and building the internal structural and systemic frameworks necessary to support ongoing local development processes. I suggest that the importance of integrating the social capital approach with sustainable community development theory is the latter's emphasis on interrelatedness and co-responsibility, both within communities, and between communities and the broader society.

Wilkinson's (1991) notion of the community field – which stresses the importance of locating development at the intersection of differing interests or objectives – is useful in illuminating the need for enabling structures and systems to support sustainable community development. While the sustainable community development paradigm, which emphasizes the interdependence of economic, social, and environmental factors, enhances our understanding of the role of social capital in rural community renewal, it does not, in my view, give adequate attention to the cultural dimension of sustainability. I discuss this, and the issue of conflict, in some detail in the latter section of this chapter.

The ideas outlined in this chapter are based on an in-depth review of the emerging body of international and local case study literature on rural community regeneration. This is supplemented by data collected from semi-structured interviews with state-government-employed field staff involved in rural community development in six regions throughout the Australian state of New South Wales (NSW), and observational research in one small rural NSW community that is attempting to respond to the profound effects of deregulation of the dairy industry. This research is preliminary, and forms part of a larger comparative study, "The Role of Community Organisations in Rural Community Sustainability," which is currently underway.

Factors Impacting on Rural Australia

In recent years, Australia – like many nations – has experienced significant economic, social, and political change. Rapid advances in communication and transport technologies have provided the impetus for major global economic restructuring, including the restructuring of markets and the nature of employment (National Institute of Economic and Industry Research 1999). Global economic shifts have been accompanied by neo-liberalist domestic policies, which have sought to capture new economic advantages through market deregulation and promotion of free trade (Davidson and Grant 2001). Finally, increased understanding of the economic and social consequences of environmental degradation has led to greater demands for ecologically sustainable industrial processes (Frawley 1994).

While the effects of global economic restructuring and domestic economic rationalism have brought about significant increases in Australia's overall wealth, they have also led to greater disparities between rich and poor, socioeconomic advantage and disadvantage, and access to opportunities in the so-called information economy. The experience of disadvantage is by no means confined to rural communities. In fact, some of the starkest experiences of socioeconomic exclusion are occurring in our urban centres. However, global economic trends and domestic policy frameworks have had specific impacts on rural and regional Australia.

These trends have led to increased concentration of investment, employment, and occupation in metropolitan centres, and consequent marginalization of areas that are disconnected from centralized economic growth and knowledge flows (National Institute of Economic and Industry Research 1999, 25). Rural Australian communities have traditionally relied on the agricultural industry, which now constitutes a significantly smaller proportion of national economic output (although recent improvements in commodities prices suggest at least some relief from this trend in the longer term). Reduced profitability and the restructuring of many farming practices have limited direct and associated agricultural employment opportunities (Productivity Commission 1999). The absence of local employment opportunities, combined with increased employment and educational opportunities in urban and regional centres, has led to significant out-migration, particularly of young people, from many rural communities (Baum et al. 1999; Productivity Commission 1999).

The problem of rural decline should not be overstated, nor attributed to all rural and regional areas. Many small communities and regional centres are successfully responding to change through local economic diversification and effective community development activities (for examples see Kenyon and Black 2001; Tabart, Fulton, and Clark 2001). Nevertheless, there is a strong body of theoretical and empirical research which suggests that, overall, rural and regional Australia is experiencing disproportional disadvantage across a range of economic and sociocultural indicators (Duff and Tonts 2000; Black et al. 2000; Smailes 1996) and that smaller communities are bearing the brunt (Baum et al. 1999; Collits and Gastin 1997).

Davidson and Grant (2001, 6) have defined the regional marginalization associated with uneven development trends as a structural condition that implies a diminishing economic base and an increasing alienation from the mainstream of society. As they have pointed out, the very real challenges faced by rural communities, combined with growing rural disaffection with major political parties since the early 1990s, have rendered public policy responses to this issue a political imperative. The notion of "rural renewal" is now at the forefront of policy discourses at both federal and state levels.

Policy Responses to Rural Development

Within this context, significant political attention is now being paid to the need to build rural communities' capacity to respond to economic, social, and environmental challenges. Traditional development approaches in this country – such as the Regional Economic Development scheme initiated in the 1970s and the Regional Development Organisations established under the Labor government's 1994 Working Nation strategy – have focused primarily on regional rather than local strategies, with an emphasis on economic development alone. While the regional approach continues through a range of current federal and state government programs, there is also an emerging emphasis on developing integrated approaches to rural renewal at a local community level. This is apparent particularly in state government development programs but also in federal strategies oriented toward community service provision.

This focus on the local reflects a growing argument that the role of local communities in development outcomes has become increasingly important in an environment where nation states are influenced by global forces and less able to control their local effects. It also acknowledges an increasing acceptance by theorists, policy makers, and development practitioners alike that effective approaches to rural development must address the issue of community sustainability by addressing the interdependence of economic, social, and environmental factors (see Dale 1999; Roseland 2000). In the Australian context, Herbert-Cheshire (2000, 203) identifies this emerging focus on local activity as a shift away from the traditional political conflation of agricultural development and rural development, toward an emphasis on rural communities as a whole.

As Herbert-Cheshire suggests (204), the community approach to rural development is underpinned by a significant change in the popular ideology of governing in this country. She argues that the renewed focus on community self-sustainability implies a shift in governing styles, away from formal interventionist powers of government and toward a "governance" framework, in which communities are increasingly encouraged to govern themselves. This renewed focus on community self-reliance suggests a blurring of the boundaries between state and civil society, which places increased responsibility for community success on community networks and organizations within a given locale.

It is within this context that the concept of social capital has gained increasing attention from policy makers and development practitioners concerned with building rural communities' capacity to renew themselves. The range of Australian case study literature (see, for example, Onyx and Bullen 2000; Falk and Kilpatrick 2000; Hase et al. 2000; Onyx and Leonard 2000) suggests that strong stocks of bonding, bridging, and linking social capital enhance community capacity for regenerative or development activity.

As a number of these writers acknowledge, however, the developmental benefits of social capital include the extent to which the micro processes of social capital building at the local level facilitate effective engagement with the broader set of social, economic, and political relations and institutional frameworks in which communities are located. That is, the value of social capital to community renewal rests not in its presence but in the way in which it is mobilized to coordinate action – both within a community, and between the community and the broader society – to achieve developmental objectives.

Community Self-Reliance and Structural Influences: Recognizing Co-Responsibility

The social capital approach to community renewal is predicated on the valuing of community self-reliance through individual and collective agency. As Onyx and Bullen (2000, 109) put it, "social capital refers to people as active agents and creators of their social world, not as passive victims of fate or government policy."

While constructing communities as sites of developmental action appears persuasive, there are a number of potential dangers in this approach. In a recent discussion of prospects for regional renewal in Australia, Gray and Lawrence (2001) criticized the community self-reliance or social capital approach to regional development on the basis that it denies the structural elements of rural and regional marginalization. They suggest that the emerging policy discourse of community self-reliance reflects a rise of the neoliberal focus on the individual, which has the effect of characterizing community challenges in terms of individuals (and individual communities), with no recognition of the effects of structural relationships on regional sustainability. For example, they identify that community-led responses to skills and educational development within particular locales do nothing to challenge structural inequality in the Australian education system between urban and rural/regional areas.

In the case of the community in which I am currently conducting research, significant restructuring of its principal industry, which has been spearheaded by the federal and state governments in the name of market freedom, has had a significant impact on local economic and social resources, as well as providing the impetus for changing the way in which natural resources are managed and utilized. Farmers in the area are adjusting to changing contractual arrangements, which encourage increased competition at the local level. These changes are creating new economic pressures in the area, which necessarily impact on social interactions at the level of the family and the community. While mobilization of bonding and bridging social capital may well enhance this community's capacity to respond to restructuring through economic diversification and innovation, the very need for a response has been determined by economic policy decisions well outside the community's sphere of control. Just as significantly, to the extent that industry deregulation is affecting patterns of cooperation, competition, and succession planning within and between farming families, it seems to be undermining traditional sources of social capital within this community. Boydell's chapter in this book (Chapter 13) further explores, within another context, the effects of government policy and practice on social capital development.

Critics of the growing focus on social capital as the panacea for community sustainability characterize this approach as being based on an individualistic prescription which, by focusing on the capacity of individuals to act together in furthering their interests, absolves government of responsibility for redressing socioeconomic inequity (Gray and Lawrence 2001; Herbert-Cheshire 2000). As Herbert-Cheshire (2000, 210) has observed, the danger of the ideology of community self-reliance privileged in current approaches to rural development is that it ignores the very real "structural barriers to self-help which exist in communities with declining levels of social, economic and physical capital," while at the same time placing responsibility for failure on communities themselves. While more recent work on social capital and community development has emphasized the importance of linking social capital – that is, the quality of relationships between local communities and broader political, professional, and economic institutions and networks – this work still places the onus for building such links on the community.

These arguments are suggestive of the problems of a social capital approach to rural renewal where it positions community as the site of action without recognizing the impacts of macro political, economic, and social systems on the local. Gray and Lawrence (2001) state that what is missing from this approach is a recognition of the structural dimension of rural renewal. I would expand this to say that such an approach ignores the relational dimension of effective community development within a broader regional, national, and global context. In this sense, a development approach that emphasizes the role of social capital will be effective only where it recognizes the interdependence of factors within local communities (including local economies, social infrastructure, and ecosystems) and the interdependence of communities and the broader networks, ecosystems, and institutional frameworks in which they function.

Community Sustainability and Social Capital: Recognizing Co-Responsibility

It is here at the local level that the notion of community sustainability plays an important role. In broad terms, sustainable community development may be seen as the synthesis of sustainable development principles and community and local economic development practices. That is, sustainable community development draws on conceptualizations of sustainable development popularized since the publication of the Brundtland Commission report, *Our Common Future,* in 1987, and the theory and practice of community development and local economic development popularized in the 1970s and 1980s, respectively.

As has been emphasized in the growing body of literature on sustainable community development (see, for example, Hart 1999; Roseland 2000; Bridger and Luloff 1999), community sustainability emphasizes an integrated response to economic, social, and environmental imperatives within a given locale, and an emphasis on intergenerational equity with regard to resource use. While the focus on interdependence in the community sustainability literature has been on the internal functions of the sustainable community, the contribution of sustainable development theory more broadly is the recognition of the importance of interdependence within any given ecosystem.

As Bridger and Luloff (1999) point out, sustainable development theory emphasizes ecological interdependence, and the interdependence of human beings and the natural environment. If we view the local community as an organism operating within a larger ecosystem comprising political, environmental, economic, social, and cultural dimensions, we begin to recognize the interdependence between individual organisms, and between individual organisms and the broader ecosystem. The significance of introducing the notion of sustainability to a social capital approach to community development then becomes twofold. First, and more commonly discussed, it focuses our understanding of development on the interactions between the various resources (environmental, social, human, financial, and so on) present in a given locale. Second, it stresses the importance of co-responsibility – that is, the responsibility of local communities and the broader systems and institutions with which they necessarily interact – in achieving constructive outcomes at the local, regional, and societal level. This overcomes the tendency of the social capital approach to locate agency, and therefore responsibility for development, entirely within a given community.

Enabling Structures for Sustainability: Building the Community Field

So far I have discussed the importance of recognizing the interrelatedness of rural communities and the broader structural frameworks in which they function. Perhaps equally important is to consider the role of enabling structures and processes in practising sustainability within local communities. As I have discussed above, policy shifts toward the local in rural development strategies in Australia in recent years have placed a renewed emphasis on community capacity for coordinated action. While the sustainable community development approach has been identified as important at state and, to a lesser degree, federal government levels, little attention has been paid to the internal systems and structures required to manage this approach over time.

A common concern raised by government-employed field staff who participated in our interviews was how innovative projects could be sustained in communities once their own participation ceased. For the most part, this was not a concern about the level of community energy or talent to maintain these projects but about the absence of systems or structures to embed them in the day-to-day functions of the community. This reflects a common dilemma of development programs oriented toward the management of place.

Drawing on the work of Wilkinson (1991), Sharp (2001) identifies the capacity for coordinated action as being directly connected to the presence of a community field within a given locale. A community field may be described as an emergent structure for collective action that cuts across a range of specific social fields, or interest areas (Wilkinson 1991). Sharp (2001, 410) defines a community field as "a purposefully organized sub-network that increases the capacity of local actors from diverse social fields to achieve their respective goals." In the context of community renewal, he describes this field as providing a structural base for coordinating action between special interest fields (such as social services provision or economic development) that facilitates broad community awareness of local concerns and improves the flow of knowledge and financial resources between various social fields.

In terms of social capital theory, we may view the community field as providing the structural, or institutional, framework for the development and/or mobilization of social capital. As Onyx (2001) argues, the formalization of enabling structures, including but not limited to community-based organizations, is an important aspect of social capital building and mobilization in the process of community renewal. Such structures have the potential to harness bonding social capital – characterized by dense multifunctional ties and high levels of localized trust – within a community. Also critical to the community renewal process, the community field provides a structural base for the development of bridging social capital, or diverse networks within communities, and links between communities and external networks and institutions. As Onyx (2001, 85) points out, successful community renewal requires the mobilization of bonding social capital as well as "the development of bridging links to outside expertise and resources."

Bridger and Luloff (1999) have described the community field not as harmonizing diverse interests or completely bridging different perspectives but, rather, bringing common interests into focus. They suggest that, in the context of sustainable community development, purposive actions to build the community field should be focused around drawing together those social fields that they define as constituting the five dimensions of sustainable communities. These include:

- increasing local economic diversity
- developing economic self-reliance (where self-reliant communities are linked to larger economic structures)
- reducing the use of energy and careful management and recycling of waste
- protection and enhancement of biodiversity and natural resources
- commitment to social justice and equity. (Bridger and Luloff 1999)

Bridger and Luloff's five dimensions focus on the importance of economic, environmental, and social aspects of community well-being to sustainability. As I will discuss in detail below, I would call for an additional aspect – that of culture – to be explicitly considered in our understandings of community sustainability.

If we transpose the concept of the community field onto this model of community sustainability, the community field becomes the site in which the interactions between social, environmental, economic, and cultural development are systemically addressed (see Figure 4.1). The community field does not constitute the sum total of development activity, as the range of activities in any given locale is likely to be diverse and variously focused on one or more of the four dimensions of sustainability. Rather, the community field provides the systemic framework in which interactions between such activities is deliberatively addressed. As Figure 4.1 suggests, neither the community field nor the sustainable community as a whole operates in isolation from the broader society, rather, it is in interaction with and influenced by the range of institutional factors determined by public policy and broad socioeconomic trends.

Figure 4.1

Institutional factors

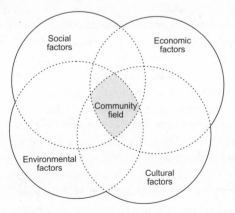

The community field notion illuminates the significance of enabling structures in building and sustaining community capacity for coordinated action. Where those structures are inclusive of diverse community interests and needs, they provide the framework for the efficient flow of information and resources, the building of networks of trust and reciprocity, the sharing of power, and the communicative mechanisms necessary to build "whole of community" approaches to growth or change. Bearing in mind the importance of linking to external networks, institutions, and social systems, the community field may also be conceived as the site in which linking social capital is fostered and mobilized.

From the sustainable community development perspective, building the community field means establishing the systems or structures necessary to manage and legitimize decision making regarding economic, social, and environmental objectives. Community based organizations and organizational networks have a critical role to play in developing the community field. Before considering this in further detail, however, I wish to explore the importance of the cultural dimension of community sustainability and its omission from the current paradigm.

Community Sustainability and Culture: A Missing Dimension?

Bridger and Luloff (1999) have discussed the importance of purposive action to build a community field that encompasses the social, economic, and environmental features of sustainable community development. What is interesting in this, and other, constructions of community sustainability which appear in the literature and policy discourses is the absence of a fourth dimension, that of culture, in the sustainable community development paradigm. While some writers (see Onyx 2001; Falk and Kilpatrick 2000) do identify supporting cultural activity as an important feature of sustainable communities, the cultural dimension has largely been subsumed by discussions of the social dimension in the literature. The lack of distinction between social and cultural dimensions of sustainable community development within the theoretical literature has been transferred into policy discourses, where the importance of cultural experience and activity has to date been ignored or highly marginalized in relevant development programs.

A detailed discussion of the broad ranging and highly contested debate on definitions of culture is beyond the scope of this chapter. However, if we consider culture in a generic sense as the aggregate of symbolic and learned aspects of human society, then cultural experience becomes a critical filter through which we interact with society, economy, and environment.

The absence of an explicit discussion of cultural aspects of sustainable community development is notable, given that an emerging body of case study literature on rural community renewal in Australia (see Onyx and Leonard 2000; Hase et al. 2000; Kenyon and Black 2001) is consistent in recognizing the impact of cultural experience and activity on renewal efforts. On the basis of this literature, and from my own research, I would suggest that the cultural dimension of community life plays a significant role in supporting community sustainability on three levels.

First, engagement with cultural activity (such as community festivals, heritage projects, artistic endeavour, and so on) is frequently identified as an important factor in building social capital. Participants in research conducted by Hase et al. (2000, 23) noted the importance of a long-running community festival in "pulling people together." As Onyx (2001) has suggested, celebrations of local culture serve to kindle people's energy and enthusiasm for the community and its development activities, reinforce a community's understanding of its own richness, and generate new ideas and action. Perhaps even more significantly, celebrating or promoting cultural identity provides a constructive forum for the recognition of diversity within a given community. That is, festivals, music, art, and so on provide people with opportunities to engage with and learn about cultural and social experience across age, gender, ethnicity, and other forms of diversity. This isn't an argument for reducing all engagement with diversity to the level of cultural celebration. Indeed, to do so would run the risk of ignoring the root causes of socioeconomic exclusion that affect people from marginalized groups, and which must be redressed if we are to build socially just and inclusive communities. What is important to note here, however, is that engagement with diverse cultural experience through cultural celebration can provide a productive avenue for the development of bridging links between diverse peoples and interests within the local community. As the case study literature suggests, building bridging social capital is critical to ensuring the long-term viability of a community and its development processes.

The second way in which culture interacts with the other dimensions of community sustainability is the increasing significance of cultural product in local economies in the so-called knowledge economy. In brief, the knowledge economy can be described as emphasizing knowledge, intellectual property, branding, and other intangible assets as the basis for competitive advantage and value. The case study literature identifies the range of ways in which rural communities are engaging with the knowledge economy, including niche marketing and value adding to agricultural and manufacturing products at source, building local employment through creation of telecentres, and stimulating tourism through marketing local (environmental, historic, and cultural) advantages. It is this latter activity that illustrates the increasing economic importance of cultural activities and icons to rural communities. To the extent that cultural identities are commodities that distinguish one community from another, marketing such identities has become an increasingly important feature of stimulating local economies.

Finally, our experiences of culture both inform, and are informed by, our experiences of environment. In the words of Nassauer (1997, 3), "We cannot stand apart from nature, and now nature as we know it cannot stand apart from us." Cultural experience and understanding plays a significant role in the way in which we interact with and manage our natural resources.

The three levels on which culture impacts on local community activity are suggestive of the importance of the cultural dimension of the sustainable community development paradigm. If we accept the inclusion of the cultural dimension in community sustainability, then the community field must provide a systemic framework for addressing social, economic, environmental, and cultural imperatives.

Building the Community Field: Organizations, Power, and Conflict

Across the range of community development, local economic development, and sustainable community development literature, the role of community-based organizations in facilitating development is widely acknowledged. In brief, observations in the literature suggest that, to the extent that community-based organizations are driven by community need and have a specific (if not necessarily articulated) objective of building social capital and civil society, they may be ideally placed to provide the enabling structures for building the community field.

The organizational structure of the community field can take two forms. The first is an umbrella organization – such as Broken Hill Community Inc., described by Jenny Onyx and Lynelle Osburn in Chapter 10 – which provides an overarching framework for developing and resourcing diverse community projects, and which provides the face of negotiation between the Broken Hill community and external political, business, and educational institutions. The second structure, which is typified by the Strategic Alliance Group in the community of Maleny in Queensland, is a coordinated network of organizations representing different interests in the community. Rather than provide the forum for conducting sustainable community development projects, the Strategic Alliance group facilitates identification and articulation of strategic issues to inform the development process. Both of these organizational forms are reflected in the development of so-called community coalitions, or community collaborations through partnerships and networks, which have gained popularity in the United States over the past decade (see Chavis 2001; Himmelman 2001).

These two forms – the singular umbrella organization and the coordinated network of multiple organizations – suggest different approaches to community organizing that may inform, or be informed by, different power structures at work within a given community.

Drawing on existing typologies of community power structures, Sharp assesses the contributions of four power structures – representing a spectrum from highly centralized to highly decentralized decision making – to the development of the elements making up a community field. These power structures are:

Pyramidal structure   where power is concentrated in a single leadership
                        group (for example, an umbrella organization)
Factional structure   where power is concentrated in two or more durable
                        and competing factions
Coalitional structure   where power is dispersed and actors and organiza-
                        tions work together in fluid coalitions (for example,
                        a network of multiple organizations)
Amorphous structure   where power is diffuse and there is no pattern of co-
                        alition building or central leadership. (Sharp 2001,
                        406)

On the basis of exploratory comparative research in four rural communities in the American Midwest, Sharp (2001, 421) concludes that pyramidal and coalitional structures – which most closely describe the umbrella organization and networked organizational forms respectively – are the most likely to generate community field-like interaction and capacity. Sharp tends to favour the pyramidal over the coalitional model, on the basis that it is more efficient to maintain small numbers of links to a central node or subnetwork than it is to cultivate and maintain multiple links with potential coalitional partners. However, as he rightly points out (418), a significant concern with the pyramidal structure is the extent to which concentrated power can lead to the exclusion of broad community interests, or the privileging of the narrow interests of core clique members. I would argue that, to the extent that community self-help both relies on and needs to include the satisfaction of diverse community interests, a coalitional structure is more likely to achieve long-term community field effects than a pyramidal structure, which is by its very nature an exercise in exclusivity. Further, the coalitional structure suggests a greater level of flexibility in the articulation and development of specific activities. It would seem that a flexible system – such as an interorganizational network in which network actors shift and change – would provide greater possibility for innovation through accessing the diverse intellectual, professional, and human resources available within a given community.

While it is useful to consider the way in which organizational structures may support or erode the community field, it is important also to recognize that structure alone is not a predictor of positive outcomes. The way in which social capital is manifest within a given organizational structure is also a critical issue. For example, in the community in which I am currently conducting research, the efficacy of establishing a comprehensive umbrella organization explicitly oriented toward building a community field is significantly undermined by the factional power relations at work within the town. In this case, all the organizational structure in the world will not assist this community to meet its objectives while warring factions continue not to speak to each other.

This raises the significant issue of the role of conflict in rural regeneration, and how conflict is addressed in social capital and sustainable community development discourses. A number of field staff interviewed in our research emphasized community conflict as a key inhibitor of successful development activity. In some cases, this was conflict that evolved around the best way to do specific projects, but more often than not, these conflicts were steeped in much deeper historical conflicts between individuals or social groupings within the local community. Chapter 5 by Suzanne Benn and Jenny Onyx, and Chapter 10 by Onyx and Osburn also illuminate the effects of historical conflict on community capacity for collective action.

It is important not to assume, however, that all forms of conflict are unproductive and to be eradicated from the development process. Indeed, as Flora, Sharp, and Flora (1997) have observed, healthy communities are those where controversy (and the diversity it implies) is accepted as part of community life, and where individuals can take specific positions in a controversy without negative personal consequences. The type of controversy described by Flora, Sharp, and Flora, however, is predicated on interaction and engagement with difference, rather than factionalization and disengagement. This requires collective commitment to engagement, and explicit management of traditional relations of power that serve to silence already marginalized groups.

Both the social capital and sustainable community development approaches to rural community development are based on the assumed value of consensus over conflict. Social capital is, by definition, a resource generated through cooperation. Sustainability, in Dale's (2001) terms, will occur only where environmental, social, and economic imperatives are reconciled. My research, and the work of others such as Flora, Sharp, and Flora (1997), suggests that it is important to qualify these terms with a recognition that some types of conflict or controversy are functional, and necessary for communities to manage the development process in the face of diverse community interests and needs. If we recognize that consensus, in the traditional community development use of the term, describes a decision or situation that all can live with, rather than a decision or situation that all agree with, then supporting consensus remains a useful development approach.

Conclusions

In this chapter, I have considered the contributions of social capital and sustainable community development approaches to rural renewal. In brief, the value of the social capital approach is that it identifies the significance of the breadth and quality of networks – between individuals, between organizations, and between communities and their broader environments – in making the transition from community vulnerability to crisis to community strength and well-being. The value of the sustainable community development approach is that it acknowledges the interdependence of social, environmental, cultural, and economic factors within communities of place, and emphasizes the relationships between local communities and the broader social, environmental, and economic systems in which they operate. By linking the insights of social capital and sustainable community development, it becomes apparent that the development of a strong community field – a structural framework that systemically integrates social, environmental, cultural, and economic objectives – is a potentially critical factor in ensuring successfully coordinated approaches to sustainable community development.

Acknowledgments
My thanks to Dr. Suzanne Fraser for her research assistance in conducting and transcribing interviews with NSW regional coordination field staff.

Note
1   There is no universally agreed-upon definition of what constitutes a region in Australia. For the purposes of this chapter, I define a region as a geographical area that has some natural or cultural boundaries. While all areas of Australia form part of a region, this article focuses on regions located outside metropolitan boundaries.

References
Baum, S., R. Stimson, K. O'Connor, P. Mullins, and R. Davis. 1999. *Community Opportunity and Vulnerability in Australia's Cities and Towns: Characteristics, Patterns and Implications.* Brisbane: University of Queensland Press.
Black, A., J. Duff, S. Saggers, and P. Baines. 2000. *Rural Communities and Rural Social Issues: Priorities for Research.* Canberra: Rural Industries Research and Development Corporation.
Bridger, J.C., and A.E. Luloff. 1999. "Toward an Interactional Approach to Sustainable Community Development." *Journal of Rural Studies* 15: 377-87.
Chavis, D.M. 2001. "The Paradoxes and Promise of Community Coalitions." *American Journal of Community Psychology* 29(2): 309-20.
Collits, P., and B. Gastin. 1997. "Big Town, Small Town: The Centralisation of Services and Economic Activity, the Decline of Small Towns and the Policy Response in New South Wales." *Regional Policy and Practice* 6(2): 9-21.
Dale, A. 1999. "Sustainable Development: A Framework for Governance." PhD. diss., McGill University, Montreal.
Davidson, A.P., and B. Grant. 2001. "Rural Australia: Neo-Liberalism or a 'New Feudalism'?" *Journal of Contemporary Asia* 31(3): 289-303.
Duff, J., and M. Tonts. 2000. "Comparative Perspectives on Regional Development Policy in Australia and Ireland." *Rural Society* 10(3): 301-17.
Falk, I., and S. Kilpatrick. 2000. "What is Social Capital? A Study of Interaction in a Rural Community." *Sociologia Ruralis* 40(1): 87-110.
Flora, J.L., J. Sharp, and C. Flora. 1997. "Entrepreneurial Social Infrastructure and Locally Initiated Economic Development in the Nonmetropolitan United States." *The Sociological Quarterly* 38(4): 623-45.

Frawley, K. 1994. "Evolving Visions; Environmental Management and Nature Conserva-tion in Australia." In S. Dovers, ed., *Australian Environmental History,* 55-78. Melbourne: Oxford University Press.

Gray, I., and G. Lawrence. 2001. "Neoliberalism, Individualism and Prospects for Regional Renewal." *Rural Society* 11(3): 283-97.

Hart, M. 1999. *Guide to Sustainable Community Indicators,* 2nd ed. North Andover, MA: Sustainable Measures.

Hase, S., R. Phelps, A. Graham, and M. Wallace. 2000. *Kyogle: Capable Community or Social Statistic? A Report on Factors Which Assist Rural Communities to Deal with Social Disadvan-tage.* Lismore: School of Social Sciences, Southern Cross University.

Herbert-Cheshire, L. 2000. "Contemporary Strategies for Rural Community Development in Australia: A Governmentality Perspective." *Journal of Rural Studies* 16(2): 203-16.

Himmelman, A.T. 2001. "On Coalitions and the Transformation of Power Relations: Col-laborative Betterment and Collaborative Empowerment." *American Journal of Community Psychology* 29(2): 277-84.

Kenyon, P., and B. Black. 2001. "Small Town Renewal: Overview and Case Studies: Report for the Rural Industries Research and Development Corporation." Publication No. 01/ 043. Barton, ACT: Rural Industries Research and Development Corporation.

Nassauer, J.I. 1997. "Culture and Landscape Ecology: Insights for Action." In J.I. Nassauer, ed., *Placing Nature: Culture in Landscape Ecology.* Washington, DC: Island Press.

National Institute of Economic and Industry Research. 1999. *State of the Regions 1999.* Sydney: Australian Local Government Association.

Onyx, J. 2001. "Third Sector as Voice: The Importance of Social Capital." *Third Sector Review* 7(2): 73-88.

Onyx, J., and P. Bullen. 2000. "Sources of Social Capital." In I. Winter, ed., *Social Capital and Public Policy in Australia,* 105-35. Canberra: Australian Institute of Family Studies.

Onyx, J., and R. Leonard. 2000. *Rural Renewal and Social Capital: The Case of Sweden and Australia.* Working Paper No. 46, Centre for Australian community Organizations and Management, St. Leonards, University of Technology, Sydney.

Productivity Commission. 1999. *Impact of Competition Policy Reforms on Rural and Regional Australia.* Report No. 8. Canberra: Ausinfo.

Putnam, R., R. Leonardi, and R. Nanetti. 1993. *Making Democracy Work: Civic Traditions in Modern Italy.* Princeton, NJ: Princeton University Press.

Roseland, M. 2000. "Sustainable Community Development: Integrating Environmental, Economic, and Social Objectives." *Progress in Planning* 54: 73-132.

Sharp, J. 2001. "Locating the Community Field: A Study of Interorganizational Network Structure and Capacity for Community Action." *Rural Sociology* 66(3): 403-24.

Smailes, P.J. 1996. "Accessibility Changes in South Australia and the Country Town Network." In G. Lawrence, K. Lyons, and S. Momtaz, eds., *Social Change in Rural Aus-tralia.* Rockhampton: Rural Social and Economic Research Centre, Central Queensland University.

Tabart, T., A. Fulton, and R. Clark. 2001. "Taking the Future in Their Hands: Local Develop-ment Practice Around the World." *Rural Society* 11(1): 5-21.

Wilkinson, K.P. 1991. *The Community in Rural America.* New York: Greenwood Press.

5
Negotiating Interorganizational Domains: The Politics of Social, Natural, and Symbolic Capital
Suzanne Benn and Jenny Onyx

In Australia, the costs of remediation of massive environmental degradation[1] and the challenges of the sustainable management of remaining resources are such that policy making has required collaboration between numerous stakeholders. Interorganizational domains have tended to form between various levels of government, nonprofit and community organizations, corporations, small- and medium-sized enterprises, and expert advisors in an attempt to address the issues. In Canada, the forestry industry has led the way in forming collaborative arrangements with other sector organizations such as NGOs in order to further understanding of sustainability standards and certification. However, it is recognized that these arrangements will not effect change for sustainability unless the community is engaged (Robinson 2002). In British Columbia, where the harvesting of primary resources is a mainstay of the economy, resource companies are increasingly working with government and communities to ensure benefit for all stakeholders (British Columbia 2001).

This chapter aims to explore the role that social capital plays in the power relations of interorganizational domains that form around policy making for sustainable natural resource management. The implications of these power relations for the engagement of local communities are then assessed. One way of approaching this problem is to examine the distribution of social capital within domains that include community-based organizations as stakeholders.

Theoretical Understandings of Multi-Stakeholder Cooperation for Sustainability

Sustainable development and sustainability are now generally accepted as complex and ambivalent concepts, which attempt to integrate both radical and reformist perspectives on environmental and social issues (Robinson 2001). Ann Dale, in Chapter 1, points out that sustainable development is characterized by conditions of deep uncertainty. What are the characteristics of interorganizational domains that deal effectively with these challenging concepts?

In a seminal article, Emery and Trist (1965) argue that the appropriate organizational structure for turbulent organizational fields (fields characterized by complexity, uncertainty, and multiple interconnections between component systems) is not a single hierarchical organization. They put forward the case that an interorganizational domain, held together by shared values, is the most appropriate organizational form. In such domains, social order is negotiated between the stakeholders rather than imposed at the outset (Hardy 1994).

This question of multi-stakeholder relationships for sustainability can also be explored from the perspective of reflexive modernization (Beck 1992, 1995, 1999, 2000; Giddens 1994; Lash, Szerszynski, and Wynne 1996). The main focus of this theory is the increasingly self-critical nature of society as it learns to cope with its own side effects. Recognition of the social and ecological threats associated with industrial society results in diminished trust in the capitalist state and the organizations associated with industrial capitalism, forcing a rethinking of organizational structure and the need for new and interorganizational forms (Beck 1992, 1995). Conflict over accountability develops and new forms of regulation emerge to deal with such side effects. This study focuses on informal reflexive regulation, such as networks and informal interorganizational arrangements between corporations, state agencies, NGOs, and communities (Benn 2004). According to Beck (1999, 37-38), such forms of regulation are "shaping society from below" and their dynamics, and those of attendant disputes, are examples of "subpolitical" arrangements of the "risk society."[2] Although issues of trust are crucial to an understanding of the conditions of the "risk society," its leading theorists have not examined the role social capital plays in the formation and success of "sub-political" arrangements for sustainability.

We argue here that the concept of social capital is particularly relevant to the consideration of the subpolitics of an interorganizational domain formed around policy making for sustainable natural resource management. Social capital is increasingly recognized as a source of influence and power. An emerging and key distinction, important for the relationship between social capital and power is between bridging and bonding social capital. Bonding social capital appears to be characterized by dense, multi-functional ties and strong but localized trust. It refers to the internal links within collectivities, to empowerment, and to solidarity. What is implicit throughout most discussions of bonding social capital is a sense of personal and collective efficacy through the development of group norms. This requires the active and willing engagement of citizens within a participative community and is quite different from the receipt of services, or even from human rights to the receipt of services, though these are unquestionably important. Social capital refers to people as creators, not as victims (Onyx and Bullen 2000). Conversely to institutionalization theory, this aspect of social capital theory focuses on the way lower-level aggregates get to influence higher-level aggregates through the diffusion of norms and beliefs (Adler and Kwon 2002). Social capital can therefore act as a source of symbolic power because of its role in the diffusion of meaning (Morgan 1997). Theorists of late modernity argue that, in a discursive and uncertain environment, organizations need to develop symbolic power as well as economic power. In other words, organizations build symbolic as well as economic capital (Tsoukas 1999). In this chapter we argue that bonding social capital can act as a source of symbolic capital.

Bridging social capital refers to the external links within networks (Adler and Kwon 2002). It is shown to be important in "the search (by local communities) for, and acceptance of[,] outside assistance" (Onyx and Leonard 2000, 27) and appears to be usually mediated by trust in expert systems (Giddens 1998). Bridging social capital can act as an important resource for both individuals and groups, facilitating their actions by linking them in social networks (Adler and Kwon 2002). In terms of power, actors in networks can build up sets of obligations that they can use when needed as a source of influence. Where bridging capital is low and groups are disconnected, Burt argues, power will flow to the broker who can negotiate across these structural holes (Burt 1992).

Adler and Kwon shows that while the benefits of bonding social capital include influence, control, and power, it can also be associated with deficits. For instance, communities high in bonding social capital may become too embedded and unable to develop the bridging social capital necessary to form links to external networks or actors (Adler and Kwon 2002).

In the subpolitical arena, the assumptions and prejudices of the different stakeholders are exposed to wider scrutiny, particularly as sustainability issues are often associated with sociotechnical uncertainties. In these conditions, lay knowledge is more likely to challenge established or expert science and to be the source of a newly reflexive consciousness (Irwin 2001; Wynne 1996). Thus, the role played by different forms of knowledge and rationality as it relates to the social capital of interorganizational domains also needs to be investigated. Studies of the micropolitics of community response to environmental risk show that expert knowledge, science, reason, and rationality may not be the basis for good decision making and that lack of trust between differing rationalities is a major issue (Welcomer et al. 2000; Wynne 1996). Local community groups may be marginalized by expert discourse in subpolitical decision-making arrangements (Benn 2004). Presumably this situation would be exacerbated if bridging social capital is low.

Background to the Case Study

This chapter suggests that the Landcare movement in Australia offers a rich source of data on the relationship between social capital and power in the subpolitical decision making of interorganizational domains. Landcare is a Commonwealth-government-sponsored, grassroots movement that has spread to encompass numerous autonomous groups and local and regional networks across Australia. With the primary aim of building local capacity for sustainable land management and improved environmental risk communication, Landcare has developed varied relationships between these groups and networks, experts from all levels of government, and corporate sponsors (Hill 1999). Here we report on an intensive qualitative analysis of Landcare as a multi-stakeholder, networked, organization that is currently undergoing major shifts in relations of power. The lens of social capital can both illuminate our understanding of these shifts and enable us to postulate implications for local communities.

Methodology

Our research involves participant-observation in public meetings and in some of the individual and collective discussions and organized and impromptu activities of a local Landcare group, its relationship with the local Landcare network and with a regional Landcare network.[3]

We also conducted a study at the macro level of key stakeholders of the Landcare movement in Australia. The researcher attended meetings of the peak Landcare body, the Australian Landcare Council (ALC), and Landcare conferences at the state level. Following this typology, participant observation at this stage can be classified as observer-participant (Gold cited in Punch 1998) or moderator (Spratley 1980).

In both studies, key respondents from community, business, and government were questioned in semi-structured and open-ended interviews. Respondents were selected from the primary stakeholders of Landcare: corporate sponsors and local and other levels of governments, representing bureaucratic interests such as National Parks and Wildlife, the Environment Protection Authority, and the Rural Fire Brigade.

As a balance to the participation-observer work, data were also collected from other Landcare groups in New South Wales and Victoria selected for their interorganizational nature. Material was gathered by attending public meetings, by semi-structured and open-ended interviews with Landcare members, and from documents produced by the various groups, associations, and networks, as well as from other local documents.

Research Findings

The Subpolitics of Landcare

Landcare was created with the stated aim of raising local awareness and fostering cooperation between land managers and farmers in order to develop more sustainable natural resource management practices. Its origins lie in a partnership formed between the National Farmers Federation and the peak conservationist group, the Australian Conservation Foundation (ACF). Since then, the National Landcare Program has been largely funded through the sale of the national telecommunications facility. The Natural Heritage Trust allocates public funding through grants, tax deductions, and property management programs. The funding also covers the employment of coordinators, whose responsibilities include networking and developing community understanding of technical and other issues. However, the Landcare movement is largely volunteer-driven and the various groups have, until 2002, remained autonomous organizations. There are now more than 4,500 local autonomous groups across Australia. In 2000-2001, approximately AUD$82.6 million was dispersed to these community-based groups, funds being administered at the state, territory, or catchment level (Cary and Webb 2001).

Individual groups have recently tended to come together in networks. For instance, there are seventy shire networks in the state of New South Wales, with shire networks also coming together as regional and catchment networks (Marriott et al. 2000). The ALC is the government's key advisory body on Landcare matters. The council is a multi-stakeholder body, comprising community members, various levels of government, community organizations such as Greening Australia, and representatives from the ACF and the National Farmers Federation.

Partnerships have formed between the Landcare groups and networks, environmental groups, Greening Australia, industry sector organizations such as the various state farmers organizations, the Commonwealth government, the state governments and other state and territory governments, local government, and universities. Local government often offers a supporting role in terms of resources, and sponsorship by corporate interests is common. State governments also play a role. Landcare Australia Limited (LAL) is a Commonwealth government corporation whose function is to raise funds and awareness for Landcare.

The official rhetoric of Landcare is that the movement brings together diverse and sometimes opposing factions of society into networked relationships. Recent research shows that Landcare networks build new social capital through shared experiences in learning and communication and that this form of social capital contributes to the success of networks in developing ecological sustainability (Cary and Webb 2000; Sobels, Curtis, and Lockie 2001). The numbers of Landcare groups formed across Australia represent an unusual success rate, at a time when participation in community organizations in the developed world is apparently decreasing (Putnam 2000). As well, LAL has been very successful in its cause marketing campaign, and there are now approximately forty corporate sponsors (Landcare

Australia 2002). Although critics have argued that corporate sponsorship of Landcare represents nothing more than corporate greenwash (Lockie 1999), it is undeniable that the Landcare image holds considerable meaning for the Australian public.

Recently, the accountability of Landcare has been questioned. In 2001, an Auditor General's Report criticized the Commonwealth government funding scheme which contributes funding to Landcare through the Natural Heritage Trust, for vague target-setting, loose reporting, and monitoring arrangements, and for its inability to prove that it has made a significant contribution to the environment (*Sydney Morning Herald* 2001).

Evidence of Tensions in the Interorganizational Domain of Landcare

Our research indicates that the Landcare interorganizational domain is in fact two quite distinctive subpolitical decision-making arenas whose relationship is characterized by a number of tensions. The bureaucratic decision-making arena contains the formally constituted, tightly organized bureaucracies such as state and federal government departments, catchment management authorities, and corporations, including the commercial arm of Landcare, LAL. These organizations are in a "discourse coalition"[4] with natural resource management professionals and with a number of academics who have made the social and political aspects of natural resource management their academic sphere of expertise. This coalition has formed based on the general argument that "local" Landcare should only be an aspect of wider catchment management and planning.

The other arena is the local arena. It contains the members of looser community-based networks, the local Landcare groups and the local Landcare network coordinators, local government officers, local business organizations, academics, and other actors who support the grass-roots approach. This coalition has formed based on the perception that change for sustainability emanates from basic community-building processes that develop and recognize the success of small, local projects (Hill 1999).

The ALC offers an opportunity for representatives of the two arenas to negotiate; its discourse reflects the tensions between them. Regional representative forms of Landcare may also present such an opportunity in the future, but their role currently is unclear and dependent on context, such as individual skills and other capacities, as well as on their relationship with the bureaucratized catchment management authorities. As well, it is predictable that the community elites may shift to the bureaucratic arena.

Voices for Planning and Integration

Senior bureaucrats and natural resource management professionals are critical of the local activities of Landcare: "Landcare is not working. The farmers plant trees where their bank is eroding. They should really be planted higher up or the river needs to be addressed as a whole," said one Sydney member of the Healthy Rivers Commission, in September 2001. The activities of the local Landcare coordinators are referred to as "odd-jobs" by a government representative on the ALC.

A corporate relations manager at a major international company that is a sponsor of Landcare commented on the community's and bureaucratic arena's different ways of operating: "The people here would not understand the stop-start pattern of community-based project work, lots of enthusiasm and then nothing in between projects." This manager was asked to support the local group studied but refused on these grounds: "I prefer to deal with the regional level. [Local] Landcare seems very disorganized" (interview, 15 December 2001, Singleton, NSW).

The state Landcare manager (a state government employee) sees the culture and priorities of corporate sponsors as quite different from that of local business enterprises, as he explained in a telephone interview, 20 June 2001: "The corporate sponsors really only get involved in the big projects organized at the state level; there is not much money down at the group level ... Corporations are all urban-based, their volunteer ethic does not fit with the Landcare model which is more about self-determination. At the local level it is the local agribusiness which is getting involved." Scientific planning and productivity priorities are also linked. The major push for productivity in the following dialogue at an ALC meeting comes from the representative of a scientific institution linked to both the state and to a commodity sector – the Grain Research Development Corporation (GRDC):

We need to increase productivity by 30 percent over the next five years. We need to get productive solutions to environmental problems. (GRDC representative)

What is the point given the price of sorghum? (Community member)

Twenty-five percent of our research and development is in the environmental area. (GRDC representative)

How much of the 25 percent R and D for environmental research can be related to chemicals and weed management? I'm making a comment about public projection of an image. (National Landcare facilitator)

The environmental debt is building up. Will the Grain Research and Development Council fund environmental work in areas which have no relation to productivity? (Community member)

A successful outcome for R and D has to enable farmers to be neutral or better off. (GRDC representative)

The issue is short term versus long term. (Chairman, ALC)

The problem is a research culture based on wheat. Cultural change needs to be factored in. (Greening Australia community representative)

The Grain Research Development Corporation is taking an expedient approach towards its constituents. (Community member)

The Research Development Corporations represent big money – the farmers relate to them. How can we get them to devote more money to sustainability, rather than to productivity? Good sustainable farm management must support further production. The government puts in dollar for dollar into a Research Development Corporation – this is for public benefit. There is need for further awareness that the Research Development Corporation is also obliged to move its focus from commodities to natural resource management. (Chairman, ALC)

Voices of Community Actors in the Landcare Domain

According to one local Landcare coordinator, "it will not work in helping other people's land management. Projects will not work if the community have no role in developing the projects – unless there is a sense of ownership." Another local coordinator describes how the local group works differently from other voluntary associations concerned with environmental or social issues: "Landcare is less political, more local." The strong identification with the local can be related to the "embeddedness" of bonding social capital (Adler and Kwon 2002) and has implications for the development of bridging social capital. Many local group members can see no benefit in working away from their own direct area. As one local group member puts it, "what have we got to do with the region?"

At the local level, community perceptions of the corporate-Landcare relationship are of a distant, exploitative entity:

I don't want anything to do with Rio Tinto and the Queen of England. (Community member of a Landcare group)

Why shouldn't they pay back some of the damage they have done to the environment?" (Community member)

Local Landcare groups have a diverse membership. Within the group of relatively new settlers in one local Landcare group are a number of "experts" in sustainability who are trusted and accepted as comembers of Landcare. Such groups fulfill the original aim of Landcare to act as a forum for different perspectives on natural resource management. This is demonstrated by the following exchange between community members at a Landcare group meeting:

> What is the group's suggestion about the wombats and their effect on the trees just planted along the creek banks? They will end up destroying half the new plantings. (Community member A)
>
> Wombats were here before us. (Community member B)
>
> I don't give a damn about that. (Community member A)
>
> Why don't we try putting in wombat gates and pathways? I've heard about that being done. (Community member C)
>
> That hardly seems a natural solution for the wombats. (Community member A)[5]

Problem Definition in the Domain of Landcare

In underorganized interorganizational domains, disagreement of one kind or another between stakeholders impedes the development of shared values and of a more structured cooperative arrangement (Hardy 1994). The research reported on here shows Landcare as an underorganized domain, characterized by considerable tension between two distinct subpolitical arenas for decision making. Recently, the tensions have intensified into a struggle for power as the discourse coalition representing the bureaucratic arena has stepped up attempts to colonize the local. The power of each arena and its coalition of interests can be analyzed in terms of the relationship between social capital and influence, control, and power. This relationship has implications for control over the problem definition of sustainable development and, thus, has implications for local communities.

The Power Relations of the Bureaucratic Definition of Landcare

The source of influence of this discourse coalition is technocratic expert power. Their discourse is linked by an instrumentalist perspective on sustainability and a shared emphasis on broad-based planning for ecological rationality. Also pulled into this coalition are academics critical of the volunteerism of Landcare as just another example of the neo-liberal determination to dismantle the state (Martin and Ritchie 1999). Other members are peak environmental organizations and green political groups (Lockie 1999). For instance, one community member of ALC commented that "when the Australian Conservation Foundation member of the ALC is here, feathers tend to fly a bit."

Bridging social capital comes into play in the power and influence of this arena, enabling the development of the discourse coalition at conferences, meetings, committees, working groups, research funding schemes, and alliances, and other decision-making fora characteristic of the risk society. Our field research indicates that the elements of this coalition are linked by a shared techno-instrumental rationality that enables the building of trusting reciprocal relationships between organizations and different professional groups. This is the so-called revolving door between big business, big science (such as the various agricultural sector research foundations, which are partly funded by government and partly by the particular agricultural sector), and government (Beder 2000; Rose 2000).

The Power Relations of the Local Definition of Landcare

The local group is a major source of social capital, particularly in areas where there are many "new settlers." One group we studied has acted as an organizing basis to oppose unwanted developments in the area, drawing in to their cause a number of locally based experts in sustainability and environmental planning. Members of Landcare groups say their reason for joining Landcare was to "mee[t] people."

Importantly, this discourse coalition is not as bound as the bureaucratic arena by language interaction resulting in a similar interpretation of the problem of sustainable natural resource management. Its disparate community members (which may include farmers, environmentalists, rural residential, bushcarers, dunecarers and other locally based groups) are linked by considerable mistrust of state and federal governments, big science, and big business. Many local Landcare members expressed mistrust to our researcher of governments or of "bureaucrats." Local coordinators expressed anger and a sense of betrayal at corporations moving their sponsorship to a more "high-profile" site after just a year or so of funding. The shared norm at this level is that of collective efficacy, in an organization the community members "can have a say in."

The great source of influence and power held by the local arena is the symbolic power of the bonding reputation of Landcare: the green linked hands of its logo are a symbol of the perceived power of Landcare to bring together disparate elements of Australian society under one "apolitical" roof. This symbolic capital of Landcare is sourced in the capacity of Landcare to build social capital. Landcare's reputation is built on its ability to bring disparate actors together in the name of sustainable natural resource management. It is this reputation concerning collaboration for sustainability that corporations purchase when they take up cause marketing arrangements with Landcare. At a time when rural community life and spirit is well

Table 5.1

Sources of power

Bureaucratic arena	Local arena
Bridging social capital facilitates expert and technocratic power acting through professional and corporate networking	Symbolic capital derived from the reputation of Landcare as an unique organization
Bridging social capital facilitates potential to generate economic capital through sponsorship	Local knowledge empowered through social capital and community renewal
Bridging social capital linking government networks to foster support for top-down planning	Bonding social capital can enable effective and cohesive local action

recognized as diminishing in Australia (*Sydney Morning Herald* 2002), Landcare has survived. The local arena has power in that it can withdraw in solidarity, leaving government with no volunteers and corporations with no Landcare image of the "shared hands" to sponsor. As government representatives themselves admit, the resources will never all be able to be provided by government.[6] The sources of convening power (Dale 1995) for Landcare are identified in Table 5.1.

The Colonization of the Local

As Hajer (1996) has so clearly shown in his work, members of a discourse coalition share a rationality and, thus, an interpretation of a particular problem. As well, each member may directly benefit from the selected problem definition and associated solution of his or her coalition. This case study reveals a situation where government is possibly challenged by the anarchic and autonomous grassroots organization of Landcare, academics are possibly politicized by the increasing need for universities to find external sources of funding, and natural resource management professionals are possibly marginalizing local groups from the decision-making process to ensure their professional future.

Both Jo Barraket and Tony Boydell point out, in Chapters 4 and 10 respectively, that sustainable development is dependent on the local. It requires a decentralized structure that will "let people get on with it." Landcare was established to develop local awareness. Yet the competing discourse of the bureaucratic arena has acted to shift the problem definition associated with the Landcare domain away from the local. Sustainable natural resource management in Australia is moving away from rather than toward this ideal of local action. As shown in Table 5.1, each arena has sources of power that relate to the distribution of social capital. The "colonization" of the local is currently being enabled through a number of surveillance mechanisms that are moving to institutionalize a hegemonic definition of the requirements for sustainable natural resource management in Australia.

Surveillance Mechanisms in the Colonization of the Local

Bureaucratic standardization is the surveillance mechanism employed in the "colonization" of the local arena. Management according to measuring and monitoring systems are now key elements in the government-driven agenda for Landcare. This discourse at an ALC meeting highlights the contrast between this agenda and the community perspective:

> The need for a strategic approach is recognized but a community bottom-up approach is essential. (Community representative, Greening Australia)

> But we need to manage in bite-sized chunks. (Intergovernmental committee representative)

> From a community perspective, a holistic approach is necessary, not bite-sized chunks. (Community representative, Greening Australia)

The attempt by the bureaucracy to establish control systems over the local arena is evident as the government departments look to establish greater surveillance systems over on-the-ground Landcare staff:

> There are more strategic returns from investment in human resources than from technology. We need standardization in the training of Landcare staff. (Representative, Australian Government, Agriculture, Fisheries and Forestry)

Personnel employed at the Landcare regional network level recognize their roles as potential intermediaries between the local and the bureaucratic. Yet they describe a role of the Landcare regional network that involves surveillance, and thus a power differential between themselves and the local:

> We need to come up with evaluation-gathering information without annoying on-the-ground Landcare groups. The issue is accountability – with the Natural Heritage Trust being too loose. That is why the state agency has been given carriage.

Community representatives perceive the community arena to be in need of defence against encroaching government influence. One community member of ALC commented, "It's a shame you can't pick up on the government agenda – they tend to be pretty quiet around the table." Another community member complained, "I think the worst thing is that we now have projects divided into Bushcare, Coastcare, Rivercare, and Landcare – all with different objects described by the government." Another objects to local Landcare coordinators now being called Community Support Officers: "If we accept that, we are being conned by the federal government."

Problem Definition and Different Forms of Knowledge
Tension is evident between different forms of knowledge and control of problem definition. In this discussion, community representatives on the ALC defend local capabilities:

> Local people need to recognize their own capacity. (Community member)

> Farmers don't always understand that it means sustainability of the natural resource base – not whether they can pass it on to their children. (Representative, Australian Government, Agriculture, Fisheries and Forestry)

> National Resource Management is placing an increasing emphasis on Environment Management Systems – most farmers don't understand it. (Chairman, ALC)

> Who decides the indicators? What is sustainable farming? (Community member)

> Catchment is becoming a dominant word, but its meaning is not really understood. (Community member)

The struggle for control is most obvious in the determination to rationalize the funding process of the previously autonomously acting local groups. In the following exchange, a representative from the federal Agriculture, Fisheries and Forestry department is questioned by community members of the ALC. The topic is the proposed rationalization of Landcare funding to less than four bids per region (in other words, local groups are no longer to be the autonomous managers of their own funds).

> The situation has the potential to become top-down. People's sense of the environment depends on what they can see. How can community volunteering involvement be married with a single bid? (Community member of ALC)

> The process will be a bid within a bid, say within the Catchment Management Authority. (Representative, Australian Government, Agriculture, Fisheries and Forestry)

Table 5.2

A new negotiated storyline of sustainability

From	To
Landcare coordinator	Community support officer
Local	Regional
Landcare organization	Landcare ethical principles
Holistic	Strategic
Farm	Catchment
Local awareness raising	Priority projects

The question of how Landcare groups can relate to the Catchment Management Authority is very important and there will be a workshop on this question at the next ALC meeting. (Chairman, ALC)

Environment Australia [a federal government department] has been coming in at the last minute with directives to communities on corridor [wildlife] width. Formal organizations lose the community this way – an agency comes in with an arbitrary figure – preaching to people who really know the area. (Representative, Australian Government, Agriculture, Fisheries and Forestry)

A manager of Landcare at the state level (a government employee) puts it bluntly: "The regions will have more say. Lowering the water tables is a huge task. It requires more targeted approaches."

The effect of the power struggle is the emergence of a new storyline of sustainable natural resource management (see Table 5.2).

Discussion

There are clearly very different modes of discourse adopted by the various stakeholders of Landcare. These different forms of discourse reflect the operations of Landcare as a segmented organizational domain consisting of two communicative arenas, each favouring a particular storyline (Hajer 1995) concerning the interpretation of sustainability in relation to natural resource management.[7] One arena is tightly structured, the other decentralized. Each needs the other, but the arenas have fundamentally different discourses, reflecting different rationalities. At this stage, it is unclear what role the regional forms of Landcare will take and how they will negotiate between these arenas.

It is tempting to allocate all power to the bureaucracies and their professionals: the national and state governments, the National Heritage Trust, academics, the large scientific research organizations associated with big science, and corporate sponsors. The bureaucratic arena generates considerable expert power as well as having the bridging social capital to link to economic power and bureaucratic control. However, the discourse of the local arena reflects the relations of another source of power at the grassroots. The arena containing the local group, the local network, and local coordinator exerts considerable power through the development of bonding social capital. This grassroots aspect of Landcare is also a powerful source of symbolic capital (Tsoukas 1999). It is this aspect of the Landcare movement that has a strong and unique public identity. The community arena contains the actors who are the source of the prestige and recognition given to Landcare and sought by the corporate sponsor.

There is clear evidence from this study that the people are drawn to Landcare for a variety of motivations, of which the desire to adopt more custodial attitudes to the land is a common and dominant one. In this process the local Landcare groups generate considerable social capital, which they are able to mobilize for the creation of new and creative solutions. In practical terms, this means increased levels of trust, better networks, and an enhanced capacity to work collectively for mutual gain. This commitment at the local level is grounded; it refers to this time and this place as experienced in the everyday reality of life in this environment. The rationality expressed is the rationality of the immediately lived experience (Dryzek 1997; Tsoukas 1999).

The key action underpinning these tensions appears to be the colonization of the local, community arena by the "discourse coalition" of the bureaucratic arena as it attempts to take over the social and symbolic capital developed by the local group. The surveillance mechanisms of standardization and monitoring employed by the actors of the bureaucratic arena facilitate the acceptance of the new taken-for-granted understanding of the storyline of sustainable natural resource management (see Table 5.2) (Foucault 1972, 1977). Power relations observed in this study of Landcare thus support an analysis of the fluid nature of power, and its shifting, dynamic characteristics (Clegg 1989; Hajer 1995; Livesey 2001).

A major source of tension is the emerging challenge to the local knowledge and capacity that has developed in association with the bottom-up process of community-based decision making and face-to-face consensus negotiation in decentralized networks. This is currently threatened by top-down concerns over accountability and ecological irrationality, and challenged by bureaucratic understandings of whole-of-catchment planning, involving centralized decision making and funding.

In this sense there is a discordance between the development of social and ecological capital. The vision of sustainability since the 1992 UNCED Conference has been for the integration of social and ecological concerns. This study has highlighted some barriers in the implementation of this vision. Whole-of-catchment planning is necessary for progress to be made in

Australia on major issues such as salinity. In terms of ecological rationality, integrated bureaucratic planning at the catchment level offers a more appropriate form of governance than existing political boundaries. The weakness, and the frustration experienced by those operating at the local level, is that the experience, the collective action, and the access to resources, are all bounded to the local. While social capital is certainly generated, it is largely bonding rather than bridging social capital. The commitment to the commons is locally understood, and does not extend beyond the boundaries of the local group.

While local resources can and are mobilized in the form of local knowledge, equipment, and volunteer labour, this only becomes really effective when used to leverage outside expertise and funding sources. Yet the external agents who could provide such expertise and funding are not necessarily sympathetic to the local agenda. As pointed out, these agents are focused on the ecological dilemma: the need for a catchment-wide perspective. For the corporation, the issue is that the symbolic capital is associated with the image of the local group; the problem becomes how to access this capital, the community domain operating as it does, a world to itself. Relationships are also influenced by corporate demands for high project visibility and the need to be seen as legitimate participants in the scientific debate and planning for sustainability.

Still another area of tension is that between productivity and sustainability. Here the influence of big science – the alliance between the state, industry sectors, and science – becomes evident (Rose 2000). In place of the lived local experience, we have a language that reduces the issues to a technical and scientific set of problems to be resolved, in the name of productivity, by expert knowledge and direction. The research has shown the community frustration at being marginalized by big science. As Wynne (1996) points out, it is not that local or lay knowledge is lost or submerged but, rather, silenced by the dependency of the local on the expert institutions. Yet there is a growing cynicism born of distrust of those expert and centralizing institutions.

The tensions observed may reflect the strength rather than the deficits of Landcare as it relates to local communities. According to Hardy (1994), a fragmented domain may lead to a more creative result. In this case, the tensions and contradictions between the two arenas of operation highlight some of the profound challenges of sustainability (Chua and Clegg in Hardy 1994). As well, the "structural holes," (Burt 1997, 340) or spaces between the local and bureaucratic networks, provide opportunity for effective and powerful action. Creative and contextually based solutions may be achieved at the regional and ALC representative levels of Landcare. As Szerszynski (1997) has pointed out, voluntary associations such as Landcare provide the glue on which sustainability can be built but, more importantly, engagement with such challenges can provide a quality of life.

Notes

1 In Australia, 5.7 million hectares of land are currently considered at risk from dryland salinity, with the figure projected to be 17 million hectares in fifty years (Land and Water Resources Audit 2000).
2 Ulrich Beck (1992) uses the concept of subpolitics to describe the decision making, disputation, and negotiation that takes place outside the traditional representative realm of politics. It involves new relationships and alliances in the management of society.
3 This research was supported by a research grant from Innovative Collaboration, Alliances and Networks (ICAN), University of Technology, Sydney.
4 Hajer (1995) describes discourse coalitions as groups of actors who take up a similar interpretation of a multi-interpretable concept. Development of a storyline by this coalition requires a certain loss of meaning as other interpretations of the concept are discarded in the process of language interaction. The discourse becomes hegemonic when it is translated into policies.
5 LRLC Group meeting, Bloodwood Valley, 6 January 2002.
6 Agriculture and Resource Management Council of Australia and New Zealand (ARMCANZ) representative on the ALC.
7 Hajer (1995, 63) interprets a storyline as a generative narrative, or an analytical device that pulls together (the "discursive cement") a discourse coalition (the group of actors and the practices associated with a particular discursive activity).

References

Adler, P., and S. Kwon. 2002. "Social Capital: Prospects for a New Concept." *Academy of Management Review* 27(1): 17-40.

Beck, U. 1992. *The Risk Society.* Trans. Mark Ritter. London: Sage.

–. 1995. *Ecological Politics in the Age of Risk.* Cambridge, UK: Polity Press.

–. 1999. *World Risk Society.* Cambridge, UK: Polity Press.

–. 2000. "Risk Society Revisited: Theory, Politics and Research Programs." In B. Adam, U. Beck, and J. Van Loon, eds., *The Risk Society and Beyond,* 211-29. London: Sage.

Beder, S. 2000. *Global Spin.* 2nd ed. Melbourne: Scribe Publications.

Benn, S. 2004. "Managing Toxic Chemicals in Australia: A Regional Analysis of the Risk Society." *Journal of Risk Research* 7(4): 399-412.

British Columbia, Ministry of Community Development Cooperatives and Volunteers. 2001. "The Changing Resource Development Paradigm: Maximising Local Benefits from Resource Development." Prepared by Wayne Dunn and Associates, Mill Bay, BC.

Burt, R. 1997. "The Contingent Value of Social Capital." *Administrative Science Quarterly* 42(2): 339-365.

Cary, J., and T. Webb. 2000. "Community Landcare, the National Landcare Program and the Landcare Movement: The Social Dimensions of Landcare." Canberra: Bureau of Rural Sciences, Agriculture, Forestry and Fisheries.

–. 2001. "Landcare in Australia: Community Participation and Land Management." *Journal of Soil and Water Conservation* 56: 274-78.

Chua, W., and S. Clegg. 1989. "Contradictory Couplings: Professional Ideology in the Organizational Locales of Nursing." *Journal of Management Studies* 26: 103-27.

Clegg, T. 1989. *Frameworks of Power.* London: Sage.

Dale, A. 1995. "Multistakeholder Processes: Panacea or Window Dressing." Address given to the University of Victoria, Victoria, BC, February.

Dryzek, J. 1997. *The New Politics of the Earth.* Oxford: Oxford University Press.

Emery, F., and E. Trist. 1965. "The Causal Texture of Organizational Environments." *Human Relations* 18: 21-32.

Foucault, M. 1972. *The Archaeology of Knowledge and the Discourse of Language.* New York: Pantheon Books.

–. 1977. *Discipline and Punish.* New York: Random House.

Giddens, A. 1994. *Beyond Left and Right: The Future of Radical Politics.* Cambridge, UK: Polity Press.

–. 1998. *The Third Way.* Cambridge, UK: Polity Press.

Hajer, M. 1995. *The Politics of Environmental Discourse: Ecological Modernisation and the Policy Process.* Oxford: Clarendon Press.

–. 1996. "Ecological Modernisation as Cultural Politics." In S. Lash, B. Szerszynski, and B. Wynne, eds., *Risk, Environment and Modernity,* 246-68. London: Sage.

Hardy, C. 1994. "Underorganised Interorganisational Domains: The Case of Refugee Systems." *Journal of Applied Behavioural Science* 30(3): 278-96.

Hill, S. 1999. "Landcare: A Multistakeholder Approach to Agricultural Sustainability." In A. Dragun, and C. Tisdell, eds., *Sustainable Agriculture and Environment.* Cheltenham: Edward Elgar.

Irwin, A. 2001. *Sociology and the Environment.* Cambridge, UK: Polity Press.

Land and Water Resources Audit. 2000. *Dryland Salinity in Australia.* Natural Heritage Trust, Commonwealth of Australia.

Landcare Australia. 2002. <http://www.landcareaustralia.com.au/GoodBusiness/Introduction.htm> (28 August 2002).

Lash, S., B. Szerszynski, and B. Wynne. 1996. "Introduction: Ecology, Realism and the Social Sciences." In S. Lash, B. Szerszynski, and B. Wynne, eds., *Risk, Environment and Modernity,* 1-26. London: Sage.

Livesey, S. 2001. "Eco-identity as Discursive Struggle: Royal Dutch/Shell, Brent Spar, and Nigeria." *Journal of Business Communication* 38(1): 58-92.

Lockie, S. 1999. "Community Movements and Corporate Images: 'Landcare' in Australia." *Rural Sociology* 64(2): 219.

Marriott, S., T. Nabben, L. Polkinghorne, and R. Youl. 2000. *Landcare in Australia: Founded on Local Action.* Chatswoor: Landcare Australia.

Martin, P., and H. Ritchie. 1999. "Logics of Participation: Rural Environmental Governance under Neo-liberalism in Australia." *Environmental Politics* 8(2): 117.

Morgan, G. 1997. *Images of Organization.* Thousand Oaks, CA: Sage.

Onyx, J., and P. Bullen. 2000. "Measuring Social Capital in Five Communities." *Journal of Applied Behavioral Science.* 36(1): 23-42.

Onyx, J., and R. Leonard. 2000. "Rural Renewal and Social Capital: The Case of Sweden and Australia." Working Paper Series No. 46. Sydney Centre for Australian Community Organisations and Management.

Punch, K. 1998. *Introduction to Social Research.* London: Sage.

Putnam, R. 2000. *Bowling Alone.* New York: Simon and Schuster.

Robinson, J. 2002. "Squaring the Circle? On the Very Idea of Sustainable Development." *Ecological Economics* 48(4): 369-84.

Rose, H. 2000. "Risk, Trust and Scepticism in the Age of the New Genetics." In B. Adam, U. Beck, and J. Van Loon, eds., *The Risk Society and Beyond,* 63-77. London: Sage.

Sobels, J., A. Curtis, and S. Lockie. 2001. "The Role of Landcare Group Networks in Rural Australia: Exploring the Contribution of Social Capital." *Journal of Rural Studies* 17(13): 265-78.

Spratley, J. 1980. *Participant Observation.* Fort Worth, TX: Holt, Rinehart and Winston.

Sydney Morning Herald. 2001. Editorial, "Green Spending," 5 June.

–. 2002. Editorial, 20 October.

Szerszynski, B. 1997. "Voluntary Associations and the Sustainable Society." In M. Jacobs, ed., *Greening the Millennium?* 148-59. Oxford: Basil Blackwell.

Tsoukas, B.H. 1999. "David and Goliath in the Risk Society: Making Sense of the Conflict between Shell and Greenpeace in the North Sea." *Organization* 6(3): 499-528.

Welcomer, S., D. Gioia, and M. Kilduff. 2000. "Resisting the Discourse of Modernity: Rationality versus Emotion in Hazardous Waste Siting." *Human Relations* 53(9): 1175-1205.

Wynne, B. 1996. "May the Sheep Safely Graze? A Reflexive View of the Expert-Lay Knowledge Divide." In S. Lash, B. Szerszynski, and B. Wynne, eds., *Risk Environment and Modernity,* 44-83. London: Sage.

6
Modelling Social Capital in a Remote Australian Indigenous Community
Paul Memmott and Anna Meltzer

This chapter reports on the application of the social capital construct to Indigenous communities in Australia, and the adaptation of a methodology for measuring social capital in a particular remote Indigenous community.[1] Anthropological evidence suggests that Indigenous societies traditionally had well-adapted, flexible governance, effective for small-scale hunter-gatherer societies.[2] These institutions accorded primacy to rights in land and its resources, derived from inheritance and united by a system of religious knowledge. Such governance was robust while allowing for a degree of contestation and negotiation. The challenge faced by Aboriginal groups and communities today is how to mesh these traditional modes of governance with alternate forms and structures of governance and corporatization imposed by the Australian Commonwealth and state governments (ATSIC and Reconciliation Australia 2002, 5).[3]

Traditional forms of Indigenous governance can and have been analyzed using the new social capital framework (see Chase 1980; Kesteven 1984; Martin 1995; Martin and Finlayson 1996; Hunter 2000; Altman 2001; Smith 2001; Schwab and Sutherland 2001). In many contemporary Indigenous situations, social capital appears to exist in a robust form though it is localized and closely linked to kinship rather than to community or being regionally oriented. A number of researchers have argued that Indigenous people actually invest significant time and energy into building social capital; however, it often manifests in ways that are not registered in terms of "economic development" or that do not match the mainstream criteria of "good governance" (Altman 2001, 3; see also Martin and Finlayson 1996; Schwab and Sutherland 2001; Smith 2001.)

A recurring theme in the Australian ethnographies is the operation of conflicting processes of autonomy and relatedness in Aboriginal domains. A number of studies (Martin 1993, 1995; Myers 1986; Sutton 1978; von Sturmer 1978) point to the strong emphasis on personal autonomy and distinctiveness within the Aboriginal domain, where styles of political and social process, such as decision making, can primarily work toward the preservation of individual independence. Similarly, a strong value is often placed on individual and local-group rights. This frequently means that sustaining cooperation and coordinating effort over a broad social or geographical field can be quite difficult; "in such a system, achieving political unity or even the semblance of common purpose can be a significant accomplishment in itself" (Martin and Finlayson 1996, 6). The processes that facilitate autonomy are juxtaposed with a strong emphasis on relatedness and extensive webs of interconnection through kinship and family. Relatedness is realized and defined through forms of shared identity, particularly kinship and social group membership (Martin 1995, 6). Political and social process can also serve the purpose of establishing, negotiating, maintaining, and extending the internal social and political relationships, or social capital, that are of significant concern to Aboriginal people; "unfortunately, internal goals are usually achieved at the expense of organisational outcomes" (Finlayson 1997, 145).

This chapter draws on two other technical reports by one of the authors (Memmott 2002; Memmott in UQ, SERC 2002) that were part of the "Community Strength Indicators and Measurement Project" undertaken by the Australian government's Department of Families and Community Services (FaCS) as part of its current "Stronger Families and Communities Strategy."[4] This strategy is concerned with capacity building to support and strengthen Australian families and communities, particularly those that are deficient in the characteristics of strong communities and therefore vulnerable to changing economic circumstances that may result in the breakdown of family and social structures. Basic precepts of the strategy were developing firm community leadership and groups of volunteers, developing community capacity for self-help, and facilitating useful partnerships of various sorts between public and private sectors (Australia, Department of Family and Community Services 2002, 4).

Black and Hughes (2001) had previously carried out a comprehensive review and analysis of the literature for FaCS on indicators of "community strength," resulting in its definition as "the extent to which resources and processes within a community maintain and enhance both individual and collective well-being in ways consistent with the principles of equity, comprehensiveness, participation, self-reliance and social responsibility" (3). They also developed a framework of four community strength domains for methodological use: (1) natural capital, (2) produced economic capital, (3) human capital, and (4) social and institutional capital. The Social and Economic Research Centre (SERC) at the University of Queensland was in turn engaged by FaCS to develop and test indicators and measures of strength for Australian communities based on the Black and Hughes conceptual framework. A small team of geographers and sociologists from SERC addressed this task in metropolitan and urban settings. One of the current authors, Paul Memmott, was engaged as an anthropologist and social planner to see if and how the SERC test-and-measure instrument might be relevant to a discrete remote Aboriginal community, particularly in terms of social and institutional capital.

FaCS selected the remote Aboriginal community of Wadeye (formerly Port Keats Mission) for the pilot study. It is located in a remote corner of northwest Australia, between Darwin and Wyndham. The settlement was established as a Catholic mission in 1935 within what became the Daly River/Port Keats Aboriginal Reserve. It received adverse publicity in the late 1980s and mid-1990s, being characterized as dysfunctional due to a variety of reasons, including alcohol abuse and inept council administration (Thamurrurr Inc. 2000, 40, 41). In 2001, the community had a young Aboriginal population profile, with 66 percent under the age of twenty-four (Australian Bureau of Statistics 2002, I01). Estimates of the community population size varied from 1500 to 2500.[5] This discrepancy was probably because of a decentralized system of smaller communities and outstations in the region, with high mobility between these places and Wadeye as a regional centre.

This chapter describes the adaptation of the survey instrument on social and institutional capital for use in the Aboriginal community, as well as presenting the fieldwork findings on such. It then attempts to position these findings within the current literature on governance in Aboriginal Australia.

Preparing for Fieldwork: Adaptation of the SERC Questionnaire on Social Capital

Social capital is defined by SERC as being generated from social networks characterized by norms, particularly those of trust and reciprocity, as well as norms of unity (a sense of belonging to a group/community) (UQ, SERC 2002, 37-39). Two dimensions of social networks are inherent in this definition: (1) a structural aspect, in which social relations between people can be mapped or counted, and (2) a normative dimension that encapsulates the qualities or content of these networks. Network structures and norms are likely to vary according to the type of network in which a person engages. For example, the structure and norms present in a family are likely to be different to those in friendship groups and different again at a community level.

Expanding on this definition by drawing on the international literature on social capital (Black and Hughes 2001; Christakopoulou, Dawson, and Aikaterini 2001; Health Development Agency 2001; Krishna and Shrader 2000; Onyx and Bullen 2000; Stewart-Weeks and Richardson 1998; Stone 2001) and on the basis of pilot surveys, SERC constructed four primary scales of social capital in addition to four measures of the outcomes of social capital. The social capital scales were informal structures, formal structures, informal norms, and formal norms. Each primary scale comprised a number of subscales. The subscales for informal structures were community divisions and particularized social agency, whereas for formal structures they were participation in the local community, generalized agency, and friends in institutional networks. The subscales for informal norms were particularized trust and informal reciprocity and exchange, while those for formal norms were openness to and tolerance of diversity, confidence in and trust of links, community spirit and place attachment, formal reciprocity and feelings of trust and safety, and generalized trust. The four outcome scales were anomie, perceived quality of life and well-being, perceived natural and human capital, and perceived economic capital (UQ, SERC 2002, 121).[6]

The SERC project team modelled this conceptual framework for social capital in the form of a matrix, with the scales arranged along two axes (see Table 6.1). The x-axis includes the structural dimension and the normative dimension. The y-axis lists a number of types of networks categorized as either informal or formal network types. The various components in each

Table 6.1

Social and institutional capital matrix (from SERC methodological notes)

Dimensions of social capital according to network types	Structural dimension (size of the network, capacity to draw on the network, density of the network, openness of the network, homogeneity of the network[1])	Normative dimension (trust, reciprocity, unity or a sense of belonging)
Informal networks (family, kin, intimates, friends, and neighbours)	• Onyx and Bullen's Factor F (2000) • Stone (2001b): size	• Stone (2001b): trust, reciprocity
Formal networks (non-group civic participation, participation in civic groups and associations, work associations, associations with formalized bodies[2])	• Onyx and Bullen's Factors B & C (2000) • Stone (2001b): size	• Onyx and Bullen's Factor A (2000) • Stone (2001b): trust, unity

1 "Homogenity of the network" pertains to the similarity (as opposed to diversity) of people in the network according to various dimensions such as age, education, gender, religion, and occupation.
2 The terms "non-group civic participation" and "formalized bodies" used in terms of "formal networks" raise the issue of the definition of "formal." This term is used here in the sense of referring either to (a) a formal structure, such as an incorporated cooperative, or (b) a formal purpose, such as attending a political march or rally.

of the four scales and their subscales were measured using a set of questions assembled and/or designed by SERC (2002, App. 5.1). A fifth set of questions was devised for outcomes of social capital. These together comprised the survey instrument for modelling and assessing social and institutional capital. The other three domains of community strength (natural, economic, and human capital) were assessed with a different methodology. There is insufficient space to explore this latter methodology here; see the SERC report for further details (2002, Chapter 3).

SERC recognized at the outset that because of the cultural differences and social structures in a remote Indigenous community, the survey instrument would not be suitable without modification.[7] The SERC questionnaire was thus taken through several redrafts by the field researcher, Paul Memmott, in order to simplify the English, eliminate excessively abstract terms and constructs, and make the questions relevant to the experience of remote and rural Indigenous communities – or to cull those questions that were not. We also decided to distribute the survey during group workshops. The limited budget allowing a field visit of only three days precluded conducting a large number of one-on-one interviews to achieve a statistically viable sample in the same way that was done by SERC in urban centres through phone interviewing. The dimensions of the SERC matrix (Table 6.1) were retained as a useful way to model social capital, albeit adapted into more readily understood concepts and in relation to the bicultural setting (see Table 6.2), discussed below on issues of quantification and measurement.

One of the adaptive changes in Table 6.2 is the omission of the dimension of formal versus informal networks, as used in Table 6.1. Within the social capital literature there is a certain lack of theoretical resolution about this property. The definition of "formal" may pertain to either the structural clarity and/or stability of the network, the common sense of purpose or the role of the network, or the entry requirements for membership of the network. Even an informal spontaneous group activity, once demonstrating some purposive behaviour, takes on a degree of formality. Formal versus informal networks should be seen not as a binary model but as a series of gradations involving multiple properties of formality within such networks.

The authors (Memmot and Meltzer) presented with both Aboriginal and Anglo-Australian type networks in the study community. At first the Anglo-Australian type networks were classified as formal, often being corporations, companies, trusts, and so on, formed under different parliamentary acts, whereas the Aboriginal networks were referred to as informal networks because they were, for the most part, not recognized as corporate bodies in the day-to-day matters of Australian law and because they had been ignored, even suppressed, by missionaries and government officials from colonial times until at least 1976, when land rights were first given legal recognition. However, after reflection, this position was abandoned by the authors, for the combination of Aboriginal kinship, the system of social classes or divisions (subsections, sections, and so on, or "skins"), and the land tenure system are all formal structures that generate multiple social and even corporate networks in Aboriginal societies – as anthropologists well know. To model these networks as informal would be to gloss over their mathematical beauty and formal precision. The authors eventually decided to omit the property of formality versus informality in Table 6.2 (in the manner in which it was portrayed in Table 6.1) and to replace it with a binary of "Aboriginal cultural networks" versus "whitefella type organizations" (meaning Anglo-Australian networks). This was a far stronger dimension of network character encountered in the field. Once again, in reality, there is a gradation of types between the two extremes, with most if not all contemporary networks at Wadeye demonstrating a mix of properties drawing on both cultural contexts.

The workshops at Wadeye were designed for community groups to reflect on and externalize their community strengths and weaknesses and to formulate self-strengthening strategies and actions. This implied that interviews with individuals became a secondary data collection technique.[8] The advantage of this approach is that it would have a degree of operational repetition for discrete communities with the types of groups found in remote communities such as Wadeye (but would have to be piloted again for metropolitan urban communities). A first step in the fieldwork that proved to be particularly valuable was presenting the nature and aims of the study in an introductory talk to the local council, the peak community body. This provided an opportunity to place the survey in the local context and obtain support for further community contacts. A second step was explaining the content of Table 6.2.

A core concern was the need to recognize and appreciate relevant cultural differences. The use of language is a particular example, with preferred terminology and expressions having to be identified. Techniques for discussing change in community strength over time were also devised. Active engagement with individuals, groups, and organizations in the community was necessary, as was the gaining of an understanding of community history, social dynamics, and cultural character. A methodology emerged that depended less on the questionnaire as a single instrument than on a combination of techniques for use in a short time frame (but still including the questionnaire). A triangulation of techniques was developed: open-ended small-group workshops, formal interviews with key informants, and interviews while touring the town with these informants.

Strengths of the Aboriginal Networks

Customary Aboriginal networks are relatively strong and continue to operate at Wadeye. These include kinship, social classes, seven language groups,

Table 6.2

Understanding community strength in relation to Indigenous community networks

Network type	The two parts of social strength	
	1 Amount of strength	2 Type of strength
	Number of networks Size of networks Access to network (open or closed) Interconnectedness and overlapping networks Mixing together of networks	Trusting people Giving back (reciprocity) Belonging together (unity)
A **Aboriginal cultural networks** Family Extended family Skin relations Ceremony partners Friends Neighbours	A1 How much community strength comes from Aboriginal cultural networks?	A2 What sort of strengths come from the Aboriginal cultural networks?
B **"Whitefella-type" organizations** Community organizations Workers organizations Clubs and societies Government departments	B1 How much community strength comes from the "whitefella-style" organizations and networks?	B2 What sort of strengths come from the "whitefella-style" organizations?

about twenty-five land-owning clans or descent groups, and three sociospatial residential/ceremonial groups. These various group structures also generate multiple coexisting systems of social identity. Elders and clan heads more or less continue to maintain their customary leadership roles. The pervasive nature of kinship as the social glue of the Aboriginal community is particularly apparent and reflected in the responses to questions on social homogeneity and the causes of social divisions. Kinship, together with the other Aboriginal social networks, contributed to a high degree of community unity or social cohesiveness.

The issue of social integration was pursued during one-on-one interviews. It was found that people mainly mixed with members of their own extended families, though there was some mixing on the basis of "skin" (social class) relations. Customary avoidance behaviour cut across these patterns; for example, brothers could not talk to sisters.[9] Men and women usually mixed together socially. There was a general feeling that if a person required help with a problem, there were many people whom such an individual could turn to. Senior family members were regarded as strong leaders for their respective descent groups in the community. A view was put forward that people could obtain help from many quarters and that tribal or language group membership was not a barrier. One-on-one interviews indicated that the issues that most divided the community were alcohol, jealousy, pay-packet size, and arguments over children, the last item being seen as the most common issue triggering divisiveness.

No fine-grained analysis was carried out of the respective strengths and roles of the elements of this traditional social organization system and how certain parts may have been weakened because of colonial impact and directed cultural change. But a measure of their combined resilience was the capacity of the community to respond to serious social and leadership problems and to address community change, often through the expression of customary ceremony and ritual. To test the social capacity of informal Aboriginal groups, inquiries were made about community activities that had occurred in response to stressful situations and without any (or with very limited) assistance from white staff or outside agencies. Seventeen responses of this type were readily recorded by the researcher as having occurred over the previous five or six years. This indicated strong informal social networks and leadership. Responses included the establishment of a night patrol by the women's group; establishment of a camp to rehabilitate petrol sniffers; initiation ceremonies; Aboriginal leaders taking responsibility for the school; and the use of informal methods for conflict resolution in the community.

A feature of these customary systems of social organization was their close structural interrelation and interlocking, which implied a high degree of mixing of networks and, consequently, a very high degree of access to and participation in such networks. Anomie appeared to be almost nonexistent as a social trait (only one individual was identified as being in this category).

Strengths of "Whitefella-Style" Organizations

The definition of "whitefella-style" networks was taken to be those organizations in the community that were established using structural models drawn from mainstream Australian institutions and society, such as local government council, cooperatives, corporations, associations, clubs, church groups, schools, business enterprises, workers unions, and professional networks. During the short period of the fieldwork, the researcher was able to identify what appeared to be eighteen such formal networks or bodies at Wadeye. (There were undoubtedly others the researcher did not detect.) The principal examples were:

- Thamurrurr, the body of traditional clan leaders, which is the community decision-making and leadership body
- Kardu Numida, an Indigenous corporation that implements many of the infrastructure and human services of a community council, such as housing construction and management, power and water, road maintenance, and the Juvenile Diversion Unit[10]
- Palngun Wurnangat, an incorporated women's group that runs educational programs, night patrol, and a second-hand clothing store
- Murrinhpatha Tribal Development, a company with Aboriginal directors that runs the store complex, arts-and-crafts industry, and art gallery, recycling profits back to community activities
- Makura Wunthay, which runs an alcohol and drug program in some ways similar to Alcoholics Anonymous
- The Catholic Church, with both Aboriginal and non-Aboriginal clergy, which provides services for Sunday worship, funerals, baptisms, and weddings, as well as counselling and a male youth education service (Kardu Kigay)
- Our Lady of the Sacred Heart School, run by an Aboriginal leader's group.

The degree to which Aboriginal versus non-Aboriginal people constituted the membership of these "whitefella-style" networks, held the power, and dictated the rules and ideology varied on a spectrum from predominantly Aboriginal-dominated to predominantly non-Aboriginal-dominated. The Aboriginal-dominated organizations include Thamurrurr, Palngun Wurnangat, and Makura Wurnthay, but even these were dependant on non-Aboriginal sponsorship and support in some form to ensure their continuity and operation (e.g., program funding, secretarial services, government reporting and auditing), although their establishment and beginnings may have been solely dependent on volunteers.

It was generally accepted that the main body of leaders in the community was Thamurrurr. It comprised the peak body of community representatives, a mix of male and female traditional owners representing all the customary land-owning groups. It was not a local government council in the usual sense but had many attributes of a community council, being a peak decision-making body. It incorporated elders in its decision-making processes.

Attempts to explore partnerships and other forms of regular interlocking between these various organizations produced only limited findings, both in terms of internal linkages (in the community) and external linkages (outside the community), although it was clear that Thamurrurr and Kardu Numida, being the local government instruments in a small community, had linkages of some sort to most other community networks. The future capacity for network interaction was enhanced through Thamurrurr possessing an all-encompassing representation in its membership of clan groupings from the region. A second level of cohesion existed in the community, albeit one that the researcher was unable to measure in the short term. Through the widespread extent of community membership, both Aboriginal and non-Aboriginal, in the Catholic Church, it appeared that most non-Aboriginal staff positions were filled by persons of Catholic faith. The networking capacity of the Catholic Church was also evident in ties and linkages external to the community.

Despite these network linkages, there appeared to exist in the community a high degree of social separation between a substantial number of non-Aboriginal staff and the Aboriginal residents. At best this allowed for separate lifestyles and value systems to be respected, but at worst it fostered poor cross-cultural communication, misunderstandings, anger, fear, and racism. Several respondents raised concerns about some of the non-Aboriginal staff at Wadeye; they felt that there were sometimes serious communication problems and that some of these non-Aboriginals didn't fit in, having come to the community without adequate preparation. Other respondents, however, held more positive views.

Norms in the Aboriginal Networks

The starting points for the testing of norms were the values of *trust, unity* and *reciprocity,* as given in the SERC sociological matrix. Of these, *trust* and *reciprocity* clearly had high currency in the social capital of the Aboriginal cultural networks of the community, whereas unity was less utilized and less predictable in its application and manifestation in daily social problems because of the complex informal system of crosscutting social organization.

There were still other norms of social capital in the Aboriginal cultural networks that were found to be rich and strong, extending beyond the threefold set of the sociological literature. These were *respect, kindness and concern, motherly love, tough love, personal and community sharing,* and *belief in self-capacity.* Although some of these values may seem to be personal rather than social, their meaning and application at Wadeye was clearly social.

Respect was seen as a key social value in the community, one inherent in aspects of local Aboriginal law. Examples were that the young must respect the elders of the community, brothers must respect sisters (both biological and classificatory siblings) and vice versa, and the possessions of a dead person must be respected. Some people commented that respect was not maintained as strongly as it should have been among many younger people.

There was a strong value of *reciprocity* within the Indigenous sector of the community, partly manifested through forms of sharing. It was felt that people frequently helped one another. *Personal sharing* referred to sharing among selected kinspersons, while *community sharing* referred to the spreading of resources across the whole community. The only apparent distrust within the Indigenous sector was from local Wadeye people toward relative newcomers from other Aboriginal communities in the wider region. The latter were accused of being a cause of disharmony and conflict at times, at least until they married in and became an accepted part of the community.

Motherly love pertained to the collective matriarchal bond held by the female elders with the younger generations of the community. *Tough love* referred to the necessity for older adults to deny the efforts of behaviourally dysfunctional youths who were in the practice of aggressively demanding money to purchase intoxicating substances, this being for the youths' protection and best interest, albeit in contradiction to the sharing values.

A more in-depth analysis would demonstrate that many of these concepts are embedded in the customary cognitive system. Once again, kinship is the social glue that facilitates the sharing of these values. Many of the non-Aboriginal staff in the community would not necessarily be in touch with the full subtleness and pervading nature of these Aboriginal norms, potentially adding to any cultural barriers that may already exist.

Norms in the "Whitefella-Style" Organizations

Of the values emphasized in the "whitefella-style" networks, *taking ownership of the problem* was strikingly pervasive and reflected the change during the late twentieth century in the community, from one of mission and government control and dominance to one of Aboriginal control and leadership. This value in itself had the capacity to generate strong levels of social cohesion and leadership in all those organizational networks where Aboriginal control existed, providing that the necessary checks and balances concerning power were kept in place. Here we also find an Aboriginal value of homogeneity or *levelling* being invoked at times, whereby all members be viewed as equal, without overdominance by some leaders.

There were several impressive examples of *taking ownership,* namely the establishment of Thamurrurr, the new school leadership group, and the women's group (Palngun Wurnangat). Thamurrurr had come about in response to the crisis of the collapse of a previous council body. The new organization of Thamurrurr was constituted and being run using traditional governance principles of decision making and authority. Nevertheless, we suspect that the *unity* necessary for these Aboriginal-controlled networks to operate successfully was still being explored and tested by the Aboriginal leaders within the new sociospatial structures and social boundaries of post-contact settlements. There is always the possibility of fracturing along family and clan lines.

The findings on this process of change indicated something about how community action was triggered. Although individuals becoming stressed by social and health problems was one important way, a second and related way was by individuals being "shamed," as occurred as a result of the previous council's collapse. The converse was individuals achieving, being proud, and restoring local control, power, and *ownership of problems*. This had been partly achieved through the use of ceremony (an inherently Aboriginal technique), which had been synthesized as part of the reinvigoration of corporations, and used as a symbol of "Aboriginalization."

Findings on Outcomes of Social Capital

The experience of moving from a state of social stress, violence, and partial chaos in the mid-1990s to one of social prospering and creative achievement in the early 2000s had left the community with a well-developed sense of perceived self-strength (Memmott 2002). Many changes for the better had been achieved. People perceived that many aspects of their lifestyle were culturally enriching. Examples of this increase in strength are that there was less fighting, less crime because of the operations of the night patrol, more respect for elders, and high involvement in local governance. There were a number of obvious expressions of community pride (for example, a prominent sign at the local airport listed the eleven awards won by the community, including Territory Tidy Towns Winner; Best Store Large Community; Best Women's Centre; and Best Waste Reduction).

This change has been largely achieved by drawing on traditionally derived networks and norms and applying them to the more formal "whitefella style" networks. However, much of the perception was inextricably tied to the Aboriginal sense of natural capital (to use the terminology of the community strength paradigm). This draws on and is defined by a belief system of Dreamings, totems, story places, sacred histories, and fertility concepts about plant and animal species, which in turn contributes in a positive way to Aboriginal constructs of person or self. The Indigenous concept of social capital is therefore not easily analyzable separate from natural capital; the two are mutually interdependent in an epistemological sense.

This social strength was in stark contrast to the community's abject poverty in the economic and human (health) capital domains. Items such as anomie, quality of life, perceived natural capital, and perceived economic capital were tested with a number of respondents. Many problems could be listed, but those that were emphasized by residents include the acute housing shortage, affordability of store food, lack of educational and recreational opportunities, substance abuse, and the need for government infrastructure support. Nevertheless, any brief assessment of the physical state of the town, with its images of inadequate housing and social problems, would fail to detect the strong social capital within the community.

Adaptation of the Survey Technique

The survey findings from Wadeye would not be unexpected for any experienced researcher of community development working in Aboriginal Australia. Most remote communities of this type are characterized by strong customary social networks (which in turn facilitate successful land claims), and a set of incorporated organizations established under the *Aboriginal Councils and Associations Act 1976* (Cth). Wadeye is perhaps somewhat different to many in that it has integrated aspects of customary social structure and norms into its peak decision-making body, Thamurrurr. Other Wadeye corporations that have "Aboriginalized" their operations in culturally distinctive ways have been mentioned above.

The study has shown that it is possible to measure the concept of social capital in an Indigenous community with broadly similar concepts to those used in a non-Indigenous community. The Wadeye findings confirmed that concepts from the standard literature such as trust and reciprocity were valid constructs of social capital and understood in the Indigenous community. Significantly, a number of other values generally held in the community were also identified.

Given the cross-cultural context of the Wadeye data, sensitivity is needed to recognize the range of network types that draw from different cultural frameworks, and to recognize that these networks cannot be conflated into a simple dichotomy of formal versus informal networks. Rather, the networks should be seen as involving multiple properties of formality as well as of cultural origins. The bicultural model of social networks adopted by the authors (Memmott and Meltzer) appears to be a useful way to describe social capital within an overarching construct of community strength in Australian Indigenous communities where both customary Aboriginal social organization and Anglo-Australian governance, economic, and other cultural systems (e.g., education, religion) coexist and syncretize in various forms.

The methodological steps and findings of the study also draw attention to the unique features of measuring community strength or weakness in an Indigenous community. There is a need for researchers to work with clearly developed protocols that recognize community structures and enable attention to be drawn to their strengths and weaknesses in a non-offensive manner.

The conclusions drawn above indicate the type of results that might be obtained when the properties of social and institutional capital are explored in a remote Indigenous community. Field adjustments need to be made to ensure key literature concepts are understandable in the Indigenous social context and to accommodate a range of English literacy skills. New data items might need to be included or existing ones given greater emphasis in accordance with local cultural and geographic context. The adapted SERC framework of social capital provided data collection techniques with a useful method to model that aspect of community strength in a qualitative way. Although a structured questionnaire application, in the sense of one-on-one interviews, was not appropriate as a single data collection technique in a short time, a mixture of group and resident discussions and interviews provided an assessment of social capital. However, quantitative assessment of social capital would only be possible by increasing the number of structured interviews to obtain a statistically significant sample and by following the analytic procedures used in the main SERC study of metropolitan and urban centres. But this would require a considerably larger commitment of research resources than those used in this study.

Broad changes in community social strength could be measured by (1) carrying out the survey technique diachronically, (2) by then inspecting and comparing the contents of the various cells of the social capital framework or matrix and their constituent items, (3) by making judgments concerning obvious changes that have occurred in each of the cells and for individual items, and then, (4) presenting back to the community for comment and verification.

The Wadeye community leaders recommended that government departments incorporate into the design of all programs for Indigenous communities capacity-building goals, norms, networks, and strategies drawn from the findings of a community strength survey, such as the one carried out at Wadeye, especially in communities experiencing severe dysfunction problems or being targeted with large-scale multiprogrammed services through government partnership approaches.

Social Capital in Aboriginal Australia

An important theoretical issue is whether social capital is a phenomenon associated with all human cultures or particular to only some. In the context of this chapter, the question can be put, did social capital exist in traditional Aboriginal societies? Or did the existence of pervasive kinship rules, obligations, and associated punishments generate a social system in which help was always available from particular kin, rendering the construct of social capital irrelevant or at least nonviable, given the simultaneous emphasis on individual independence mentioned previously? We believe that social capital most certainly existed. Many daily activities required levels of social cooperation that went beyond the formal structure and networks of Aboriginal social organization. The most striking from the ethnographic data were the widespread large gatherings of people for ceremony, trade, intermarriage, rituals to resolve grievances and other emotional imbalances

(Elkin 1931), and joint economic activity. Examples of the latter include large-scale fireburns,[11] game drives, and the formation of bands for dugong netting. All these events require social leadership, goodwill, and cooperation to operationalize people into large-scale coordinated patterns of activity. These principles also apply to the region between the Daly and Fitzmaurice rivers in which the township of Wadeye is now centrally located, and where some twenty or more tribal groups were located at the time of early European contact (Stanner 1933a, 1933b).[12] Another category of behaviours requiring social capital is that involving the breaking of institutional rules for a common purpose, whereby a temporary alliance of people will facilitate, for example, a "wrong-skin" marriage, or provide asylum to a neighbouring tribesperson condemned to death by his own people for some religious sacrilege (Strehlow 1970, 122).

Indeed, the very independent and equitable nature of land-owning groups within an overarching system of religious philosophy, together with their relatively small size, denied any hierarchical power structure that could achieve regional goals but, rather, forced local groups to rely on forms of social capital to achieve them. Thus, in central Australia, among the Arrernte,

> all marriage arrangements and all large-scale religious activities hence de
> pended on the manipulation of the permanent social and religious links
> that existed with other [nyinangka] section areas, which however, had their
> own authorities. Thus, the Western Aranda area alone was divided into ten
> "politically independent" [nyinangka] section areas ... Again, since all ma
> jor totemic sites [pmara kutata] in these [nyinangka] section areas were
> deemed to rank equally in importance, and since these major sites were
> linked according to the nature of their totems with the totemic sites of
> other subgroups and even of other tribes, not one of them was fitted in any
> sense to act as a sort of central "capital" site for a whole tribal subgroup or a
> whole tribe. (Strehlow 1970, 129)

Another interesting category of social capital behaviour during the early contact period was the cooperative banding of individuals to implement forms of guerrilla warfare against the encroaching colonizers on the frontier. Of pertinence here were the famous feats and accomplishments of a warrior from the Wadeye area named Nemarluk, who not only formed a band of resistance fighters in the early 1930s but also forged an alliance with two other bands which together killed European and Japanese intruders into their countries, which stretched from the Victoria River to the Daly River, a distance of about two hundred kilometres. The ability of these men to evade police patrols depended on the social goodwill of other Aboriginal people throughout the region: to pass on strategic information about such patrols as well as to provide shelter, food, and weapons. As the popularity of

Nemarluk's political ideology waned, so too did his social capital, until many of his countrypeople became antagonists to his cause and provided intelligence to the police on his whereabouts (and thereby reorganized the network membership holding the local social capital) (Idriess 1946; Pye 1973, 8-20).

In traditional Aboriginal society, as in all human groups, people took on different personalities, personalities took on characters, and different human characters took on different social roles. In Aboriginal societies there were wise people, fighting people, expert hunters, philosophers, specialist scientists, religious leaders, peacemakers, social critics, and comics. To achieve worldly goals among such diverse personalities and roles, it was necessary to compile social capital.

Now let us consider the contemporary problematic relation between the traditional Aboriginal social capital on the one hand and, on the other hand, the institutional capital of Indigenous community governance corporations in the contemporary community context. With the growing recognition of the failures of the welfare state, a number of Australian Aboriginal leaders, academics, and policy writers have been looking toward new analytical and policy models with the goal of stimulating increased social and civic engagement (e.g., Pearson 2000, 2001). Recent critiques of Indigenous affairs policies by Pearson (2000, 2001) and Sutton (2001) have highlighted the effects of dysfunctional Aboriginal communities, where traditional behaviours and shared values have become distorted, effectively counteracting personal responsibility, and in turn limiting the growth of social capital and the possibility for sound governance (ATSIC and Reconciliation Australia 2002, 6). The value of community is being espoused, with new vigour, as the vehicle by which responsible and engaged citizenry can be activated. Though not always explicitly stated, Pearson and Sutton are calling for the cultivation of what others have called social capital. However, social capital is a concept that needs careful consideration when applied to Aboriginal contexts.

Rowse (1992, 89) encourages us to be skeptical of the commonly held assumption "that community power is, or should be made to be, a unified, centralised sovereignty." He continues (90), "If there is one lesson that must be drawn from an anthropological consideration of Aborigines' emerging instruments of self-determination, it is that 'autonomy' refers not only to Aborigines' relationships with non-Aboriginal society, but, just as important, it refers to their relationships with one another." It is well recognized in the Australian anthropological literature that the movement of traditionally disparate social groups into geographically bounded missions and reserves under past assimilationist policies has resulted in many contemporary Indigenous settlements in which there is an uncohesive and often fractured social field (Memmott and Moran 2001). Nevertheless, within such discrete settlements, customary social networks are often strong and can provide the fertile soil for the growth of social capital. However, these networks can also be the source of conflict and factionalism.

Given the history of Aboriginal affairs policy and the recent policy movement away from the welfare state, issues of governance and corporatization are eminently important. Across Australia tentative, unstable, and awkward balances are being struck between the Aboriginal domain and "welfare colonialism," as the legacy of the deeply structural colonial encounter (Rowse 1992, 58). Rowse argues that future government policy must be sensitive to these cultural dualities (35). He asserts that the task of the government policy of self-determination should be to sympathetically manage the cultural dualities that underlie these precarious balances. He calls for the administrative imagination to be further informed by ethnographic understandings of the concerns and preferred modes of Aboriginal collectivity (vii), and notes (1993, 68), "One potential for an anthropological account of 'Aboriginal politics' is therefore to query the 'state-centred' framework assumed by a political scientist ... and to see the duality of 'Aboriginal politics,' which involves facing not only outwards to the state (with its laws, policies and welfare benefits) but also inwards to the perpetuation of one's own 'mob' and its dealings with neighbouring mobs." Martin (2002, 2), in writing about Aboriginal corporations, notes, "The reality of distinctive Aboriginal values and practices must be accepted as a basic premise in institutional design." He believes that the key to developing appropriate Aboriginal institutions lies not in "resolving" potential conflicting values and practices but, rather, in establishing institutional structures and principles that can encompass and engage the divergent values and practices of Aboriginal and non-Aboriginal origin. He asserts,

> It is no longer defensible to resort to the mantra of "cultural appropriateness," or to that of "Aboriginal tradition," in determining the core principles by which effective Aboriginal institutions should be established and operate. Rather, the challenge is to develop distinctively Aboriginal institutions which nonetheless facilitate effective engagement with the dominant society rather than limiting it. From this perspective, "culturally appropriate" institutions will not just draw their forms, principles and goals from the Aboriginal domain. While they must take account of specific Aboriginal values and practices, they must also have to engage directly – and even on occasion challenge them. (Martin 2002, 2)

As has been seen through the bicultural analysis of social capital in this chapter, this endeavour has been progressed at Wadeye in recent years.[13] Rowse (1992, 35) notes that culturally ambiguous Aboriginal organizations are a necessary and unavoidable historical feature.

The ongoing tensions between the expression of individual rights and family and communal responsibilities can be understood as the conflicting themes of autonomy and relatedness present in many Aboriginal domains (Martin 1995). So while some groups may see economic development as particularly important, others may ascribe significance to cultural vitality and diversity at the expense of the former (ATSIC and Reconciliation Australia 2002, 6). Given the variety of cultural and historical experiences across Aboriginal Australia, different priorities need to be given to different aspects of governance, corresponding to the way different groups value process, form, and outcomes (ATSIC and Reconciliation Australia 2002, 5). It is incumbent on the government to defend both the heterogeneity and the exercise of choice that will mitigate against the effective integration of Indigenous people into mainstream economic and political institutions. Public policy is not in the habit of accounting for diversity and tends toward uniformity. However, developing social capital and building community capacity are localized activities, and in no other context is this more evident than Australian Aboriginal communities. Public policy, in the goal of promoting and developing social capital, must be place- and people-specific and deeply grounded in local values, needs, and circumstances. Uniform, public policy will not work because of the nature of social circumstances and concerns that are local and non-uniform (Stewart-Weeks 2000, 291).

Notes

1 The term "Indigenous" as used in this chapter refers to both the Aboriginal and Torres Strait Islander peoples of Australia. If the context shifts to only Aboriginal peoples, then the term "Aboriginal" is used.

2 We use the construct of governance in the sense defined by Plumptre and Graham (1999, 3): "governance involves the interactions among structures, processes and traditions that determine how power is exercised, how decisions are taken, and how citizens or other stakeholders have their say. Fundamentally, it is about power, relationships and accountability; who has influence, who decides, and how decision-makers are held accountable."

3 In order for an Indigenous group or association to legally receive government funding and then to administrate this funding, using it to perform group or communal functions in response to decision making on behalf of the group or a wider community, such a group or association must be legally incorporated. The most common way that this has occurred in Australia during recent decades is under the Commonwealth's *Aboriginal Councils and Associations Act 1976.*

4 Acknowledgment to Kardu Numida staff at Wadeye, Dale Seaniger and Terry Bullemore; the middle managers of Wadeye, especially Leon Melpi, Tobias Nganbe, and William Parmbuk; the women of Palngun Wurnangat, especially Theodora Narndu; community elders, including Felix Bunduk, Boniface Perjerdt, and George Cumaiyi; FACS staff who participated in the project, especially those who worked in Wadeye with Paul Memmott: Suzie Lodder, Catherine Phillips, and Fiona Carberry; support staff of the AERC, including Lee Sheppard, Catherine Chambers, and Carroll Go-Sam; SERC colleagues John Western, Bob Stimson, Scott Baum, Pat Mullins, and Yolanda van Gellecum; fellow contributors, for their critical feedback, especially Frank Vanclay; and Dr. Nicolas Peterson of ANU for his collaborative advice.

5 Lower estimates are from the 1996 and 2000 census findings (Australian Bureau of Statistics 2002). Upper estimates are by community organizations at Wadeye.

6 SERC was able to show in its mainstream study (2002, 115) that the primary scales and subscales and the four outcome measures had acceptable levels of reliability and validity: "The validity of the measures was attested to by item content, their selective use by other researchers in other contexts and the results of focus group discussions and key informant interviews."

7 One methodological issue was the use of the first or third person in questioning. That is to say, would people be asked questions framed in terms of their personal responses as individuals, or in terms of what the community thought as a whole? After consideration and consultation with a linguist, it was decided that the third person would be used because of the primacy of the group workshop approach. (However this was not always successful; see Memmott 2002 at <www.aboriginalenvironments.com>.)

8 A total of twelve workshops with small groups of representatives of organizations took place, as well as eighteen one-on-one interviews, although the latter interviewees were all members of one or several of the former organizations.

9 Anthropologists have attempted to explain customary avoidance behaviours in Aboriginal Australia with a number of social theories, including incest avoidance and familial obligation to maintain cultural law through reciprocity. For an introduction to these theories see Merlan (1997).

10 This organization has been the centre for community planning over the last six years (see Kardu Numida 1996, 1998, 2000; People of Port Keats/Daly River Region 1997; Bullemore 1999; Thamurrurr 2000, 2002).

11 Aboriginal fireburns are a form of regular traditional land management practice that fulfills multiple functions including preventing uncontrollable high-risk bushfires, concentrating game, and propagating certain plant species.

12 Stanner's ethnographic profile of these groups includes accounts of inter-tribal initiation ceremonies proceeding over many weeks; pan-tribal initiation songs extending over hundreds of kilometres; the ritual capture of initiates, who were then entrusted for a period with a distant tribe; hunting areas shared by several hordes; shared rights of access between several tribes to the resource-rich Daly River; and cooperative fishing and hunting activity involving up to five hordes. These activities were facilitated by widespread multilingualism (Stanner 1933b, 401, 403, 11, 13, 18). There was also a system of inter-tribal ritual exchange that joined all these tribes together (and beyond) and consisting of many human links in chains of personal gift exchange. Each person established over time, through either friendship or kinship or both, a minimum of two lifelong partners with whom to carry out delayed economic exchanges. Stanner (1933a) concludes that this system constantly enriched the social side of individual, family, and group life.

13 At Wadeye we also find syncretization of customary Indigenous religious elements and processes (a sacred site, dreaming of knowledge, gift of powerful song, ritual healing) with Catholic Christianity (pilgrimage, Holy Mother, shrine).

References

Altman, J.C. 2001. *Sustainable Development Options on Aboriginal Land: The Hybrid Economy in the Twenty-First Century*. CAEPR Discussion Paper No. 226/2001. Canberra: Centre for Aboriginal Economic Policy Research, Australian National University.

ATSIC and Reconciliation Australia. 2002. "The Importance of Indigenous Governance and its Relationship to Social and Economic Development." Paper presented at the Indigenous Governance Conference, Reconciliation Australia and ATSIC, Canberra.

Australian Bureau of Statistics.' 2002. *2001 Census of Population and Housing, Community Profile Series*. Canberra: [Wadeye and others, ILOC 3100501], Australian Bureau of Statistics.

Australia, Department of Family and Community Services. 2002. "Stronger Families and Communities Strategy, 'Targeting Strategy for the Northern Territory.'" Canberra: Department of Family and Community Services, 3-5 April.

Black, A., and P. Hughes. 2001. *The Identification and Analysis of Indicators of Community Strength and Outcomes.* Occasional Paper No. 3. Canberra: Department of Family and Community Services.

Bullemore, T. 1999. "Provision of Local Government and Other Services on Aboriginal Land, Wadeye, Northern Territory." Wadeye, NT:

–. 2002. "Busy times at Wadeye" [on the induction ceremony of the Indigenous leadership at Our Lady of the Sacred Heart School], in *Koori Mail,* 6 March.

Chase, A. 1980. "'Which Way Now?' Tradition, Continuity and Change in a North Queensland Aboriginal Community." PhD thesis, Department of Anthropology and Sociology, University of Queensland, St. Lucia, Brisbane.

Christakopoulou, S., J. Dawson, and G. Aikaterini. 2001. "The Community Well-Being Questionnaire: Theoretical Context and Initial Assessment of its Reliability and Validity." *Social Indicators Research* 56: 321-51.

Elkin, A.P. 1931. "The Kopara, The Settlement of Grievances," *Oceania* 2(2): 191-98.

Finlayson, J. 1997. "Aboriginal Tradition and Native Title Representative Bodies." In D.E. Smith and J. Finlayson, eds., *Fighting Over Country: Anthropological Perspectives,* 141-52. Canberra: Centre for Aboriginal Economic Policy Research, Australian National University.

Health Development Agency. 2001. "United Kingdom General Household Survey: Assessing People's Perceptions of Their Neighbourhood and Community Involvement (Part 1)." London: Health Development Agency.

Hunter, B. 2000. *Social Exclusion, Social Capital, and Indigenous Australians: Measuring the Social Costs of Unemployment.* Centre for Aboriginal Economic Policy Research (CAEPR) Discussion Paper No. 204/2000. Canberra: CAEPR, Australian National University.

Idriess, I. 1946. *Nemarluk, King of the Wilds.* Sydney: Angus and Robertson.

Kardu Numida Inc. 1996. *Wadeye Community, Community Management Development Strategy Overview.* Wadeye, NT: unpublished report.

–. 1998. *Submission for Funding through the Local Government Development Programme.* Wadeye, NT: unpublished report.

–. 2000. *Annual Report 1998-99 Financial Year, Operational Report 1999 and Recommendations for Future Operations.* Wadeye, NT: unpublished report.

Kesteven, S. 1984. *The Impact on Aborigines of Money Deriving from Uranium Mining: Social Impact of Uranium Mining on Aborigines of the Northern Territory.* Canberra: Australian Institute of Aboriginal Studies.

Krishna, A., and E. Shrader. 2000. "Cross-Cultural Measures of Social Capital: A Tool and Results from India and Panama." In *Social Capital Initiative.* Washington, DC: World Bank.

Martin, D. 1993. "Autonomy and Relatedness: An Ethnography of Wik People of Aurukun, Western Cape York Peninsula." PhD thesis, Australian National University, Canberra.

–. 1995. *Money, Business and Culture: Issues for Aboriginal Economic Policy.* Canberra: Centre for Aboriginal Economic Policy Research, Australian National University.

–. 2002. "Developing Strong and Effective Aboriginal Institutions." Paper presented at the Indigenous Governance Conference, Reconciliation Australia and ATSIC, 3-5 April, Canberra.

Martin, D., and J. Finlayson. 1996. *Linking Accountability and Self Determination in Aboriginal Organisations.* Centre for Aboriginal Economic Policy Research (CAEPR) Discussion Paper No. 116/1996. Canberra: CAEPR, Australian National University.

Memmott, P. 2002. *Community Strength Indicators and Measures Project – Phase 2, [for the Department of Family and Community Services],* Indigenous Pilot Study Findings. Aboriginal Environments Research Centre, University of Queensland.

Memmott, P., and M. Moran. 2001. *Indigenous Settlements of Australia.* Technical Papers. Canberra: Environment Australia. <http://www.ea.gov.au/soe/techpapers/indigenous/introduction.html> (19 March 2002).

Merlan, F. 1997. "The Mother-in-Law Tabloo: Avoidance and Obligation in Aboriginal Australian Society." In F. Merlan, J. Morton, and A. Rumsy, eds., *Scholar and Sceptic.* Canberra: Australian Studies Press.

Myers, F. 1986. *Pintupi Country, Pintupi Self: Sentiment, Place, and Politics among Western Desert Aborigines*. Washington and London: Smithsonian Institution Press.

Onyx, J., and P. Bullen. 2000. "Measuring Social Capital in Five Communities." *Journal of Applied Behavioural Science* 36: 23-42.

People of Port Keats/Daly River Region. 1997. "Memelmel, a submission to Gatjil Djerrkura OAM, Chairperson of the Aboriginal and Torres Strait Islander Commission and the ATSIC Act Review Team," Wadeye, NT, 18 December.

Pearson, N. 2000. *Our Right to Take Responsibility*. Cairns, Qld: Noel Pearson and Associates.

–. 2001. "Rebuilding Indigenous Communities." In P. Botsman and M. Latham, eds., *The Enabling State: People Before Bureaucracy*. Annandale, NSW: Pluto Press.

Plumptre, T., and J. Graham. 1999. *Governance and Good Governance: International and Aboriginal Perspectives*. Ottawa: Institute on Governance. <http://www.iog.ca/publications/govgoodgov.pdf> (18 March 2003).

Pye, Brother J. 1973. "The Port Keats Story." Kensington, NSW: privately printed.

Rowse, T. 1992. *Remote Possibilities: The Aboriginal Domain and the Administrative Imagination*. Darwin, NT: North Australia Research Unit, Australian National University.

–. 1993. *After Mabo: Interpreting Indigenous Traditions*. Carlton, Vic.: Melbourne University Press.

Schwab, R., and D. Sutherland. 2001. *Building Indigenous Learning Communities*. Centre for Aboriginal Economic Policy Research (CAEPR) Discussion Paper No. 225/2001. Canberra: CAEPR, Australian National University.

Smith, D.E. 2001. *Community Participation Agreements: A Model for Welfare Reform from Community-based Research*. Centre for Aboriginal Economic Policy Research (CAEPR) Discussion Paper No. 223/2001. Canberra: CAEPR, Australian National University.

Stanner, W. 1933a. "Ceremonial Economics of the Mulluk Mulluk and Madngella Tribes of the Daly River, North Australia: A Preliminary Paper." *Oceania* 4(2): 156-75 and 4(4): 458-71.

–. 1933b. "The Daly River Tribes: A Report of Field Work in North Australia." *Oceania* 3(4): 377-405 and 4(1): 10-29.

Stewart-Weeks, M. 2000. "Trick or Treat? Social Capital, Leadership and the New Public Policy." In I. Winter, ed., *Social Capital and Public Policy in Australia*. Melbourne: Australian Institute of Family Studies.

Stewart-Weeks, M., and C. Richardson. 1998. *Social Capital Stories: How 12 Australian Households Live Their Lives*. Sydney: Centre for Independent Studies.

–. 2001. "Measuring Social Capital: Towards a Theoretically Informed Measurement Framework for Researching Social Capital in Family and Community Life." Research Paper No. 24. Melbourne: Australian Institute of Family Studies [draft manuscript].

Strehlow, T. 1970. "Geography and Totemic Landscape in Central Australia: A Functional Study." In Ronald M. Berndt, ed., *Australian Aboriginal Anthropology: Modern Studies in the Social Anthropology of the Australian Aborigines*, 92-140. Nedlands, WA: University of Western Australia Press.

Sutton, P. 1978. "Wik: Aboriginal Society, Territory and Language at Cape Keerweer, Cape York Peninsula, Australia." PhD thesis, Department of Anthropology and Sociology, University of Queensland, St. Lucia, Brisbane.

–. 2001. "The Politics of Suffering: Indigenous Policy in Australia Since the 1970's." *Anthropological Forum* 11(2): 125-73.

Thamurrurr Inc. 2000. "Background Presentation: A Historical and Cultural Overview to the Re-emergence of Thamurrurr, a Traditional Form of Governance for the People of Wadeye Region" [prepared by the people of Wadeye on behalf of Thamurrurr Inc. with assistance from Xavier Desmarchelier], Wadeye, NT, 8 December.

Thamurrurr Local Government Council. 2002. *Draft Thamurrurr Local Government Constitution*. Darwin, NT: NT Department of Community Development, Sport and Cultural Affairs.

University of Queensland (UQ), Social and Economic Research Centre (SERC). 2002. "Assessing Community Strength – A Proposed Set of Indicators and Measures." Brisbane,

Qld: Social and Economic Research Centre (SERC) in association with the Aboriginal Environments Research Centre, University of Queensland.

von Sturmer, J. 1978. "The Wik Region: Economy, Territoriality and Totemism in Western Cape York Peninsula, North Queensland." PhD thesis, Department of Anthropology and Sociology, University of Queensland, St. Lucia, Brisbane.

7
Stones: Social Capital in Canadian Aboriginal Communities
Lesley Moody and Isabel Cordua-von Specht

This chapter explores research work conducted in nine First Nations communities in Northwest British Columbia, as well as in eight communities in Nunavut. The goal of the research was to investigate the presence of an environmental contaminant in these communities and to determine its real and perceived impacts on health (for a more detailed examination of the underlying research on the link between the evidence of and health consequences of environmental contamination, see Moody 2002). It became evident that a disconnect existed between the management of waste in these communities and their traditional relationship with the land. At the same time, the initial research suggested that the concept of social capital might provide a means to understand this disconnect. Little work has been done to date to understand the role of social capital in Aboriginal health and sustainable development. This chapter focuses on that relationship, and tries to better understand, from the perspective of the First Nations people themselves, the nature of social capital within their communities and how changes in social capital have affected the health of their communities, including their social and ecological health, and cultural integrity.

Social capital has been described in different ways in this book, often in the context of measuring it at a given moment. In the Aboriginal communities observed here, social capital is explored across time, to explore the effects of change in the nature of social capital – in the nature of the networks and the relationships of trust, reciprocity, and unity within and across those networks. Relationships change and evolve, within and between social groups, naturally. However, in the observed Aboriginal communities, change has often occurred suddenly, dramatically, and not necessarily because of natural evolutions in the communities themselves.

Memmott and Meltzer discuss in Chapter 6 the evidence of social capital in the Australian Aboriginal community of Wadeye, which parallels in many ways the experience of Canadian Aboriginal communities. They distinguish between formal and informal networks, while noting that these concepts should be viewed as a continuum. Indigenous networks are largely described as informal, based on kinship associations, as opposed to more formalized institutional or civic associations. Similarly, the Canadian Aboriginal communities Lesley Moody has worked in can be described as consisting of predominantly informal networks. However, in using the term "informal," we would like to make clear that there is no value judgment associated with its use. "Informal" by no means implies an inferior status – it signifies only that the structure and dynamic is based on kinship associations, which are no less complex, sophisticated, or valuable than more formal arrangements.

In trying to further understand the nature of these networks and how the concept of social capital might apply to Aboriginal communities, Moody interviewed several elders, asking them to share their understanding of social networks in their communities and the importance of these networks. Their accounts give insights into social capital in traditional life and ways in which it has changed, although, of course, this is not the term they use.

Social Capital and Traditional Aboriginal Life

One particularly illustrative account of the changing nature of social capital in Aboriginal communities comes from Marianno Aupilardjuk, a highly respected elder among the Inuit, known across the Arctic, and recognized for his wisdom and traditional knowledge. Aupilardjuk currently sits as one of a six-member elder council to the Nunavut government, and works to build bridges between his culture and modern Canadian society. He is also a carver, and, to illustrate his conception of social capital, he showed and described three of his stone carvings:

> The first stone, black and smooth, represents traditional Inuit life – how the Inuit so connected to the land that they knew exactly what to do to survive, using their knowledge and experience and the resources around them. Everything came from the land and the animals.
>
> The second stone is white and rough, showing what happened when the outside qallunaq culture encroached on the Inuit. The stone sits uneasily on an unstable base – a wooden peg loosely held in a small stone base that is too small to properly support the stone. It illustrates loss of balance, as rapid change and modern life challenged traditional Inuit way of life.
>
> The third stone, green yet multicoloured, is highly polished and sits on a very finely fashioned, stable wooden base. The wood is of southern origin. This carving represents the hope of a new world the Inuit are creating with the coming together of the two cultures, building new connections and sharing knowledge. (Aupilardjuk 1997)

The first stone, and Aupilardjuk's description of its significance, represents key aspects of social capital that existed in Inuit communities prior to white contact. The first stone represents a time when, living in a subsistence economy – hunting, trapping, and fishing, the Inuit's knowledge of and living with the land was fundamental to their survival. Their culture was adapted to the challenges of the harsh northern environment and responded to the rhythms of the seasons and hunting activities. Interestingly, the Inuit did not have a word for "environment" in their language. Similarly, certain remaining cultures on Earth today have no words to mean the environment, the implication being that peoples of these cultures do not treat or regard the environment differently from but rather in and of themselves (Rees 2000). By contrast, the presence of the concept in non-Aboriginal cultures might signal their separation.[1]

The Inuit relationship to the land and their environment can be characterized by oneness or unity. Their traditional culture was grounded in the basic survival needs of a way of life integrated intimately with the land. A critical part of survival also entailed passing on of knowledge to the younger generations. Elders were responsible for sharing this traditional knowledge, for teaching the Inuit youth the Inuit way of life and demonstrating by example the integrity of Inuit culture. Communal life was such, via hunting and fishing activities as well as life in their traditional shelters (igloos, or other forms of communal housing), that opportunities for knowledge sharing and transmission were part of everyday life. These stories and myths were a powerful way to share and diffuse knowledge between generations.

The value of traditional knowledge is echoed by Jim Angus, a hereditary chief of the Gitksan people, of the Kispiox community in northern British Columbia. Angus is well known throughout the Aboriginal community of British Columbia and has represented his people in national meetings. In a personal communication discussing traditional ecological knowledge (TEK), Angus uses an example from his childhood to illustrate a fundamental value of respect for all life, communicated by tradition from his elders. His grandmother instructed him to hunt for three rabbits, but he brought back four rabbits instead. His grandmother responded by telling him, "Be thoughtful that we are part of the earth and all that's on it, take only what you need" (Angus 2001). As well, she reminded him of the need for gratitude for the moose and salmon. That gratitude is a genuine expression of the notion of reciprocity extended to animals, and, indeed, the whole natural world (Berkes 1998; Dudgeon 1998; Knudtson and Suzuki 1992). Animals were viewed as equals in terms of the respect they merited and the debt that was owed when a life was taken.

When asked about the meaning of TEK, Angus stated that the Gitksan believe they are part of the earth and as such spirituality is an inherent part of the life cycle. Fikret Berkes (1993, 3) defines TEK as "a cumulative body of knowledge and beliefs, handed down through generations by cultural transmission, about the relationship of living beings (including humans) with one another and with their environment." As with Angus's account above, this definition encompasses both the social and ecological relationships in a community and illustrates the interwoven nature of these relationships. The bonds and bridges in these communities were in part dependent on this relationship to the land. This also suggests that a loss in one relationship – the social or ecological, might affect the other.

Further understanding of the nature of social cohesion in First Nation communities is garnered through an account by another Aboriginal elder, Dora Wilson, Wet'suwet'en chief (both hereditary and elected) of the community of Hagwilget, Gitxsanmx for Tse Kya, meaning "place of the quiet people" (Coull 1996). When asked to share her perspective on social capital in her community, she opted to share the particulars of a stone raising feast.

A feast is an occasion to come together to do business. There are different kinds of feasts, each serving a specific purpose. Chief Wilson described a feast for her family members who will receive a head stone for their gravesites. As per tradition, Chief Wilson had hired members of her father's clan to provide the services for the stone raising. (Chief Wilson's parents are of two distinct clans – her father is Wiget, or Fireweed, and her mother is Wolf. As social structure in this nation is matriarchal, Chief Wilson belongs to the Wolf clan.) The purpose of the feast was to officially repay those hired for their services; and about five hundred community members attended. Chief Wilson recalls the event:

> The feast is opened with prayer. The family head (chief) stands to announce the business of the feast. My house group (a smaller kinship unit than a clan) calls out all that has been prepared in terms of food, money, and gifts. Each house is identified as to how much was contributed. The food, money, and gifts are prepared and placed on the fourth table, which sits in the centre of the room for the host clan to show the material expression of their generosity.
>
> At stone feasts it is expected that the spouses of the host clan sing while the food, money, and gifts are presented at the host table. The material goods are either tied on tree branches or limbs of presenters, and the host spouses are taunted in good humour as they dance toward the host table to place their offering. All items on the table are called out for all to witness what has been provided. Each material item is presented in the fashion of gift giving to those hired to perform the tasks associated with the purchase, transportation, and placement of the headstone.
>
> Two clans not related to the host clan are invited to officially count the amount of material goods and money. One person from each clan performs the witnessing of repayment. Seating arrangements are highly guarded, as it would be "taboo" to mis-seat a high-ranking member whose duty it is to be a witness for the host clan.

Once the transaction is complete, the host clan stands and asks if they have forgotten anything. Several minutes elapse, then the two witness clan members verify that all has been done, and it is considered that full payment has been made. Should there be any remaining material goods or money, these are presented to all the general witnesses present. The head chief then sings and drums after the presentation. Once all the singing, drumming, and talking is completed by the host clan, invited clan members and members of the community, the head chief of the host clan stands to speak about those for whom the stone raising feast has been given. The head chief thanks everyone in attendance while this last acknowledgement is made, this ensuring that all is paid and no conflict should arise thereafter.

Berries play a significant roll at stone feasts, with huckleberries regarded by the Wet'suwet'en people of Tse Kya as the most honourable of berries. In ancient days the head chief brought ladles for the berries, and would have been regarded as inhospitable if he attended a stone raising feast with a small-sized ladle, as ladles are associated with the large heartedness of the host clan. Today, containers replace ladles, but the attitude remains the same, with regard to the size of container betraying the spirit of generosity of the host clan. (Wilson 2001)

The feast shares many commonalities with other feasts, or potlatches, in other First Nations communities and is fairly representative of the types of the relationships described. These feasts are grounded in principles of reciprocity and trust, where clan relationships carry concomitant duties which, at the same time, can be expected to be repaid, usually with great generosity. The conduct of these feasts illustrates both the source and strength of social networks in these traditional communities – originating in kinship groups, family and extended, with strong intergenerational ties. And they serve an economic purpose as well, in that they are an informal trading system.

In general, the feasts can have different purposes, serving as a means of establishing a family's generosity and wealth, thereby affirming status, while also serving an important economic purpose by redistributing wealth (Piddocke 1965; Cole 1991). They play significant social and cultural roles in affirming kinship and communal relationships (Ringel 1979). Feasts, or potlatches, also affirm a notion of "what comes around goes around"; that is, giving and sharing in circular fashion, ensuring survival of the group. The values expressed are inimical to a modern economy in certain ways – placing emphasis on social bonds over economic gain, and communal needs over individual profit. Social capital is the primary capital, grounded in the ecological.

Storytelling is also part of these ceremonies, and is an action that can be used to affirm a group's connection to the territories it inhabited. Storytelling is regarded as legal tender or the deed to property, and bespeaks the living connection Aboriginal peoples have with the earth and all that is borne of it. To illustrate, storytelling of geographic locations and the experiences had by Aboriginals dwelling thereon is powerful leverage in determining land claims among differing Aboriginal Nations (Guno 1996).

Through his artistic representation, Aupilardjuk offers glimpses into these dimensions of Inuit, and Aboriginal, life: their relationship to the land, traditional knowledge, social connections, and ultimately their cultural integrity and identity. Their unique way of life was captured in their language, in their traditions, and was conveyed through generations, thereby firmly establishing a cohesive community, as illustrated in the smooth black stone.

Social Capital and Aboriginal Communities Today

Much has been written about the impact of white contact and the imposition of modern ways of life and government policies on Aboriginal peoples. In the context of this research, our interest is in better understanding the impacts on social capital as a result of government policies, specifically with respect to the health of Aboriginal communities and individuals.

The communities under study have experienced a series of dramatic events and processes that have fundamentally changed their way of life. Initial contact with Europeans brought decimation from exposure to new disease. Estimates of the Aboriginal population pre-white contact vary widely, so the exact impact of introduced disease is unknown. But all sources agree that the effect of disease was catastrophic. For instance, population losses in British Columbia were as high as 90 percent, with some communities wiped out altogether (Galois 1994; Boyd 1999). Undoubtedly, this extent of human loss had profound effects on the social structure of Aboriginal communities, with families and kinship networks decimated.

As territorial control extended over Aboriginal territories, Aboriginals increasingly came under the influence of governmental policies determined to assimilate and "civilize" the Aboriginal peoples. Aboriginal groups were moved to reserves, and, in the case of the Inuit, many were resettled in new communities, for health (threat of polio and tuberculosis) and economic (resource extraction) reasons (Aupilardjuk 1997). This meant either a severe limiting of the traditional territories originally occupied, or relocation to new, unfamiliar territories. For a culture so grounded in its experience and understanding of the ecological wealth and rhythms of their traditional land and territory, these relocations impact on multiple levels.

Aupilardjuk, twelve years old when he first saw a white man, recalls the resettlement of Inuit families when he was a young man in the 1950s. Whole families were taken to an airstrip, separated by number, and herded on planes, often never to see one another again. Aupilardjuk was put on a plane destined for Rankin Inlet, the site of the newly opened nickel mines. Some members of his family remained in Pelly Bay, some were sent to various other newly established communities, as well as to white communities south of the sixtieth parallel.

These resettlements led to irrevocable changes in family structures, norms, and ways of life. The resettlement of Inuit into houses in villages and the encroachment of other cultural ways of life fundamentally transformed the Inuit connection to the land, as well as to each other. Inuit were resettled into houses, leaving their traditional shelters and nomadic way of life. With modern amenities, the Inuit were no longer wholly dependent on the land for survival, and their survival was no longer intimately connected to the cycles of nature. As well, Inuit knowledge and traditional activities of hunting and fishing were considered mere subsistence activities and not part of mainstream economic development.

In First Nations communities, traditional potlatches were banned for several generations, from 1884 to 1951, denying not only the actual ceremonies but also the contributory artistic and cultural pieces that accompanied such events – carvings, songs, dances, legends, and histories. This in effect prevented Aboriginals from practising a ceremony that played a central role culturally, legally, politically, economically, and spiritually, though some communities continued to hold potlatches clandestinely, under threat of prosecution and imprisonment. Potlatches played a fundamentally integrative role, connecting all facets of life; thus, their banning had serious ramifications at all levels.

As well, over a number of decades until the 1960s, affecting several generations of Aboriginals, Aboriginal children were forcibly removed from their homes and communities and sent to residential schools. Policies at these schools varied, but it was common practice for the children to be forbidden to speak their native languages or pursue their cultural and religious practices. Run by Christian missionary bodies, the children were instructed in Christian religion. As well, girls and boys, including siblings, were often separated and forbidden contact. For some it was possible to return to their communities over the summer months, for others not.

The impacts of residential schools – psychologically, emotionally, and culturally – have been well documented and bear evidence to the enormous abuses, disconnections, and losses of language, traditional knowledge, and practices suffered by these generations. It should be recognized that the loss of language connects integrally with the loss of traditional knowledge. As the First Peoples' Cultural Foundation notes,

> language, developed over this long period of time, is an intimate interactive reflection of the bioregion in which it was born and contains knowledge of technologies and life's rhythms of that specific place – within Indigenous culture the natural world is respected and loved like a close

relative – knowledge of the natural world is lucid in all its subtlety and vast experience of sustainable activities is spectacular. Indigenous language then is nothing short of a living, working, practical toolkit for survival in that specific region. (First Peoples' Cultural Foundation 2003)

As well, the bonds of family and kinship ties were weakened. The role of elders in teaching the young declined, and authority and justice shifted from elders to the RCMP and white teachers, fundamentally altering the social structure. Aupilardjuk, speaking of Inuit youth, believes that they have lost their sense of identity – they do not know who they are.

At the same time, new social problems have arisen with the introduction of alcohol and drugs. The combination of social dislocation, poor economic conditions, and substance abuse has been deadly. Suicide rates among Aboriginals is three times higher than in the white population, while for Aboriginal youth it is an alarming five to six times higher (Royal Commission on Aboriginal People 1995). These rates are even higher if one accounts for the numerous "accidental deaths" that are in fact suicides (ibid.). It seems that those Aboriginal communities that have retained a greater degree of their traditions have a lower suicide rate (Coulthard 1999). Apparently, suicide was practically nonexistent in traditional Inuit life – with the exception of the elderly or sick, who might have seen themselves as burdens on the nomadic community (Aboriginal Peoples and the Criminal Justice System 2002).

This level of suicide might be a measure of the level of anomie in Aboriginal society. Anomie, in Durkheimian terms, is defined as a state where social or moral norms are confused, unclear, or not present, or as "normlessness" (Durkheim 1893; Babbie 1995). Suicide has been described, both from a sociological and criminological perspective, as a response to conditions in a larger society that lacks legitimate authority and social structures to mediate the needs of the individual within a community (Durkheim 1893; Merton 1938). Thus, suicide may be an indicator at an individual level of the larger social disconnections occurring as a result of great social and cultural change (Dale 2000).

Aupilardjuk depicts this state of imbalance with his second stone. The imbalance exists in all the dimensions identified above: in the state of the Inuit's relationship with the land, the strength of their social connections and networks, and the integrity of traditional knowledge and cultural identity. In academic language, all of this can depict a decline in social capital.

The source of social capital in Inuit communities sprang from the informal networks of family and extended family. Given their strong relationship to the land, the bonds and bridges in these communities were in part dependent on this relationship to the land. Woolcock (2001) describes bonds and bridges as the adhesive for the family, close friends, and neighbours in a given geographic area. In Aboriginal communities, this adhesive was dissolved, with a break in the way of life, family structure, and relationships. This resulted in a loss of knowledge of a way of life, a concomitant loss of identity, and a collapsing of social capital in those communities.

The Health Connection

Aboriginal communities have also suffered a tremendous health impact as a result of the dramatic changes in their way of life. Aboriginal peoples in Canada have the poorest health of any people living in British Columbia and in Canada as a whole (Canada Department of Indian and Northern Affairs 1996). The report of the Royal Commission on Aboriginal Peoples (1996) states that the average life expectancy is twelve years less for status Indians than for British Columbians or other Canadians. Chronic diseases – respiratory system diseases such as pneumonia and influenza – are twice as prevalent in Aboriginal populations, and the incidence of digestive system diseases are three times higher compared with other Canadians. Injuries from accidents are responsible for about 25 percent of all deaths in the Aboriginal population, compared with only 6 percent in the mainstream population. According to a recent *Report on Plans and Priorities,* Health Canada (Canada 2000) has designated healthy First Nations and Inuit communities as a high priority. As well, the report states that there is an urgent need to improve the health status of Aboriginal populations.

Health status is measured by using health indicators. Current indicators of health status for all Canadians include life expectancy, incidence of disease, demographics, population size, degree of isolation, lifestyle, level of education, level of employment, and vital statistics.

While some reasons for the health status disparity between Aboriginal and other Canadians can be identified, still other reasons remain somewhat nebulous. The Skeena Native Development Society (2000) identified these reasons: fear of discrimination; seasonal opportunities only; isolation; limited local funding; lack of transportation; lack of training, education, and skills; lack of economic planning; low self-esteem; and dependency on social assistance. These reasons appear to focus on employment opportunities for Aboriginal people. The list illustrates the challenge facing a people to create a healthy lifestyle and retain its Aboriginal culture and belief system. In other words, the Aboriginal people of Canada living in local communities are caught between a world expressing a strong economic imperative (foreign influence) and their own local world (once consisting of an inalienable link with the land).

In an interview, Rod Raphael, director general of the Safe Environments Program, Healthy Environments and Consumer Safety Branch, Health

Canada, stipulated that social support networks, social environments, and culture become determinants of health, in addition to traditional factors (Raphael 2002). These determinants focus on the social dimensions of health, particularly relevant to Aboriginal societies.

In order for a determinant of health to be useful, a precise list of indicators must fall within each determinant. In *The Wellbeing of Nations,* Prescott-Allen seeks to identify human and ecosystem well-being by using a wide range of indicators for each; however, he was unable to find a suitable indicator for culture (Prescott-Allen 2001). It is clear that we are gaining understanding in what should be considered to measure, and hence promote, well-being. But there are still barriers to accomplishing this, particularly where Aboriginal people are concerned. In general, information regarding Aboriginal people is still sketchy (Kendall 1999). As well, "health" is not understood equally by all cultures. Aboriginal people view human health within a comprehensive model that embodies physical, emotional, intellectual, and spiritual well-being (Federal, Provincial and Territorial Advisory Committee on Population Health 1999). As well, health issues cannot be cast simply from a physical perspective. In this regard, the *Canadian Arctic Contaminants Assessment Report* (Canada 1997) cites the negative effects on the Inuit's cultural and spiritual well-being in relation to advising against the consumption of walrus liver, which was determined to be a health risk because of carcinogenic contaminants.

A further challenge to the determination of Aboriginal health is knowledge gaps associated with the value of health indicators to aboriginal people (Mussell and Stevenson 1999a). For example, the current Health Canada approach to the design and application of health indicators includes formal employment as one of the criteria. It omits a critical aspect of Aboriginal employment, which consists of subsistence activity – time spent hunting, gathering, and fishing for food. While not considered significant in the predominant economic system, so-called subsistence activities are highly valued among Aboriginals.

The concept of social capital suggests a starting point for developing some of these new indicators. As this chapter attempts to argue, social capital is a critical part of building and maintaining a healthy community, and, equally, healthy individuals. It entails an approach that values kinship networks, community relationships, and, as highlighted by the history of Aboriginal people in Canada, reintegrates the human connection to our physical surroundings, to nature, to land. This connection is not yet commonly recognized.

Research is underway in Canada (National Roundtable for the Economy and Environment, International Institute for Sustainable Development, as well as provincial and regional initiatives) and elsewhere to develop social capital indicators, given increasing evidence for its relationship to a range of sustainable development issues. This research is still in initial stages, but to date there does not seem to be an ecological component. Should there be?

The initial research in the seventeen Aboriginal communities suggests that the present disconnection with the land has had health consequences. The research investigated the presence of an environmental contaminant – petroleum – in Aboriginal communities in British Columbia and the North to determine the impacts, real and perceived, on health as a result of this contaminant. While 61 percent of those surveyed believed contaminants to be a problem in the community, only 1 percent identified petroleum as a problem. Yet petroleum was found to be improperly disposed of and leaking from above-ground and underground fuel storage tanks – on residential sites, on roadways next to residential sites, and on public property such as schools, community halls, and church grounds. Several of these instances posed a moderate to high risk to health (Moody 2002). Preliminary data also suggested contaminant threats from the local solid waste disposal site. It became evident that there was a lack of understanding in the communities as to the potential dangers of this contaminant and how to "read" its impact on the surroundings.

It is likely that the Aboriginal peoples' disconnection from their traditional way of life and waning connection to the land and natural world has also spelled a disconnect regarding the present dangers of pollution. Jim Angus, in his discussion of traditional ecological knowledge, related the words of his father, who expressed concern about the vulnerability of the great rivers that pass through their community and their lives: "When we came here there was no pollution, today there are fewer fish (Angus 2001)." Whether or not Aboriginal communities, through traditional knowledge, would understand the pathways of contaminants is uncertain. Nor would they necessarily be familiar with the threats that stem from a modern way of life, unknown in a traditional existence. However, in an environment in which they intimately depended on the resources around them and needed to understand the health of the plant and animal populations around them, Aboriginals were minutely attentive to the respective signs of health.[2] Present generations have lost much of their connectedness to the land, no longer needing to depend on it for survival. In turn, they have lost the traditional knowledge as well as critical skills of observation that would give them cues as to the state of their natural surrounding. Thus, today, lacking both traditional knowledge and adequate education, Aboriginal populations are vulnerable to contaminants.

Improving the health status of Aboriginal peoples, therefore, must also include, in connection with building social capital, rebuilding a relationship to the land. Not only is this crucial to rebuild the lost elements of culture, knowledge, and identity identified above – restoring community health – but it is also critical to individual health.

Conclusions

It is beyond the scope of this chapter to make specific recommendations as to incorporating social capital as a fundamental determinant in Health Canada's approach to and measurement of Aboriginal health. However, social capital must be in the forefront of future research in order to address previously ignored dimensions of Aboriginal health – culture, traditional knowledge, and identity.

Aboriginal peoples find themselves in a modern economy and way of life, only recently torn from a subsistence life with values in many ways incongruent with the demands of modern life. Their communities have not evolved in the typical sense; they have had to endure abrupt and violent change and, as a result, are caught between two worlds. Aupilardjuk recognizes this dilemma with his stones, and also raises hope for a reconciliation. His third stone evokes a sense of integration, where, through sharing knowledge with other communities and white society, new knowledge can be blended with old, new relationships and networks can be woven, and a new identity established, one that straddles the worlds and is balanced harmoniously, not precariously. This would spell the return to a healthy community, one vibrant culturally and socially, ecologically and economically.

Health Canada must support building these necessary bridges for Aboriginals in a manner that promotes reconciliation between the traditional and the new. The bridges must be developed from a sustainable development lens – reconciling the ecological, social, and economic imperatives (Dale 2001; Robinson and Tinker 1997) in a manner congruent with Aboriginal cultures and respectful of the qualities of their social capital. At the same time, this work may contribute to reawakening for "white" society a re-membering of the intimate connection that all human communities had with their natural surroundings, and re-establish our own membership within the natural world.

Notes

1 The Sapir-Whorf hypothesis puts forth the theory of language relativity that language and cognition shape each other. Whorf states that "every language is a vast pattern-system, different from others, in which are culturally ordained the forms and categories by which the personality not only communicates, but also analyzes nature, notices or neglects types of relationship and phenomena, channels his reasoning, and builds the house of his consciousness" (Whorf 1956, 252). While several elements of the theory are hotly disputed, there is understanding at a general level that that language and society shape each other (Chaika 1989).

2 The ability and importance of observing the health of any given animal was recounted in several interviews with Inuit hunters, specifically in reference to *Brucella,* parasitic bacteria in caribou that represent a human health risk if ingested.

References

Aboriginal Health Association of British Columbia. 1999. *Health Authorities Handbook on Aboriginal Health.* Victoria, BC: BC Ministry of Health and Ministry Responsible for Seniors.

Aboriginal Peoples and the Criminal Justice System. 2002. Ottawa: Canadian Criminal Justice Association.

Angus, J. 2001. Personal communication. Gitksan Nation, Kispiox, 20 April.

Aupilardjuk, M. 1997. Personal communication. Rankin's Inlet, 12 August.

Babbie, E. 1995. *The Practice of Social Research*. 7th ed. Belmont, CA: Wadsworth.

Berkes, F. 1993. "Traditional Ecological Knowledge in Perspective." In J.T. Inglis, ed., *Traditional Ecological Knowledge: Concepts and Cases*. Ottawa: International Program on Traditional Ecological Knowledge and International Development Research Centre.

–. 1998. "Indigenous Knowledge and Resource Management Systems in the Canadian Subarctic." In F. Berkes and C. Folke, eds., *Linking Social and Ecological Systems: Management Practices and Social Mechanisms for Building Resilience*, 98-128. Cambridge, UK: Cambridge University Press.

Boyd, R. 1999. *The Coming of the Spirit of Pestilence: Introduced Infectious Diseases and Population Decline among Northwest Coast Indians, 1774-1874*. Vancouver: UBC Press, and Seattle: University of Washington Press.

Canada. Department of Indian and Northern Affairs Canada. 1996. *Report of the Royal Commission on Aboriginal Peoples*. Ottawa: DINA.

–. 1997. *Canadian Arctic Contaminants Assessment Report* (CACAR). Ottawa: DINA.

–. Health Canada. 2000. *Report on Plans and Priorities*. Ottawa: Health Canada.

Chaika, E. 1989. *Language the Social Mirror*. New York: Newbury House.

Coull, C. 1996. *A Traveller's Guide to Aboriginal BC*. Vancouver: Whitecap Books.

Coulthard, G. 1999. *Colonization, Indian Policy, Suicide, and Aboriginal Peoples*, citing "Aboriginal Suicide in British Columbia," Burnaby, BC: British Columbia Institute on Family Violence Society, 1991. <http://www.ualberta.ca/~pimohte/suicide.html> (5 April 2003).

Dale. A. 2000. Personal communication, 15 March.

–. 2001. *At the Edge: Sustainable Development in the 21st Century*. Vancouver: UBC Press.

Dudgeon, R. 1998. "A Political Anthropology of TEK in the Canadian Subarctic." <http://home.cc.umanitoba.ca/~umdudgeo/polianth.html> (29 March 2003).

Durkheim, E. 1893. *The Division of Labor in Society*. Trans. G. Simpson, New York: Free Press.

Federal, Provincial and Territorial Advisory Committee on Population Health. 1999. *Report on the Health of Canadians*. Ottawa: Health Canada.

First Peoples' Cultural Foundation. 2003. <www.fpcf.ca> (16 April 2003).

Galois, R. 1994. *Kwakwaka'wakw Settlements, 1775-1920: A Geographical Analysis and Gazetteer*. Vancouver: UBC Press.

Guno R. 1996. Personal communication. Nisga'a Nation, Terrace, 29 March.

Kendall, P. 2000. *A Report on the Health of British Columbians – Provincial Health Officer's Annual Report*. Vancouver, BC: Ministry of Health Planning.

Knudtson, P., and D. Suzuki. 1992. *The Wisdom of the Elders*. Sydney: Allen and Unwin.

Merton, R.K. 1938. "Social Structure and Anomie." *American Social Review* 3: 672-68.

Moody, L. 2002. "Reasons for First Nations Lag Behind Other Canadians – Health Status." MSc thesis, Royal Roads University, Victoria, BC.

Mussell, W.J., and J. Stevenson. 1999a. *Value of Health Indicators to Aboriginal People*. Ottawa: Health Canada.

–. 1999b. *Health Authorities Handbook on Aboriginal Health*. Vancouver: Aboriginal Health Association of BC.

Pfleugger, G. 2002. Personal communication, 1 September.

Piddocke, S. 1965. "The Potlatch System of the Southern Kwakiutl: A New Prospective." *Southwestern Journal of Anthropology* 21: 244-64.

Prescott-Allen, R. 2001. *The Wellbeing of Nations: A Country-by-Country Index of Quality of Life and the Environment*. Ottawa: IDRC/Island Press.

Raphael, R. 2002. Interview cited in *Health and the Environment: Critical Pathways* 1(4): 1-35.

Rees, W. 2000. Lecture at Royal Roads University, March.

Ringel, G. 1979. "The Kwakiutl Ptlatch: History, Economics, and Symbols." *Ethnohistory* 26(4): 347-62.

Robinson, J.B., and J. Tinker. 1997. "Reconciling Ecological, Economic and Social Imperatives: A New Conceptual Framework." In T. Schrecker, ed., *Surviving Globalism: Social and Environmental Dimensions*. London: Macmillan.

Royal Commission on Aboriginal People. 1995. *Choosing Life: Special Report on Suicide Among Aboriginal People*. Ottawa: Canada Communication Group Publishing.

Skeena Native Development Society Report. 2000. Terrace, BC: Skeena Native Development Society.

Whorf, B.L. 1956. *Language, Thought, and Reality*. Boston: MIT Press.

Wilson. D. 2001. Personal communication. Wet'suwet'en Nation, Hagwilget, 26 August.

Woolcock, M. 2001. "The Place of Social Capital in Understanding Social and Economic Outcomes." *Canadian Journal of Policy Research* 2(1): 11-17.

8

Communities of Practice for Building Social Capital in Rural Australia: A Case Study of ExecutiveLink

Sue Kilpatrick and Frank Vanclay

"Communities of practice" and "social capital" are terms that have developed in separate discourses. While social capital refers to the social resources, networks, norms, values, trust, and commitment present in a group or community (Putnam, Leonardi, and Nanetti 1993; Coleman 1988), "communities of practice" refers to a specific form of the informal structures where social capital is built. Communities of practice are defined as collections of individuals bound by informal relationships that share similar work roles and a common context (Lesser and Prusak 2000). Communities of practice and social capital are interdependent – social capital needs communities of practice in order to be generated, and communities of practice need social capital to work effectively. Given the interdependence of these concepts, it is surprising that there has been so little awareness of the other concept in the discourse of each.

There are a few exceptions, of course (e.g., Lesser and Prusak 2000; Lesser and Storck 2001). But for the most part, the terms and their respective discourses have maintained a separate trajectory. This chapter seeks to demonstrate the logical interconnectedness of the two concepts, and will then provide a detailed case study of a specific community of practice to show how it generates social capital. The case study is of ExecutiveLink, a trademarked process for improving the sustainability of Australian farm businesses.

Communities of Practice

Community of (common) practice, community of (common) interest, and community of (common) purpose are concepts that have emerged in a range of different settings and disciplines with connected but not totally similar meanings. The term "community of practice" originated in the early 1990s (Brown and Duguid 1991; Lave 1991; Lave and Wenger 1991) and is perhaps currently in strongest use in the fields of management science and organizational studies. It is also strong in the somewhat related fields of information and communication technology (ICT) and knowledge management. But the concept and its related terms resonate well in the fields of human geography, rural sociology, and (agricultural) extension science, where they provide a contradistinction to the conventional term "communities of place."

While "communities of practice" was the most popular (insofar as the number of web hits), the three terms tend to be interchangeable and synonymous. However, one website did differentiate between them (Process Edge 2002):

> There are different types of community, each of which has a valid purpose. In order of decreasing longevity and stability –
>
> *Communities of common practice:* Specialist groups who share knowledge and procedures.
> *Communities of common interest:* People who enjoy knowing about, discussing and developing, a subject.
> *Communities of common purpose:* This type of community forms to take definite action.

Notwithstanding these definitions, and given that the implied order is not totally obvious, in this chapter the three terms will be regarded as equivalent. In management science, a community of practice (CoP) can be defined as

> a special type of informal network that emerges from a desire to work more effectively or to understand work more deeply among members of a particular specialty or workgroup. At the simplest level, CoPs are small groups of people who've worked together over a period of time and through extensive communication have developed a common sense of purpose and a desire to share work-related knowledge and experience. (Sharp 1997, 1)

In organizational studies, while it is understood that these informal networks are somewhat inevitable, more importantly it is believed that these networks "enable the organization to accomplish tasks faster or better than would be the case if the communication and action took place along formal organizational lines alone" (Sharp 1997, 1). In other words, they "can help organizations harness the real power in their companies" (ibid.).

CoPs are beneficial for their participants as well. Brown and Duguid (1991) describe how the sharing of experience, the swapping of "war-stories," through informal processes was essential for the successful completion of job tasks of Xerox repair staff. Many problems, technical (machine related) and personal (such as handling difficult customers), could not be solved by referring to official company documentation and procedures. It was through personal interactions developed at informal encounters at lunch and coffee breaks, at the water cooler, and away from work where the real skills needed for the job were acquired.

CoPs can be based on cross-functional teams as well as specialist teams. This implies that instead of a CoP being based on common work practices, it can be based on a common activity, where members contribute experiences based on their different roles (Sharp 1997).

In the fields of management science and organizational studies, the emphasis is on promoting understanding of the social nature of organizations and of the importance of communities of practice to the organization itself. This has implications for how organizations and staff are managed.

Sharp (1997), quoting from various online sources and from Handy (1996) notes how, in the information age, knowledge is central to an organization, and that a company's value derives from this knowledge that is embodied in people. As with the Xerox repair staff, much of the valuable knowledge of an organization is tacit knowledge; that is, it exists outside formal documentation (McDermott n.d., using a concept from Polanyi 1958). Professional knowledge workers, that is people who have a job that relies on knowledge embodied in people, also view themselves as having a commitment to a profession that is greater than to the corporation in which they work. These professional knowledge workers place a great importance on their informal networks, which iteratively nurture and are nurtured by reciprocal trust. But reciprocal trust does not automatically come from an occupational role, or from a company position; they develop out of the personal relationships. While hard to establish, they are easily destroyed, and then harder again to re-establish (Sharp 1997).

So mutual trust (which is closely related to social capital) is a feature of this area of study. The primary application of the understanding of communities of practice is what organizations should do to facilitate their development and success.

Outside the fields of organizational studies and management science, where the focus is on CoPs within a corporation (albeit with a discussion about links outside), there is also recognition of the role of learning groups. In ICT, CoPs are often virtual (usenets), being built around common issues, for example, a particular software package.

In the human geography, rural sociology, and community studies fields, communities tended to be tied to place. But with technological developments, particularly Internet applications, many now realize that communities of interest (the preferred term in these disciplines) may be more important than communities of place, especially given the low level of personal interaction frequent in geographically defined communities.

The characteristics of a community of practice (interest or common purpose) are not altogether dissimilar to the characteristics of a community of place. Wenger (1998), one of the gurus of CoP, argues that CoP has three dimensions: mutual engagement, a joint enterprise, and a shared repertoire of ways of doing things. While "place" is defined geographically, "community" traditionally (such as in human geography and rural sociology) tends to not only refer to place but also invoke notions of belongingness or shared identity, mutual involvement or shared activities, a sense of history and a notion about the future, and commonality or local culture. In other words, the concept of community of place does not differ substantially from a community of practice, interest, or common purpose.

The concept of community of practice, however, does have some additional characteristics as an "intentional community" that differentiate it from conventional place-based communities, but probably not from other intentional communities (communes, collectives, cults, and so on). These potentially include:

- bonding by exposure to common problems
- common practices and development of a specialized (unique) language
- a sense of purpose
- focus on learning – not just informal and random events such as around the water cooler but also deliberate learning processes and formal meetings
- an emphasis on creativity and innovation.

CoPs have always existed in one form or another, even though they were not identified as such. What is new now is that there is an increasing awareness of the need to give these age-old structures a legitimate role in society (Wenger 1998).

One aspect of CoPs that is not consistent in the literature is the extent to which they are informal. Much of the CoP literature refers to them as spontaneous and informal. The contradiction or irony then is the extent to which this management literature argues that corporations can facilitate the development of CoPs, and in some cases formally establish them. This contradiction is most evident in McDermott (n.d.), who argues that spontaneous communities of practice have always been the real vehicle through which technical knowledge spreads through organizations and that spontaneous communities of practice are informal, but then goes on to outline a model example of a community of practice, the Turbodudes (turbo-dudes), which have a formal procedure for making their meetings effective.

The Turbodudes are a group of people who work for Shell Oil's New Orleans operation. Although from different disciplines, the members have a common interest in turbidite, a geological structure. They have regular scheduled meetings (every Tuesday morning at 7:30 a.m.), a designated coordinator, mentors, formal presentations including by outsiders, and minutes of meetings that are retained on a website. The coordinator uses time between meetings to connect members with each other and to canvass issues for future meetings. A mentorship program actively brings in new members. ExecutiveLink, the topic of the case study reported in this chapter, functions in a somewhat similar way to the Turbodudes.

Social Capital and Communities of Practice

Theory

There is a growing body of research on social capital. A history of this research is provided in Portes (1998) and Falk and Kilpatrick (2000), as well as in other chapters in this book. Examples of applied research (as opposed to theoretical speculation) include Putnam, Leonardi, and Nanetti's (1993) study of regions in Italy, Krishna and Uphoff's (1999) study of an Indian community, Narayan and Pritchett's (1997) study of families in rural Africa, and those studies discussed in some of the other chapters in this book. These studies have led to a theoretical synthesis of how social capital works at family, community, regional, and national levels. More recent applications have been in institutional economics and business (Pennar 1997; Nahapiet and Ghoshal 1998). Human capital (knowledge and skills), it seems, is harnessed more effectively when social capital (networks and norms) is strong.

Lesser (Lesser and Prusak 2000; Lesser and Storck 2001), drawing on Nahapiet and Ghoshal (1998), argues that three dimensions emerge from the social capital literature: a structural element (such as networks), a relational element (such as norms, values, and trust), and a cognitive element (shared language, vocabulary, stories, history, and context). Although the third element, the cognitive dimension, is not common in all formulations of social capital (for example, it is not featured in Putnam 2000), the first two, networks and trust, are universal.

Social capital is defined most simply as the norms and networks that enable people to act collectively (Woolcock and Narayan 2000). It is a set of resources that resides in the relationships among people that allows them to share their knowledge and skills, or human capital. Sharing of knowledge and skills is facilitated by structures, procedures, and mechanisms that bring people together in places and environments that encourage and support interaction.

The structures that assist people to access the knowledge and skills of others can be informal, such as social networks, or formal, such as service groups, workplaces, and churches. The mechanisms are to do with how people get along with each other, including concepts such as trust, commitment to others, and shared values. Social capital is a set of resources that can exist in geographic communities and in communities of practice.

Communities of practice are (informal and perhaps formal) networks that contribute to the development of social capital (relational dimension). Membership of, or the existence of, such communities is social capital (structural dimension). Because communities of practice develop around common work tasks or common interests, there tends to be a common occupational language or common vernacular (cognitive dimension). As CoPs develop and grow, they are likely to produce their own vernacular, as well as artifacts of their identity. For example, the name Turbodudes is a strong statement of identity, belonging, and commonality.

This chapter analyzes the processes that occur in a community of practice (or learning community) of Australian family farm businesses for evidence of use, or generation, of stores of social capital. The purpose of analyzing processes that use or build social capital is to derive a framework, or checklist of stages and characteristics, that can be used to analyze the extent of social capital use and generation in other communities. An understanding of how what is identified as social capital can be built in a formalized learning program such as ExecutiveLink (EL) can be used to facilitate social capital building in other formal learning settings, as well as more widely.

This chapter is part of a series of papers that derive from work of the Centre for Research and Learning in Regional Australia (CRLRA) at the University of Tasmania into social capital. The CRLRA defines social capital as

> the product of social interactions with the potential to contribute to the social, civic or economic well-being of a community-of-common-purpose. The interactions draw on knowledge and identity resources and simultaneously use and build stores of social capital. The nature of the social capital depends on various qualitative dimensions of the interactions in which it is produced, such as the quality of the internal-external interactions, the historicity, futuricity, reciprocity, trust and the shared values and norms. (Falk and Kilpatrick 2000, 103-4)

A Rural Community of Practice: A Case Study of ExecutiveLink

Overview of ExecutiveLink

EL is a process oriented program that develops skills and facilitates change (learning) in Australian farm families and businesses (RCS 2000). It does this through establishing groups (called boards) comprising the management teams (usually husband and wife partnerships) of around six farm businesses who live in relative proximity to each other. Boards are clustered at regional/state level into chapters. The boards meet for regular structured events, which include formal training and experiential processes. Generally there are three such events per year, each lasting about three days. These activities are done at the chapter level, with the formal training involving all members of all boards in a chapter. The experiential components are undertaken at the board level. Boards are limited to a three-year lifespan, but the relationship that develops between members means that the group tends to continue on in an informal manner. The intensity of the training experience means that most boards decide to meet outside the established board meetings, for example, at the request of a member who has a particular issue to resolve.

A prerequisite for membership in EL is completion of two training courses in farm management, Grazing for Profit and GraduateLink. Therefore, a certain common culture and common purpose exists among would-be members of EL. The boards provide management advice to their members, who are free to accept or reject that advice.

EL is facilitated by the commercial consulting firm Resource Consulting Services, founded in 1985 and now operating in all states of Australia, with offices in five states. EL, developed by Stan Parsons and Terry McCosker, has been operating in Australia since 1991. Stan Parsons had run a company called Ranch Management Consultants in the United States, where a forerunner, Ranching for Profit, was developed.

EL is endorsed by FarmBis, a scheme jointly funded by the Commonwealth (National Heritage Trust) and the states. FarmBis provides assistance to develop new learning activities to enhance the business management skills of Australia's primary industry sector. In EL, one way of encouraging this culture of business management is the insistence that board members talk about their "business" rather than their farm, or their property, or their place. The approximately AUD$5,000 participation cost in EL is subsidized (about 75 percent) by FarmBis. Nevertheless, participants must make a considerable time and energy investment. There is ongoing change to public agriculture support programs, and the details given here are relevant to the time the data were collected (around 1998).

EL is not targeted at all farmers. Rather, it is targeted to top-end farmers or those who have a strong commitment to change. It is focused on grazing, especially on promoting intensive rotational grazing techniques. Sustainability (a triple bottom line of social, economic, and environmental sustainability) is an important dimension of the program. Sound business management – efficiency – is achieved not through productivity (although this is one dimension) but through an analysis of all expenditure. Personal development also forms an important part of the training and experiential dimensions of the program.

The primary goals of EL are to

- improve business performance through benchmarking and targets
- educate and motivate for change
- develop a well considered business plan over four years
- empower participants to analyze and assess their businesses according to individual needs
- develop a strong network of motivated producers who can respond to opportunities, both on and off the farm

- develop trust and skills to a point where group marketing and investment will be natural outcomes. (RCS 2000)

Case Study Methodology

The research was done through the CRLRA at the Launceston campus of the University of Tasmania. One of the facilitators of EL, aware of the significance of EL as a learning community and of the CRLRA's interest in learning communities and social capital, approached the CRLRA to develop a mutually beneficial link: CRLRA would be able to study EL as a case study, and the EL facilitators would receive an external evaluation of EL and potentially be able to improve their offerings.

The CRLRA research team was invited to attend the Tasmanian chapter training session in September 1998. The chapter comprised four EL boards, which had been operating for different lengths of time, including one just formed. The activities of one of the three more established boards (one had been operating for two years) were observed in full during the three days.

In addition to this observational component, a focus group was held at the end of the second day of training and drew on volunteers from all EL participants present. Fifteen EL participants from the three longer established boards attended the focus group. While the newly formed group was not formally part of the research, the spare time at the three-day training course provided opportunities to discuss issues with them. They decided not to participate in the focus group because they felt that they were still learning about EL themselves. They also commented that trust and commitment had not yet formed in their group, as they were still relative strangers to each other.

Some weeks after the training session, semi-structured interviews were administered to nine volunteer members from the three boards at their farm businesses. Three EL facilitators were also interviewed. The interviews and focus group were tape-recorded and transcribed, and the results analyzed using QSR International's NUD*IST qualitative data analysis software.

ExecutiveLink: A Network for Mutual Support

EL members go through a set of stages in forming their network in order to learn together and support each other as they make changes in their businesses. The sequential stages of the process are: (1) individual members acquiring a high level of personal self-confidence and a high level of interpersonal skills, including leadership skills; (2) getting to know each other as individuals (history and future aspirations), thereby developing shared values and trust; (3) coming to regard each other as credible sources of support and advice; and (4) committing to fellow members, and being prepared to help each other out.

Personal Development: Self-Confidence, and Interpersonal and Leadership Skills
Before they are able and willing to give effective support to fellow board
members, people must get to know themselves and their own strengths and
weaknesses. Members need to learn to realize that their views will be accepted and valued:

> [EL] gives you a lot more confidence in the decisions that you make ... It
> really does make you feel as if you're part of something ... and that you do
> have a contribution to make, even if it is just ... ideas which are totally non-
> farming orientated. (EL member)

Improving interpersonal skills of listening, empathy, and being able to take
on various roles in the group, such as leadership roles and keeping the group
on task, assists the group's development as well as the personal development of members:

> You've got a lot of different roles and they all work on each other and help
> each to benefit as a whole ... When the people in the group become more
> familiar with each other, then they really start doing a role reversal, so they
> give everybody else a go to develop their skills in areas that they wouldn't
> have been so certain. (EL focus group member)

The initial development of self-confidence and skills such as leadership
through a variety of interactions assists in people getting to know each
other.

Knowing Each Other
Getting to know others occurs as members share their personal histories and
future aspirations while relating their experiences during EL meetings. This
sharing establishes a climate of openness in which members feel free to challenge others and are open to constructive criticism. The boards learn effectively because all the members value the climate of openness. Responding to
the question of what makes their board effective, one member replied:

> A preparedness to speak up ... Everyone's pretty comfortable with each other
> and prepared to say if they don't agree with something ... If someone's got
> a problem, there's no holding back ... Everyone respects everyone's opin-
> ion, and that's important.

The EL members said that getting to know each other and building trust were
necessary before members would introduce or discuss sensitive issues. Changes
in these sensitive areas were the changes that permitted the businesses to

make major improvements in performance. Once they get to know each other better, members start to refer fundamental problems or issues that required decisions to the board:

> At the first couple of meetings ... everybody was so nice to each other. No one's got any problems ... whereas now, it's going [the board is working]. The people who didn't have any problems have got the biggest problems. (EL member)

Knowing that others share your outlook (or norms and values) helps because it provides support and gives confidence as you go about the overall management and operation of the businesses. Trust, along with rapport, develops as the group members get to know each other as people:

> Suddenly I was with a group of people who understood our problems because they all had the same. That was a good feeling ... now there is enough trust, trust and care. (EL member)

"Getting to know each other" emerges through interactions, just as personal development occurs through interactions. Interactional opportunities in the formal meeting sessions and during breaks before and after sessions allows members to move onto the next stage, coming to regard each other as credible courses of advice and support.

Credibility of the Group and Members as Sources of Support

Board members had to get to know each other before they could regard each other as credible sources of advice and support, and had to be prepared to use each others' knowledge and skills. Support from boards as changes were made came only after the members understood each other and had developed shared values and trust.

As people get to know each other, they develop a sense of belonging, and a sense that all group members can make valued contributions. Only at this stage are they able to decide whether fellow members and the group as a whole are credible as sources of support; that is, whether reassurance, advice, or practical help from the board is worth accepting. A member attending his second meeting commented that he was unsure how much notice he should take of advice from his board, whereas a member of eighteen months clearly regards his board as a credible source of information and advice:

> Everyone's got a strength, and why not pool your resources and say "Well, he's good at that, I'll ask him how to do it!" It's a quicker way of finding out than bumbling around trying to do it yourself!

This EL member sums up the advantages of having others who are regarded as credible sources of advice and support available for interactive learning:

> You can employ a consultant anytime you like ... but ... he only has one point of view. One-on-one consultancy is never going to be as powerful as the group consultancy because everybody in our board or in the group has got an area of expertise ... So it's got a lot more bang for your buck.

Members recognize that they can learn more efficiently and produce better outcomes if they combine their knowledge and skills. This stage is reached only after there has been a number of interactions of a sufficient quality, interactions that (1) produce personal development and (2) allow the members to get to know each other well enough to (3) come to regard each other as credible sources of advice and support. There is a final stage before the members can actually combine their knowledge and skills for a particular purpose: a commitment to the community.

Commitment (Being Prepared to "Put In")

Commitment featured repeatedly in the interviews and focus group that were held, and in conversations at the focus group meeting. Commitment confirms the presence of the norm of reciprocity. Commitment to the board is demonstrated by spontaneous actions that benefit others. One board helped one of its members establish a computerized accounting system. Other members speak more generally of actions that have helped them as they make changes to their businesses. There is acknowledgment that reciprocity is an integral part of the community:

> We went to an auction the other day, and we bought this computer for [a fellow member] ... [He's] got a lot to offer. These things work both ways ... it's a complex web, and I'm sure if you help other people then you might get someone [to help you]. (EL member)

Some boards are not as effective as others that have been established for the same length of time. The less effective boards offer less support to their members. For example, members in one particular board do not contact each other between meetings:

> There's an inclination for the board members to say, "You go away and do that." We don't really get in touch with each other and say, "How are you getting on, can I help in any way?" We could be a lot better. (EL member)

"Commitment" seems to represent the point at which personal development and "getting to know each other" sufficiently to see each other as credible sources of support combine with sufficient reserves of trust between members to result in a commitment to future action.

Outcomes of the ExecutiveLink Support Network

Many changes have been made to practice in member businesses that have increased the sustainability of those businesses in terms of the social, economic, and environmental aspects of the triple bottom line. Members spoke of the benefits to family relationships of having an articulated and shared vision for the business, including agreements on succession planning. Decisions to change enterprises or the allocation of natural, human, and financial resources improved the economic sustainability of all the businesses that remained in agriculture. Members not only began practices that would enhance environmental sustainability, such as ceasing cropping on unsuitable soils and better management of native bush, but the support of fellow members assisted as they implemented these practices. One member sums this up:

> Well, the main business changes, physical changes like stopping the cropping, cell grazing, and those sorts of things ... [and] personal changes ... we tend to seek other people's opinions within our group, and have discussions with them.

ExecutiveLink and Communities of Practice

Are EL boards typical examples of CoPs? Probably not, at least according to the CoP literature. But could EL boards be regarded as a variant of a CoP? Definitely. EL boards are formally created, and begin their life with a series of formal activities. However, the intention is to allow for the establishment of a network on which members can draw to solve future problems and to establish and reinforce their personal identity. This is particularly important in farming with the removal of many forms of social support from farming life (Vanclay and Lawrence 1995). While CoPs are often described as being informal, much of the CoP literature describes formal procedures for establishing them, facilitating them, and mainstreaming them within organizations. To that extent, we believe that EL boards are CoPs.

EL boards develop bonds and a sense of purpose through the process of sharing farm problems. Coming from a farming background, they likely start with a similar (sub)culture, and this similarity is enhanced as they work together as a group and as they inculcate norms promoted by the EL philosophy, including sustainability. In so doing, they also come to share norms and values. A strong sense of trust develops. They develop common practices (an emphasis on business management), and they develop a specialized and unique language that revolves around different components of their training. There is a strong focus on learning, both as a group and individually. And there is a focus on innovation and creativity, at least in terms of one's own business operation. Therefore, EL boards have most if not all of the characteristics of a CoP.

ExecutiveLink and Social Capital

EL builds social capital on all three dimensions – structural, relational, and cognitive. It initiates and facilitates the development of a network (structural). It enhances shared values and a sense of trust and commitment (relational). And it creates a sense of identity, shared knowledge, and language (cognitive).

Several members spoke of a feeling of commitment, which represents part of a store of social capital that can be drawn on when needed for dealing with difficult times. Knowledge of each others' expertise, strengths, and weaknesses, along with recognition that fellow members are credible as sources of support and advice, are also elements of the social capital that oils the change process for EL members. The social capital can be operationalized because there is a commitment to act for the benefit of fellow members; there is a norm of reciprocity that leads to spontaneous actions for the benefit of others.

The structure of EL facilitates the development of a support network, which is an example of social capital. It does this first by systematically providing opportunities for developing self-confidence and interpersonal skills, including leadership, in training sessions and as the board members work together; and second, by providing shared experiences in training sessions and board sessions.

In itself, the EL process recognizes (a) the crucial role played by opportunity for interactions (for example, in personal development); (b) the role of historicity/futuricity (both in the need to build a shared history and to find out and share each others' history and future visions); and (c) the manner in which growing trust indicates the building of social capital, with acts of commitment as clear evidence of the existence of group-level trust.

As they learn together, the members generate horizontal social capital (Putnam, Leonardi, and Nanetti 1993). The social capital is used as members make changes to their businesses. Consistent with the literature of social capital (for example, Narayan and Pritchett 1997; Putnam, Leonardi, and Nanetti 1993; Coleman 1988), EL members achieve better outcomes when they use their knowledge and skills along with the knowledge and skills of other members. Members use tools, such as benchmarking, and other knowledge gained from EL when making what are often major changes to the way they run their businesses. However, it is the social capital of the community that oils the process of learning and implementing new practices, and which is vital in ensuring major changes. One EL member sums up the advantage of the access to the pool of knowledge and support of the group:

There are so many farmers out there doing lots of work and putting in lots of effort, and just getting nowhere. And with a small amount of training and focusing, and a bit of backup, and a bit of support ... it just works so beautifully.

Two sorts of outcomes are possible from interactions using social capital. One outcome is some action or cooperation for the benefit of the community or its members; the other is the building or strengthening of social capital. As one member of a group who helped a fellow member make decisions about a major change in direction for the business commented,

> There was tremendous commitment to ... go to [that board member's] place ... We went on a Saturday and most of us were in the middle of shearing ... I had to get people to do my work for me and the other members of the board were in the same boat ... We just had to do it, and it worked really well and we all gained from it.

The experience is described as positive for the member who was helped – a direct outcome of the action that drew on social capital. The set of interactions was also a positive experience for the group as a whole: they built more social capital as they shared an experience, developed their decision-making and facilitation skills, and got to know each other better ("we all gained from it").

A Model of Social Capital as Knowledge and Identity Resources

The foregoing analysis of the process whereby the EL community builds social capital provides insights into the makeup, or elements, of social capital. It is possible to identify two components of social capital: knowledge resources and identity resources, both of which must be present and used in interactions if social capital is to be operationalized. Knowledge resources are the knowledge of who, when, and where to go for advice or resources (including a knowledge of the human capital of the community and accessible external human capital), and knowledge of how to get things done. Identity resources are the cognitive and affective attributes that allow community members to be able and willing (committed) to act for the benefit of the community and its members. Knowledge and identity resources together enable community members to combine their skills and knowledge (human capital) with the knowledge and skills of others. They are micro-level social capital resources; that is, they reside in the individuals within a community.

An understanding of the composition of social capital as knowledge and identity resources assists in identifying its presence in communities and in identifying possible interventions or strategies that will build social capital. Such an understanding makes it possible to develop a conceptual model of

Figure 8.1

Simultaneous building and using of social capital in interactions between individuals (Centre for Research and Learning in Regional Australia Model)

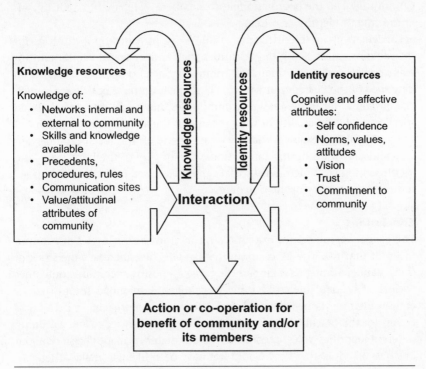

Knowledge resources

Knowledge of:
- Networks internal and external to community
- Skills and knowledge available
- Precedents, procedures, rules
- Communication sites
- Value/attitudinal attributes of community

Knowledge resources

Identity resources

Interaction

Identity resources

Cognitive and affective attributes:
- Self confidence
- Norms, values, attitudes
- Vision
- Trust
- Commitment to community

Action or co-operation for benefit of community and/or its members

Source: Falk and Kilpatrick (2000, 101).

social capital. A model of the simultaneous building and use of social capital is illustrated in Figure 8.1.

The two components of micro social capital – knowledge and identity resources – are built concurrently. This is illustrated by the description of EL members building social capital as they learn. Our case study found that getting to know each other and building trust were necessary before sensitive issues were introduced or discussed by group members. Members had to get to know each other before they could regard each other as credible sources of advice and support for sensitive issues; that is, before they would actually use each others' skills and knowledge.

EL members spoke of increasing self-confidence and personal development. Personal self-confidence, high-level interpersonal communication, and leadership skills are a part of identity resources, the willingness and ability to act for the group. As they got to know each other, they developed shared values and trust, a sense of belonging and commitment, and a sense that all group members could make valued contributions; that is, they built identity resources. Coming to regard each other as credible sources of support and advice is a further stage in the building of knowledge resources. Commitment to the board and fellow members – prepared to "put in" – is at the core of identity resources.

Participation in activities in a community provides opportunities for interactions, these being opportunities for building social capital and for using social capital to enhance economic or social outcomes, as has been described of the EL community. Not all interactions have positive or beneficial outcomes for individuals or communities, nor do all interactions build social capital. The quality of the outcome of the action and the quality of the social capital resources that are built depend on the social capital available and drawn on during interactions. The quality of the knowledge and identity resources (micro-level social capital) accessed in the interaction determines the quality of the outcome.

Conclusions

The ExecutiveLink boards examined in this study are examples of communities of practice. The EL community, like all CoPs, increases the stock of social capital among its members. EL achieves positive economic outcomes because it is adaptable and willing to change. EL members found that by combining their knowledge and skills they were able to achieve better outcomes for their farm businesses. By learning new knowledge and assuming different identities (roles) as confident actors, members made decisions about business activities that they would not have been likely to make otherwise. These decisions have improved the social, economic, and environmental sustainability of the businesses. Member businesses are more resilient because the community acts as a support network that assists businesses as they make changes to take advantage of opportunities and minimize the effects of threats. These characteristics match those attributed to social capital in the literature. There is, therefore, a strong connection between the concept of CoP and social capital.

The case study of EL has implications for research in the field. Social capital scholars may wish to further consider the role of CoPs in developing social capital, and CoP scholars should consider social capital as a useful concept. Scholars should consider the nature and level of personal skills in building networks. This applies to bonding networks, but especially to bridging networks.

By focusing on EL boards, a different type of CoP than the workplace groups normally considered, the research has shown that the CoP concept is useful in a wider range of applications than previously considered. Many parallels to EL boards can be conceived. The role of formally constructed groups in producing social capital and in becoming legitimate CoPs has also been identified and recognized in this chapter as a valuable contribution. We draw the attention of policy makers to the finding that formal structures (rather than chance informal encounters) that are flexible and have planned space for informal interaction are more likely to provide the opportunities of interaction for building social capital. This has implications for resourcing network-based initiatives of a larger scale than EL, such as Landcare (see Benn and Onyx, Chapter 5 in this book). We therefore commend the EL process as an example of creating interaction in an arena where traditional social interactions are declining.

Acknowledgments
This chapter includes a case study that has been reported in a number of other publications, including Kilpatrick (2002). Rowena Bell was involved in the interviewing for the case study. We thank ExecutiveLink for permission to report the case study, and the farmers who were involved. We acknowledge the contribution of Professor Ian Falk in the development of the CRLRA model of social capital reproduced in this chapter.

References
Brown, J.S., and P. Duguid. 1991. "Organizational Learning and Communities of Practice: Towards a Unified View of Working, Learning and Innovation." *Organization Science* 2(1): 40-57.
Coleman, J.S. 1988. "Social Capital in the Creation of Human Capital." *American Journal of Sociology* 94 (Supplement): 95-120.
Falk I., and S. Kilpatrick. 2000. "What Is Social Capital? A Study of Interaction in a Rural Community." *Sociologia Ruralis* 40(1): 87-110.
Handy, C. 1996. *Beyond Certainty: The Changing Worlds of Organisations*. Cambridge, MA: Harvard Business School Press.
Kilpatrick, S. 2002. "The Role of Group Learning in Building Social Capital." *International Journal of Lifelong Education* 21(5): 446-64.
Kilpatrick, S., R. Bell, and I. Falk. 1999. "The Role of Group Learning in Building Social Capital." *Journal of Vocational Education and Training* 51(1): 129-44.
Krishna, A., and N. Uphoff. 1999. *Mapping and Measuring Social Capital: A Conceptual and Empirical Study of Collective Action for Conserving and Developing Watersheds in Rajasthan, India*. Social Capital Initiative Working Paper No. 13. Washington, DC: World Bank.
Lave, J. 1991. "Situating Learning in Communities of Practice." In L.B. Resnick, J. Levine, and S.D. Teasley, eds., *Perspectives on Socially Shared Cognition*, 63-82. Washington, DC: American Psychological Association.
Lave, J., and E. Wenger. 1991. *Situated Learning: Legitimate Peripheral Participation*. Cambridge, UK: Cambridge University Press.
Lesser, E., and L. Prusak. 2000. "Communities of Practice: Social Capital and Organisational Knowledge." In E. Lesser, M. Fontaine, and J. Slusher, eds., *Knowledge and Communities*, 123-32. Boston, MA: Butterworth-Heinemann.
Lesser, E., and J. Storck. 2001. "Communities of Practice and Organizational Performance." *IBM Systems Journal* 40(4): 831-41.
McDermott, R. n.d. "Knowing in Community: 10 Critical Success Factors in Building Communities of Practice." <http://www.co-i-l.com/coil/knowledge-garden/cop/knowing.shtml> (26 October 2002).
Nahapiet, J., and S. Ghoshal. 1998. "Social Capital, Intellectual Capital and the Organizational Advantage." *Academy of Management Review* 23(2): 242-66.
Narayan, D., and L. Pritchett. 1997. "Cents and Sociability: Household Income and Social Capital in Rural Tanzania." <http://www.worldbank.org/research/growth/absnapr.htm> (26 October 2002).

Pennar, K. 1997. "The Ties That Lead to Prosperity: The Economic Value of Social Bonds Is Only Beginning to Be Measured." *Business Week,* 15 December, 152-55.

Polanyi, M. 1958. *Personal Knowledge.* Chicago: University of Chicago Press.

Portes, A. 1998. "Social Capital: Its Origins and Applications in Modern Sociology." *Annual Review of Sociology* 24: 1-24.

Process Edge. 2002. "Communities." <http://www.processedge.com/store/community.htm> (26 October 2002).

Putnam, R., R. Leonardi, and R. Nanetti. 1993. *Making Democracy Work: Civic Traditions in Modern Italy.* Princeton, NJ: Princeton University Press.

–. 2000. *Bowling Alone.* New York: Simon and Schuster.

Resource Consulting Services (RCS). 2000. "ExecutiveLink™." <http://www.rcs.au.com/training/execlink.htm> (26 October 2002).

Sharp, J. 1997. "Communities of Practice: A Review of the Literature." <http://www.tfriend.com/cop-lit.htm> (26 October 2002).

Vanclay, F., and G. Lawrence. 1995. *The Environmental Imperative: Ecosocial Concerns for Australian Agriculture.* Rockhampton, QLD: Central Queensland University Press.

Wenger, E. 1998. *Communities of Practice: Learning, Meaning, and Identity.* New York: Cambridge University Press.

Woolcock, M., and D. Narayan. 2000. "Social Capital: Implications for Development Theory, Research and Policy." *World Bank Research Observer* 15(1): 225-49.

9

Social Capital and the Sustainability of Rural or Remote Communities: Evidence from the Australian Community Survey

Alan Black and Philip Hughes

In the wheat belt of central New South Wales, there is a point marked on the map as Trungley Hall. Little more than a Lutheran church now constitutes that community. The school has gone. The shops have gone. The substantial numbers of people who used to gather at the tennis courts no longer gather. In fact, the chance of meeting anyone at Trungley Hall is slim.

The surrounding farms used to support a large population. Many families had ten or twelve children, and the farm supported them all. Now a farm in the area barely supports one person. Some farmers are deep in debt, waiting for a good season. Some spouses work in nearby towns to help make ends meet. A generation of children has moved away, looking for work in the cities. They are now bringing up their own children in a very different environment. The grandparents continue to work the farm at Trungley Hall.

In good seasons, the farms are as productive as they ever were. But most of the money that is generated goes out of the area, in the purchase of fertilizers and massive machinery, as well as for financial, communication, and other services. Very little money goes back into the local economy. As the economics of Trungley Hall have changed, so community life has declined. Unless there is an economic base to maintain the population, community life cannot be sustained.

Other developments are contributing to the anxiety of local farmers. New categories of people are moving into the vicinity. The farmers are concerned that these people may not contribute to the community as they themselves have done. They see these groups of people as potential threats to the quality of community life within the region.

One of the threats comes from agribusinesses that have been buying farms not far away. Large businesses owned by shareholders, many of whom live overseas, are taking over some family farms. In such cases, any profits derived from primary production will go to the shareholders, outside the local community. As part of the same trend, the committed farmers, who have spent a lifetime on their farms, are being replaced by managers who may have little commitment to the area or to the community. There are fears within the community that these managers will stay in the area only briefly before moving on to another job; that they will have little commitment to the local Landcare group or to local emergency-service organizations. Likewise, they might not support the local Lutheran church, which remains the centre of what little community life exists at Trungley Hall.

Another perceived threat comes from people on unemployment, single-parent, or other social security payments who are moving into nearby towns, attracted by cheap housing. These people and the local farmers have little in common in their ways of life. Many farmers see these newcomers as draining the limited social resources while contributing little, if anything, to the quality of community life. As long-standing family farmers are replaced by employed managers, and empty houses in the small towns nearby are occupied by social security recipients who have moved in from urban areas, many farmers fear that the remnant of social capital is under threat. In their view, the sustainability of the vestiges of community life is endangered.

As noted elsewhere in this book, there has been extensive debate on the definition of social capital. This chapter will assume that social capital includes relationships of trust, reciprocity, cooperation, and active goodwill among individuals and groups. Such relationships may be between

- relatives and close friends (these relationships are sometimes called "bonds" or "thick ties")
- acquaintances (these relationships are sometimes called "bridges" or "thin ties")
- strangers (see Cox 1995; Narayan 1999).

In contemporary societies, a further issue of importance relates to the extent to which people have confidence in the functioning of various "expert" systems or institutions, such as retail systems, public utility systems, and financial, legal, educational, health, mass media, and other systems (Giddens 1990, 83ff). Because confidence in institutions is a form of trust, some writers – for example, Stone and Hughes (2002) – include it within their definition of social capital. Thus, Stone and Hughes (2002) distinguish three realms in which social capital may be discerned:

- *informal realm,* in which there are relationships of trust, trustworthiness, reciprocity, and active goodwill among kinsfolk, friends, neighbours, and workmates
- *generalized realm,* in which there are relationships of trust, trustworthiness, reciprocity, and active goodwill among people who do not necessarily know one another personally

- *institutional realm,* in which there is confidence in the operation of various expert systems and institutions.

The general hypothesis of this chapter is that social capital contributes to the sustainability of communities. Elsewhere (Black and Hughes 2001), we have analyzed some of the conceptual literature on sustainable communities, resilient communities, healthy communities, and strong communities. Although these concepts are not necessarily identical, they have much in common.

While the notion of sustainability has arisen partly from the awareness that reserves of natural capital are being depleted in many parts of the globe, it has also been applied to other aspects of life and society. Hart (2000) says that "a sustainable community takes good care of all its capital, natural, human and social in addition to its built capital, in order to continually improve the quality of life of all its inhabitants." The main focus of this chapter is on the sustainability of the quality of life within rural or remote communities. While this depends in part on ecological sustainability, it also involves the extent to which local economic and social structures satisfy people's basic needs and embody values that are capable of being sustained for both present and future generations.

Over recent decades, many small rural or remote communities have lost some of their services. A critical mass of population is needed to retain a hospital, banks, churches, a police station, and other services. Below that critical mass, various services are likely to be closed or curtailed. This contraction of facilities may in turn lead to a further decline of population in small rural or remote communities. On the other hand, some larger regional centres might gain population as various specialized services become increasingly concentrated there.

Population size is generally closely related to the economic bases of the community, and sustainability of community life is linked to the sustainability of the economic activity of the area. It is, for example, difficult to sustain a mining community when the mine runs out. However, the social relationships that people have may also affect sustainability. Strong social links may provide the basis for people to work together to develop new economic enterprises. They may provide a quality of life that attracts new people, new ideas, and new vitality to a locality. Thus, social capital may contribute to the sustainability of community life.

We have noted in previous research that levels of trust toward local people and toward strangers vary from one type of community to another. For example, trust toward local people tends, on average, to be higher among residents of small rural or remote communities than among residents of metropolitan areas, whereas trust toward "most Australians" tends to be lower in small rural or remote communities than in large cities (Hughes, Bellamy, and Black 1999, 21).

Hesitation to trust outsiders may underlie some of the concerns felt in places such as Trungley Hall about agribusinesses buying into the area. Only time will tell whether those fears are justified. In principle, they could become either self-fulfilling or self-negating prophecies, or they may have no effect either way. Some evidence suggests that corporate farms (when compared with family farms) have a greater propensity to purchase farm inputs and services from outside the local community; are likely to employ a more seasonal, mobile, and lower-paid workforce; and are less likely to be integrated into the social life and institutions of the local community. On the other hand, they may also bring social and economic benefits to rural communities, such as increases in local employment, diversification of the local economic base, and a more cost-effective and competitive agricultural sector (Tonts and Black 2002). Tonts and Black are currently examining the positive and negative effects in five communities.

Although long-term economic, technological, and social factors have resulted in the decline of many small inland towns in Australia, other small inland towns have successfully implemented a range of survival and revival strategies. A recent publication examines the experiences of fourteen such towns with populations of less than 3,500; indeed, most have populations of less than 1,000 (Kenyon and Black 2001). Each of these towns has its own story and set of ingredients that have contributed to survival and renewal strategies. Despite their unique circumstances, size, and location, there are remarkable similarities. These commonalities relate not so much to location, weather, or proximity to the coast or to a regional centre but more to attitude, local leadership, and local action. All have strong community networks that actively support new ideas and new ways of working together. All have also been successful in cultivating allies, networking with outside supporters, and securing funding from external sources, as well as committing resources from within the community for new civic or business ventures. In other words, social capital has been important in creating, accessing, and mobilizing other forms of capital and thus contributing to the ongoing vitality of these communities.

Based on a survey conducted by researchers from Edith Cowan University and NCLS (National Church Life Survey) Research, this chapter will examine further evidence of a relationship between social capital and community sustainability.

Methods

The survey, known as the Australian Community Survey, was conducted in 1997-98. For the purpose of drawing samples from various communities for the survey, the metropolitan environment throughout Australia was divided into four socioeconomic levels. Socioeconomic indices for local areas (SEIFA), produced by the Australian Bureau of Statistics and based on a wide range of data about income, occupation, educational level, and social background, were used in categorizing all metropolitan postal codes into four strata. Random samples of the population were drawn from each of these four strata. A somewhat similar process was used in non-metropolitan areas but the criterion used here was the size of population centres. Postal codes of towns with 20,000 people or more, towns of between 2,000 and 19,999 people, towns of between 200 and 1,999 people, and areas in which there was no centre of more than 200 people were identified. In each of these four environments, random samples of the population were drawn. Questionnaires were mailed in October 1997. After two reminder letters, 8,452 questionnaires were returned completed. Taking into account those questionnaires returned to the sender without reaching the addressees, this represents a response rate of 50 percent. The responses were weighted by proportions of gender and age in each of the eight sampled strata to provide a picture of the Australian population.

Eight versions of the questionnaire were developed. Each of the versions was sent to equal numbers of people in each of the sampling strata. Some core questions were asked in all eight versions. Other questions were asked in only one version. Most of the questions used in this chapter are taken from Questionnaire 7, which was completed and returned by 1,027 people.

Two sets of questions in Questionnaire 7 provide some indicators related to sustainability. One set of questions was about the experience of change over the last five years:

We would like your thoughts on change in your local area over the past five years. How much change do you think there has been in each of the following areas?

1 Much good change
2 Some good change
3 Both good and bad change
4 Little change either way

5 Some bad change
6 Much bad change
0 Don't know

In local businesses (e.g., industries, banks, shops)	1 2 3 4 5 6 0
In local services (e.g., education, health, local council)	1 2 3 4 5 6 0
In the type of people who live in the area	1 2 3 4 5 6 0
In the strength of the local economy	1 2 3 4 5 6 0
In local voluntary activities or services	1 2 3 4 5 6 0
In neighbourliness	1 2 3 4 5 6 0
In the way of life of people in the local area	1 2 3 4 5 6 0

We will take a score of five or six as indicative of people thinking the quality of local community life is not being maintained or improved. We note that this is a subjective measure. Inevitably responses reflect how people feel about the nature of community life, and may be influenced by their personal changed circumstances or the need to draw on services they had not drawn on in the past.

A second set of questions asked people about problems in their local community.

In your opinion, how much of a problem are the following issues in your local community?

	Not a problem				Major problem
Decline in local business	0	1	2	3	4
Lack of support for the poor	0	1	2	3	4
Racist treatment of Aboriginal people	0	1	2	3	4
Crime	0	1	2	3	4
Decline in quality of the natural environment	0	1	2	3	4
Withdrawal of government services and banks	0	1	2	3	4
Loss of trust between people	0	1	2	3	4
Decline of churches	0	1	2	3	4
Lack of vision for future community directions	0	1	2	3	4
Too many people leaving the community	0	1	2	3	4
Lack of jobs	0	1	2	3	4

Some of these items refer directly to change, such as decline in local business, withdrawal of government services and banks, loss of trust between people, decline of churches, and people leaving the community. The extent to which these are rated as problems will be taken as indicative of decline in the sustainability of community life.

Within these two sets of questions are items that are often taken to refer to social capital understood in terms of the quantity and quality of relationships between people within a community, and participation in community life. Thus, in the first set of questions, perceived bad change in local voluntary activities or services and neighbourliness is indicative of a decline in these forms of social capital. Conversely, perceived good change is indicative of an increase in these forms of social capital.

In the second set of questions, the extent to which there is a perceived problem of loss of trust between people may also be taken as indicative of a decline in the levels of social capital.

Several other questions are indicative of levels of social capital in the local community:

1. To what extent do you agree or disagree with the following statement: "Generally speaking, most people in my local area can be trusted" (five-point scale from "strongly agree" to "strongly disagree")?

2. To what extent do you agree or disagree with the following statement: "Generally speaking, you can't be too careful in dealing with most people in my local area" (five-point scale from "strongly agree" to "strongly disagree")?

3. Do you know your close neighbours well enough to be aware of some of their personal concerns?
   1. No, for none of my neighbours
   2. No, for hardly any
   3. Yes, for some
   4. Yes, for most
   5. Yes, for nearly all my neighbours

4. Are you involved in community groups or organizations in an unpaid capacity?
   (For each type of group listed below, respondents were asked to use the following scale:
   1. No, I'm not involved
   2. No, I'm not involved but I subscribe or donate money
   3. Yes, I am involved
   4. Yes, I am involved in leadership of a group)

- Work-related group (e.g., professional or business association, trade union)
- Educational / school group or organization (e.g., school canteen, school committees)
- Groups for children or youth (e.g., play groups, Scouts)
- Art, music, or cultural group or organization
- Sporting group or organization
- Emergency services (e.g., SES)
- Health group or organization (e.g., hospital auxiliary)
- Environmental group or organization (e.g., ACF)
- Animal welfare group or organization
- Care, welfare, or support group or organization
- Community service group or organization (e.g., Rotary)
- Church or religious group or organization
- Hobby or recreational group or organization
- Social action, justice or lobby group or organization (e.g., human rights or resident action)
- Political party
- Any other community group or organization

These do not cover the gamut of social capital by any means. However, we take these questions as indicative of some dimensions of social capital.

Results

Much of the following analysis examines the Australian Community Survey data in terms of four types of local communities, namely those situated in

1 federal or state capital cities
2 regional cities – non-capital cities with populations of at least 20,000
3 rural service towns, with populations of from 2,000 to 19,999
4 small rural or remote communities, with no population centre greater than 1,999 people.

Higher proportions of people in small rural or remote communities than in other types of environments perceived that there had been bad change in the past five years. As shown in Figure 9.1, this was particularly so in relation to

• local businesses (e.g., industries, banks, shops)
• the strength of the local economy
• the type of people who live in the area
• local services (e.g., education, health, local council)
• local voluntary activities or services
• the way of life of people in the local area.

Figure 9.1

Residents affirming that "bad" change had occurred in their community

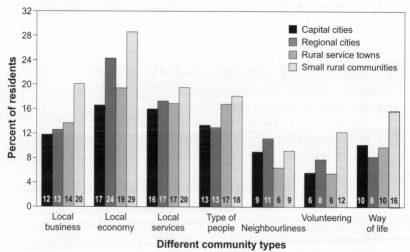

Source: Australian Community Survey, 1998.

There was a high correlation between the various perceived areas of change. Thus, those areas in which people were experiencing "bad" change in terms of the economy and business tended to be those areas in which people were experiencing a decline in voluntary activities and in valued aspects of the local way of life. While the high correlations may be explained partly by personality factors – some personality types generally feel more negative about most aspects of life than do others – they may also indicate that changes in some aspects of society have repercussions in other aspects.

Scores on these various areas of change form a scale of local change, with an alpha (reliability coefficient) of 0.83. With the scale running from 7 to 42, and a score of less than 15 indicating mostly "good" change and a score of more than 28 indicating mostly "bad" change, the mean score for the various types of communities was:

Capital cities	20.2
Regional cities	21.1
Rural service towns	21.5
Small rural communities	24.3

Figure 9.2 presents data on the extent to which people perceive that there are major problems in their local community.

When asked about problems existing in the local community, the patterns were more varied than those for "bad" change. In regional cities, there

Figure 9.2

Residents affirming that problems exist in their community

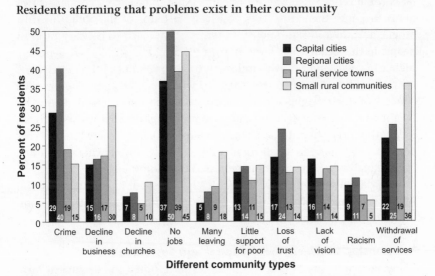

Source: Australian Community Survey, 1998.

was greatest concern about crime, lack of jobs, and loss of trust. By contrast, greatest concern about decline in local businesses, the withdrawal of government services and banks, and too many people leaving the community was expressed in small rural communities. There was also widespread concern about the lack of jobs in small rural communities.

There were high correlations between responses to most of the items listed in Figure 9.2. A scale of "local problems" developed from the list of items had an alpha coefficient of 0.84. Possible scores on the scale varied from 0 to 44. The following were the mean scores for the various types of communities:

Capital cities	19.6
Regional cities	22.0
Rural service towns	19.3
Small rural communities	19.8

While the questions on the extent of change occurring locally and the questions on local problems were somewhat different, there was a fair degree of similarity in the ways in which people responded to them. This scale of local problems had a correlation with the scale of local change of 0.207. In items referring explicitly to change, and thus indicative of a sense from residents that the quality of life was not being sustained, there was greater concern in small rural communities than in other types of communities.

Nevertheless, as shown in Figure 9.3, small rural communities also had the highest levels of "local" social capital in terms of the various indicators available in the Australian Community Survey. One indicator of social capital is the level of trust. The Australian Community Survey contained two items that measured trust, one positively in terms of the ability to trust others, and the other negatively in terms of the need to be wary of most people in the locality. The levels of trust toward local people were generally higher in rural service towns and small rural communities than elsewhere.

Another item measured the extent to which people know the personal concerns of their neighbours. This is indicative of some interaction between neighbours and may also indicate a certain level of trust between them. Again, the survey found that people were more likely to know the concerns of their neighbours in small rural communities than elsewhere, although only a small minority of people professed such knowledge.

A third item was a measure of people's involvement in voluntary groups. Again, levels of involvement were significantly higher in small rural communities than in large cities.

Relationship between Social Capital and Sustainability

Many people in small rural communities have noted the decline in business, in the local economy, in services and, indeed, in their way of life.

Figure 9.3

Residents affirming trust of locals, knowledge of neighbours' concerns, and involvement in voluntary groups

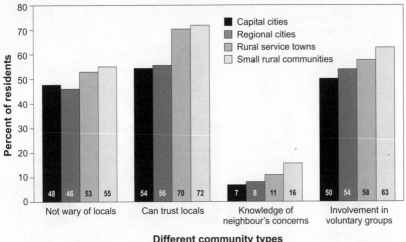

Source: Australian Community Survey, 1998.

Nevertheless, there are still high levels of social capital. The strength of social capital in small rural communities does not appear to have been sufficient to counteract other perceived negative forces of change.

The variability of the link between perceived changes in neighbourliness (one measure of social capital) and other perceived changes within the local community is shown in Figure 9.4. The height of the bars in that figure is indicative of the strength of the relationships, calculated as correlations. Figure 9.4 shows that the strength of the relationships between changes in neighbourliness and changes in local business, in the local economy, and in the type of people living in the area are much stronger in the capital cities and in regional cities than in rural service towns or in small rural communities. This indicates that decline in local business or economy is not seen as necessarily affecting, or affected by, the level of neighbourliness in small rural communities as much as in other types of communities. In some other aspects of life, there are exceptions to that pattern. The first is the relationship between neighbourliness and "the way of life" as a whole, a relationship that is strong in both rural and urban communities. Also strong in all types of communities is the relationship between changes in neighbourliness and changes in involvement in voluntary organizations.

In all types of communities, perceptions of whether there had been a loss of trust between local people tended to correlate fairly highly with perceptions about whether there had been other undesirable changes in the local

Figure 9.4

Strength of correlation between neighbourliness and other aspects of community life

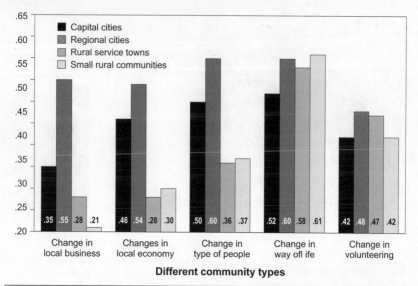

Source: Australian Community Survey, 1998.

community. Interestingly, these correlations were weaker in small rural communities than in rural service towns. Substantial numbers of people in small rural communities indicated that local business had declined, there had been a withdrawal of government services and banks, and there was a lack of jobs, but that levels of trust between people had not declined. On the other hand, there were few people living in small rural communities who said that local business, services, and jobs were fine, but that there had been a loss of trust between people. While causal links cannot be shown by such relationships, these results are consonant with the proposition that trust may be a prerequisite for healthy local business, services, and jobs, but may not be adequate for their maintenance.

Regression analysis was used to examine which factors were most predictive of lack of sustainability in a community, measured in terms of the "bad" changes explored in the Australian Community Survey. Table 9.1, based on the sample of respondents from all types of communities, shows that the strongest predictor was a perceived lack of vision for future community directions. Next in importance were population loss and decline in local business, which is not surprising since Table 9.1 includes an item on change for the worse in local businesses. The only other significant predictors in the regression equation were the extent to which the respondent is involved

Table 9.1

Predictive model of lack of sustainability in terms of "bad" change

	Zero-order correlation	Beta coefficient	Significance (p)
Lack of vision for future community directions	.248	.209	.000
Too many people leaving the community	.244	.151	.001
Decline in local business	.202	.134	.004
Involvement in voluntary group	.155	.096	.013
Knowing neighbours' personal concerns	.117	.094	.013
Withdrawal of government services and banks	.202	.066	.156
Lack of jobs	.129	.007	.873
Loss of trust between people	.102	-.025	.585
Decline of churches	.072	-.049	.264
Crime	.021	-.049	.264
Racist treatment of Aboriginal people	-.003	-.055	.196

Note: Adjusted r^2 = .130

in community groups and organizations and the extent to which the respondent knows close neighbours well enough to be aware of some of their personal concerns. In other words, these forms of social capital do not necessarily protect a community against the impact of other factors that may affect its sustainability.

When regression analysis was limited to the sample of respondents living in small rural communities, the only factors that were significant were "too many people leaving the community" and "lack of vision for future community directions." No item indicative of social capital was significant in the model. This result reiterates the importance of a sense of vision being a key factor in sustainability of community. Where there is a strong sense of vision for the future, people are far less likely to report that "bad" changes have been occurring in their community. On the other hand, the results may also indicate that in communities in rapid decline it is more difficult to formulate a positive vision for the future.

Another question asked how people felt about their neighbourhood on a scale of one to seven, from "delighted" to "terrible." Overall, the profiles of responses were fairly similar for each of the four types of communities. Although there was a slight tendency for a stronger positive affirmation of their neighbourhood in small rural communities, the differences were not great, as shown in Figure 9.5.

Table 9.2 indicates that social capital items were nevertheless significant in terms of how people felt about their communities, both in small rural communities and in other types of communities. The extent to which people

Figure 9.5

How people feel about their neighbourhoods

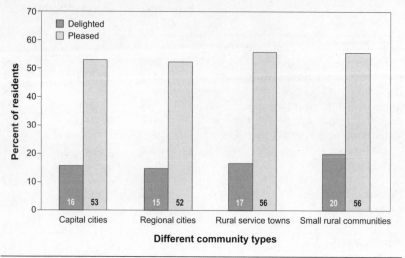

Source: Australian Community Survey, 1998.

felt they could trust other local people, the extent to which neighbours knew each other, and the overall levels of positive change were the strongest predictors of people's level of satisfaction. Respondents' perceptions that crime was not a major problem in their local community were a further predictor. Thereafter, concerns about decline in local business, lack of community services, and even lack of vision added little to the predictive power of the regression model.

Table 9.2

Factors relating to satisfaction with neighbourhood

	Zero-order correlation	Beta coefficient	Significance *(p)*
Trust in local people	.305	.227	.000
Knowing neighbours' personal concerns	.186	.163	.000
"Good" changes occurring in the local community	.157	.139	.000
Crime not a problem	.212	.099	.028
People leaving the community not a problem	.162	.080	.067
Decline in local business not a problem	.143	.025	.590
Lack of vision not a problem	.147	.023	.627
Withdrawal of services not a problem	.092	-.021	.645

Note: Adjusted r^2 = .142

Conclusions

Some of the social capital variables that were measured in the Australian Community Survey were significantly associated with how people felt about their communities. In those communities in which people said they were pleased or delighted with their neighbourhood, they were more likely to say that they felt they could trust the local people and that they knew their neighbours well. Involvement in voluntary groups, however, did not have any significant independent impact on how people felt about their communities.

The fact that people are delighted with their neighbourhood, or feel they can trust other people who live in the area, does not necessarily mean that those communities are sustainable. In terms of sustainability, the most significant aspects are the economic base and the sense of vision. When there is no longer a sense of vision, people are most likely to report that "bad" changes are occurring in the community.

Social capital may contribute to achieving that sense of vision and thus may contribute to sustainability. But social capital in terms of the levels of trust and neighbourliness in a community does not automatically produce vision. Such vision requires leadership, ideas, and an entrepreneurial spirit. It is noteworthy that a report of action-based projects to build community life in rural areas found that one of the major factors in facilitating the emergence and continuing development of beneficial projects was a positive attitude to change within the community. In many cases, the positive attitude was engendered by social entrepreneurs who could "identify, nurture, mobilise and draw on the social capital embedded in communities and groups" (Stayner, Foskey, and Ramasubramarian 2000, 15).

Nevertheless, the survey results indicate that when the local economy crumbles, and when people start moving away, there may still be a high level of social trust. Indeed, in some instances, the problems may bring people closer together and make them more reliant on each other.

Robert Putnam (2002) has noted that the disaster of 11 September 2001 has increased the levels of social capital throughout the United States. He argues that wars and other challenges bring compatriots together, strengthen the trust they have in each other, and spur them into working jointly through their problems.

The Australian Community Survey results suggest that the problems confronting rural communities have at least sometimes had similar effects in Australia. As people find ways of coping with the withdrawal of services, with the closing of businesses, and with other challenges, they work more closely with each other. They may become more interdependent than when the economy is thriving and when a good range of services is available.

On the other hand, it may also be that as very small rural communities decline, the sense of community is developed in other ways. The community life and involvement of people may become absorbed by the larger service town, for example. If the local emergency services or church closes, people may transfer their involvement to a larger centre. In such ways, social capital may be redeveloped in a new context.

There is some evidence that the level of social capital is important for local business to thrive and for community vitality to be maintained. But social capital alone is not sufficient. Social connections may provide the ground through which issues are explored and challenges confronted but do not guarantee the emergence of a strong vision for the future of the community. However, unless there are good networks of social connections and a sense of belonging, a forward-looking vision for the community is unlikely to be widely owned.

The survey results do not allow us to explore the dynamics that would be evident from case studies. The challenges for the farming communities as agribusinesses take the place of family-run farms, or for rural towns whose populations are being supplemented by people on social security benefits who are looking for cheap housing but not interested in playing creative roles in community life, were not evident in this survey. Nor would their impacts be easy to measure in a survey of a national sample of people, as such challenges to community life can bring sections of a community closer together, in response to sections of the community that are socially isolated.

The dynamics of social capital and the sustainability of communities are complex. Various types of communities need to be considered. Situations can vary widely. The survey evidence can provide only broad generalizations. The Australian Community Survey results suggest that social capital is important in sustaining community life, but is only partly determinative of it.

Acknowledgments

The 1998 Australian Community Survey, conducted by researchers from Edith Cowan University and NCLS Research, was made possible by a grant from the Australian Research Council, together with the support of ANGLICARE (NSW) and the Board of Mission of the Uniting Church (NSW). The research was jointly supervised by Alan Black and Peter Kaldor. The research team included John Bellamy, Keith Castle, and Philip Hughes.

References

Black, A., and P. Hughes. 2001. *The Identification and Analysis of Indicators of Community Strength and Outcomes*. Canberra: Department of Family and Community Services.

Cox, E. 1995. *A Truly Civil Society: 1995 Boyer Lectures*. Sydney: Australian Broadcasting Corporation.

Giddens, A. 1990. *The Consequences of Modernity*. Stanford, CA: Stanford University Press.

Hart, M. 2000. Sustainable Measures. <http://www.sustainablemeasures.com> (15 September 2000).

Hughes, P., J. Bellamy, and A. Black. 1999. "Social Trust: Locally and Across Australia." *Third Sector Review* 5(1): 5-24.

Kenyon, P., and A. Black. 2001. *Small Town Renewal*. Canberra: Rural Industries Research and Development Corporation.

Narayan, D. 1999. *Bonds and Bridges: Social Capital and Poverty.* Washington, DC: World Bank.

Putnam, R. 2002. "Bowling Together." *American Prospect* 13(3), 28 February 2002.

Stayner, R., R. Foskey, and L. Ramasubramarian. 2000. *The Continuing Effects of Action Research Projects: Final Report to the Department of Family and Community Services.* Armidale, NSW: Institute for Rural Futures, University of New England.

Stone, W., and J. Hughes. 2002. *Social Capital: Empirical Meaning and Measurement Validity.* Melbourne: Australian Institute of Family Studies.

Tonts, M., and A. Black. 2002. "Changing Farm Business Structures and the Sustainability of Rural Communities and Regions." *Sustaining Regions* 1(2): 17-23.

10
Social Capital and Sustainable Development: The Case of Broken Hill

Jenny Onyx and Lynelle Osburn

Dale (2001) and others define sustainable development as a process of reconciliation of three imperatives: (1) the ecological imperative to live within global biophysical carrying capacity and maintain biodiversity; (2) the social imperative to ensure the development of democratic systems of governance to effectively propagate and sustain the values that people wish to live by; and (3) the economic imperative to ensure that basic needs are met worldwide. Given the interconnected nature of sustainable development, failure in any one area will result in failure in the other two, particularly over the long term. If used correctly, the mobilization of one form of capital may multiply the effects of another in a positive, or virtuous, cycle. Equally, the misuse or overuse of one may reduce or destroy another.

Some Canadian scholars (Dale 2001; Robinson and Tinker 1997; CCSDR 1990) define sustainable development as a process of reconciliation of three imperatives, and there is considerable evidence that high levels of social capital may well be a prerequisite for the process of reconciliation between the ecological, the social, and the economic imperatives (Putnam, Leonardi, and Nanetti 1993). Social capital refers to the ability of people to secure benefits by virtue of membership in social networks or other social structures. Many analysts have emphasized the centrality of two factors to social capital: trust and social networks (Putnam, Leonardi, and Nanetti 1993; Woolcock 1998; Fukuyama 1995). For the purposes of this research, social capital is defined as the norms (the informal rules and values) and networks that facilitate collective action, focusing on the relationships within and between those networks.

Recent research has also distinguished between bonding, bridging, and linking social capital (Putnam 2000; Onyx and Bullen 2000; Woolcock and Narayan 2000). Bonding capital refers to relations among family members, close friends, and neighbours in closed networks. Bonding social capital appears to be characterized by dense, multi-functional ties and strong but localized trust. Meanwhile, bridging connects people or bonded groups across social or economic divides. Bridging social capital may facilitate access to resources and opportunities that exist in one network to a member of another. However, bridges across the social divides of a community may be fragile, the level of trust less certain. The work of Wilkinson (1991) and Sharp (2001) suggest that a key role in bridging may be played by community field organizations, those whose function is to coordinate other action fields into a whole (Wilkinson 1991, 90). Woolcock and Narayan (2000) argue that while localized, bonding social capital operates as effective defensive strategies against poverty, the necessary condition for real development entails a shift to other, looser networks. Thus, a shift from "getting by" to "getting ahead" entails a shift from bonding to bridging networks. Further, linking social capital involves social relations with those in authority, which might be used to garner resources of power (Stone 2001). It may be that the most effective role for governments to play is at the bridging or linking level. This raises the question of the role of government within conditions of social entrepreneurship when local communities take what has traditionally been seen to be the responsibility of government (Herbert-Cheshire 2000).

The Unique Context of Broken Hill

Broken Hill has a history of over one hundred years of mining. It is located some 1,300 kilometres west of Sydney, close to the South Australian border. It is an outback town in arid, near desert conditions, with a dry, sometimes harsh, climate. The Broken Hill mining industry has been in decline for twenty-five years, with a population drift reducing the population from 36,000 to 20,300. There are also ten villages or townships, some of them 300 kilometres from Broken Hill, as well as outback stations, which together have a further 3,000 residents who rely on Broken Hill as their service centre. The city has a company town culture characterized by the mining company's paternalistic relationship that discouraged independence and autonomy. The last remaining mine is scheduled to close in 2006. Yet despite these problems, the people of Broken Hill are fiercely proud of their heritage. Many families have been in Broken Hill for three or more generations. Those in Broken Hill are still labelled according to whether they are A groupers (those born and bred in Broken Hill) or B groupers (those who have spent much of their lives in Broken Hill but were not born there and therefore have reduced access to employment in the mines). Other, relative newcomers are identified as "from away." There is a strong tradition of community service and very high participation in community events such as St. Pat's race day, show day, and the "great barrow races" held during the 1980s. The latter were organized by Rotary, and those members are still very active in community life. They do not want their town to die. The community responded to the crisis by forming a community business partnership, with the active engagement of Rotary. This later became Broken Hill Community Inc., an umbrella community centre with ongoing community round tables to address the emerging social issues and avoid social dislocation.

Research Methodology

This chapter presents preliminary analysis of the Broken Hill round tables. This is part of the much larger study "Measuring and Enhancing Community Capacity in Outback NSW." As a case study, qualitative research methods are used to identify the common elements of networks and mechanisms and their impacts, as well as the specific and unique context of Broken Hill itself. This is part of an ongoing action research methodology in collaboration with Broken Hill Community Inc., which auspices the twice yearly round-table process. All members of the community are invited to take part in the process. At the round table itself, citizens are invited to put forward key issues or community problems for discussion. If enough interest is generated over a specific issue, a solutions task force is created to address the issue and develop an action plan.

Each round table, solution group, and project is tracked and documented. Included in this documentation is a profile of the individuals involved at each stage, and the flow-on or ripple effect over time of each action. What resources were needed and obtained, what impediments were faced, and the nature of any collaborative partnership is also tracked.

The specific indicators of social capital examined in this case study network are diversity, stakeholders, commitment (trust), leadership, and voice. The research explores in depth these research questions:

- How are decisions made? Which stakeholders are included/excluded?
- Do decisions take into consideration ecological, social, and economic imperatives?
- How are knowledges accessed and mobilized? Is there a shared commitment, a pooling of resources by stakeholders?
- What are the patterns of leadership, and at what point do they become crucial?
- Do overlapping networks facilitate the mobilization of collective action beyond the community?
- What resources are critical and where do they come from? Does existing diversity within the community contribute to creative responses to identified crises? What is the role of newcomers?
- What role is played by government at the local, state, and national level?

The model illustrated in Figure 1.6 in Chapter 1 underpins the proposed research (SSHRC research grant, September 2002 to March 2005). In this model, sustainable development, defined as the reconciliation of three imperatives – the social, economic, and natural (or ecological) – is the goal and outcome. Social capital, identified by the indicators of diversity, stakeholders, commitment, leadership, and voice, facilitates key decision making and action that will provide for the reconciliation of the three imperatives, and, hence, contribute to sustainable development.

Direct participant observation of round-table meetings and analysis of written records, where available, identified stakeholders and leaders in the network(s) as well as contributed to an analysis of the network process. Key network leaders and stakeholders were interviewed. At least two people from each solution group were interviewed where possible.

Results: The Round-Table Process
At the time of writing, Broken Hill Community Inc. had sponsored six monthly round tables. The first of these was held in February 2000, and the most recent was held in July 2002. Table 10.1 summarizes the attendance at each.

Of the total for each, roughly 67 percent of attendees were women. About a third of those attending were individual citizens. Others were volunteers from local community groups, paid community services workers, and employees from a variety of government departments. Several local government councillors also attended regularly. In addition, at each round table, one or more external experts or "mentors" were invited to speak on relevant issues. This was seen both as a marketing tool and as a means of accessing and incorporating outside knowledge.

Broken Hill Community Inc. is itself a partnership comprising many community and business groups. A representative of the chamber of commerce is currently treasurer on the management committee, and the president is a member of the Rotary Club. Rotary has played a significant role in the formation of Community Inc., and a number of businesspeople have become actively involved in various Community Inc. projects via their Rotary Club membership.

Table 10.1

Round-table attendance

Round table	Total attendance	Men	Women
1	73	30	43
2	70	21	49
3	73	29	44
4	111	31	80
5	57	23	34
6	83	32	51

Table 10.2

Solution groups formed, and number of participants in each

Round table 1		Round table 5	
Solution group	Number of participants	Solution group	Number of participants
Community centre	10	Public liability	15
Community gardens	4	Family reconnect	10
Cultural issues	12	Cool Communities	13
Employment and men's issues	18	Olive trees	5
Youth issues	9	Health services advocacy	6
Community markets	not known	Professional women	4
		Mulga Greek Walkway	not held

Note: Participant numbers are rough estimations based on existing records.

For purposes of detailed analysis of the process, two round tables were selected: the first, which focused on the establishment of the community centre, and the fifth, which was fairly typical of later round tables and dealt with new issues arising. The first author, Jenny Onyx, was present at this fifth round table. Table 10.2 summarizes the solution groups formed at each of the two round tables and the number of people participating in each.

Each of these solution groups evolved in a different way. Each tells a different story involving different people and activities. Some of them have already led to clear outcomes, while others disappeared or were shelved until circumstances allow them to be revisited. Each will be described briefly here; those relating to issues of ecological sustainability will then be explored in more detail. The research questions and social capital indicators are used to guide the analysis of each solution group. However, as each question/indicator is entailed in the others, it is not possible to provide a separate analysis of each within this limited summary description.

Community Centre

It is perhaps strange that a city the size and affluence of Broken Hill had no community centre. Many clubs and organizations had their own premises, as did churches, sporting organizations, and so on. But there was no central and inclusive centre for community. It was therefore a priority for the community in general to create such a centre. At the first round table, this issue was one of the largest solution groups, and those attending the round table included a number of Rotary Club members and businesspeople, as well as local government councillors from the original business/community partnership. They were predominantly A groupers. The solution group decided to buy rather than rent a property, and to obtain a government grant for the purpose. Following the first round table, a meeting was held with the funding body (thirty-five people attended), and a second meeting with a small group of influential local people. A subcommittee was formed to look at ten potential properties, and volunteer tradespeople examined the proposed centre buildings.

This project became the major preoccupation of the management committee of Broken Hill Community Inc. over the next two years, and came under the direct leadership of the manager. By the end of 2001, Community Inc. had successfully purchased the old bowling club near the centre of town. It provided not only ideal internal facilities but also considerable outdoor space. One of the old greens was maintained as a green for use by a disability group; by mid-2002 it was already in use for that purpose. The official opening of the Centre for Community occurred at the sixth round table in July 2002, with the governor of New South Wales as the keynote speaker for the round table and opening of the centre. The local member of parliament opened the centre on behalf of the Commonwealth government. The opening was accompanied by the symbolic planting of trees by the local member of the Commonwealth government, the local member of the state government, and the mayor of Broken Hill.

The old building requires considerable renovations to render it compliant to modern building standards. A renovation subcommittee of Community Inc. was formed to manage the process. The process is now well underway, with voluntary donations of material and labour stretching the funding dollar further. For instance, Inland Energy and Water contributed AUD$19,000 toward the total cost of AUD$29,000 for solar panels, which provide enough power for most centre uses, with surplus power fed back into the national grid. The company wanted two demonstration sites, one in Broken Hill, the other in Balranald, to promote its solar power. This display panel in a community building will encourage others to use solar power (this links with the Cool Communities agenda, discussed below). It is intended that one section of the building will be leased for commercial use, providing an ongoing source of income. Other areas will be used for community office space, for meetings, and so on. A commercial kitchen is being planned, as well as an area potentially to be used as a youth drop-in centre.

Community Gardens

Originally only five people met for the community gardens solution group. The group met at regular intervals over two years, with an average attendance of twelve people, and with approximately thirty people involved in some way. Those involved included old and young, male and female, A groupers and new arrivals, under the leadership of a young professional "A grouper" woman.

Upon purchasing the community centre property, one of the three old bowling greens was set aside for a garden. At first the group had little gardening knowledge and sought information from the Internet. The solution group designed the shape of the new garden and established basic principles for its operation, for instance, that only those who became members of the Community Gardens Group could be involved in planning, planting, and harvesting. The group formed links with the existing Silver City Garden Club. Several TAFE (state-funded Technical and Further Education College) horticultural teachers became involved, providing information and assistance by using the garden as a practical exercise for their students. The group managed to obtain an ABC (Australian Broadcasting Corporation) Open Garden grant, and another grant from Silver City Charities to erect a central pergola. Rotary Club men helped erect the pergola and TAFE students erected raised garden beds and compost bins, using discarded material from the old shed.

A newsletter was started in February 2002. The front page of the newsletter states the intended benefits of the community garden:

- revitalizing and beautifying barren land
- creating sustainable agriculture and reducing hunger
- providing fresh, healthy, cheap food
- improving environmental quality
- strengthening the sense of community
- promoting cultural understanding
- reducing crime, educating people, and developing skills.

That first newsletter also contained an article on "the low water usage garden," indicating an awareness of the special challenges of gardening in a semi-arid area such as Broken Hill.

There was some tension within the community garden project group during the first two years. This appeared to relate to a clash of cultures and leadership styles involving on the one hand those from the mines who were used to a masculine style of authoritarian leadership and on the other hand those used to a more collaborative style of leadership. At times the clash of style was difficult and distressing for those involved. Nonetheless, by August 2002, the first crop of vegetables had been harvested and sold at the community markets. The gardens had not yet engaged the active involvement of a wider cross-section of the community.

Cultural Issues

At the first round table, twelve people joined the cultural issues solution group. The group comprised several employees of local government council, as well as others interested in specific issues, such as signage. There were those interested in the eisteddfod, the visual arts, and poetry. There was general discussion about what could be done, but no emerging consensus or action plan. The group did not meet again, and several people subsequently left Broken Hill.

It is difficult to establish what happened to discourage this solution group. Certainly the diversity of interests and agendas meant that there was no clear focus. No one appeared to be prepared to take a leadership role. There was also suggestion by some of those present at the one and only group meeting that Community Inc. was usurping the proper professional role of council and other arts organizations. Whatever the reason, this solution group appeared to dissolve without a trace.

Employment and Men's Issues

It is unclear from the written record as to whether there were one or several solution groups meeting on employment and men's issues. Informants suggested several discussion foci at the first round table. The main discussion centred on the problems created for those men who were being retrenched from the mines. Broken Hill was bracing itself for increased levels of unemployment as the mines began to close. Attendees felt that while Community Inc. could not directly deal with employment generation projects, it could develop the concept of useful employment: utilizing the skills of these men in ways that were useful to the community and meaningful to the men themselves. So, for example, there was discussion of a skills register of "community builders." Two women had close experience of men committing suicide, and argued strongly that some kind of support was needed for the men in the community.

One of the discussion papers presented at the round table dealt with the possibility of creating a "men's shed." Most miners' homes in Broken Hill have a shed at the back of the house, usually made of corrugated iron and whatever materials could be scrounged from the mines. This shed became a private workshop, a home brew still, a place to write bush poetry, or just "a place to hide" from the world. The suggestion was made that a community men's shed could be built as part of the Centre for Community.

The first round-table discussion did not lead directly to concrete action. But the issue did not go away, and similar discussions occurred at the next two round tables. Then, in 2001, three men (an A grouper, one person "from away," and the centre manager) organized a men's day. This was well advertised by the local press, and offered a program including bush poetry, displays of machinery, and a home brew workshop. The purpose was to get a men's community shed up and running as a place where men could feel safe and provide mutual support. Approximately fifty men attended, a good turnout.

By August 2002, the basic structure of the shed was under construction on the other side of one of the old bowling greens. The men's shed made use of the centre's renovation fund and was built with the help of TAFE students, as part of a strategy to provide training opportunities for young people to encourage them to stay in Broken Hill.

To date there has been no strategies for ongoing action within the men's shed, nor any attempt to link these activities with employment diversification.

Youth Issues

Nine people joined the youth issues solution group, and there was a general "talk fest" about the issues confronting youth in Broken Hill. Young people have little to look forward to by way of higher education and career prospects in Broken Hill, and the demographics of the town show an increasing trough of twenty to thirty-five year olds, as young people move to the cities.

Nothing came of the first round-table discussion, but the issue was raised again at the second and the third round tables. At the second round table, some talented young people with passion and vision talked, but again there was no one to drive the process, and these young people left Broken Hill shortly afterward.

In March 2001, the Youth Active Citizenship Group was formed by Community Inc. as a pilot project. TAFE was looking to involve students in voluntary work for a short period. The community facilitator of Community Inc. worked with students during class time for six hours per week. She wished to work not with the elite kids but with the ordinary kids who are struggling at school and more likely to stay in Broken Hill. She worked with a small group of kids from TAFE and helped them organize the Youth Active Citizenship Forum at the fourth round table. The morning events were open only to people under age twenty-four and attracted a large number. In the afternoon, the young people made a presentation to the full round table. Out of this came a proposal to develop a café/drop-in space within the community centre. That project has not proceeded further, and the facilitator has left the centre. Nonetheless, the proposal remains "on the shelf," waiting an opportunity to reactivate.

Community Markets

For some time there had been talk of creating community markets. Community markets were not a part of community life in Broken Hill, but they were in the hometowns of several of Broken Hill's citizens "from away," and these residents suggested that Broken Hill have some also. There is no written record of a formal discussion of the markets until the third round table in the following year.

Once the new community centre building with the old bowling greens was acquired, the community markets quickly became a reality, held regularly on the second Saturday of each month. At first the markets were small and business was slow, with only ten or eleven stalls, borrowed tables, and few customers. By August 2002, the markets had been going for a year, the markets group had acquired its own trestles, there were regularly twenty to thirty stalls, and some six hundred shoppers came through the gates each market day.

The year had been a learning process for all concerned. At first a formal organizational structure was created, but it did not work well. Now the group meets as an informal network, with regular meetings of all interested stallholders on the Monday following the markets. The committee is made up almost entirely of those "from away," although an "A grouper" was instrumental in starting the project.

There are several couples and several older women involved. The secretary is a young woman artist who has lived in Broken Hill for most of her life.

A number of tensions are unresolved, particularly about the relationship between the markets and the management of Community Inc. Community Inc. holds all moneys and no correspondence can go out from the markets committee without the approval of the centre manager. No hot food can be sold except by Community Inc., as a fundraiser. Only Community Inc. can set the fees for stallholders. The committee finds these and related issues disempowering, and some members have become discouraged and left. Nonetheless, there is fierce interest and commitment by those remaining.

Public Liability

The public liability solution group arose out of the fifth round table in February 2002, as a direct result of the crisis in public liability insurance that has hit all Australian community ventures. Since 11 September 2001 and the collapse of several of Australia's biggest insurers, insurance premiums have increased several thousand fold in some cases, threatening many organizations and events with closure. The solution group consisted of fifteen people, mostly men of power and influence, including the local member of parliament, local government councillors, local businessmen associated with Rotary, and is chaired by the CEO of Australian Inland Energy and Water. Following the round table, community groups were asked to register their difficulties; this information was passed onto the director of the NSW Council for Social Services. The issue of public liability is ongoing, being pursued by stakeholders and governments across Australia.

Family Reconnect

Ten people joined the family reconnect solution group that followed on from the morning workshop on the same day. This was organized by a service provider, Broken Hill and District Family Support-Youth Reconnect. A solution group was formed to establish a family mediation service and was successful in recruiting volunteers for the project. Funding was then sought and obtained by Family Support, with the support and encouragement of Community Inc.

Cool Communities

Cool Communities is an Australian government-initiated program managed by the quasi-NGO Australian Greenhouse Office. Following an expression of interest from Community Inc., the Cool Communities program manager from Sydney came to the fifth round table in February 2002 and facilitated a solution group to canvas support for the program. The program aims to involve the community in reducing energy costs and greenhouse gas emissions. Thirteen people joined the group, most of them people "from away" with a commitment to sustainability, but including also employees of the local energy and water utility. Over the following six months there were several meetings of the group, but the initial enthusiasm rapidly dissipated as conflict became apparent. After nearly twelve months of negotiations between Broken Hill Community Inc. and the Australian Greenhouse Office, the first funding instalment was received.

This appeared to be a multi-stakeholder conflict involving the program office in Sydney, the management of Community Inc., and other businesses and citizens of Broken Hill. Meetings were called and cancelled, and anger and frustration expressed by all stakeholders. Much of this conflict appeared to revolve around the issue of control of the project itself. After a series of meetings, and a delegation from the Community Inc. management committee to the funding body in Sydney, a compromise was reached. According to this agreement, Community Inc. would sponsor local workshops on energy efficiency for householders with the assistance of Australian Inland Energy and Water employees (as part of their corporate volunteering initiative). In addition, a school art competition would be conducted, and the Centre for Community would be used as a demonstration site. Seed funding would be available for local groups wishing to use Community Inc. facilities to establish a recycling cooperative. The funding would be delivered in small amounts as each objective, or target action was achieved.

While the proposed action plan appears to provide a useful base for future cooperation, in fact all parties have expressed strong disapproval of the process to date, and the ordinary local citizens who expressed interest in the issue have largely withdrawn from the group, perhaps waiting for further developments. A great deal of energy by many players continues to focus on this project, but its future direction is unclear.

Olive Trees

A local doctor (a new arrival) had noticed the large number of healthy olive trees in the town, with the harvest going unused. Olive oil has many health advantages, and this was a resource that could be used for the benefit of the citizens of Broken Hill, and perhaps lead to a new local industry.

Five people joined the solution group created for this issue in February 2002. By August 2002, an early and a late harvest of existing trees had occurred, the oil pressed at Riverton (some 470 kilometres away) and the oil tested. The oil was found to be of a very high quality, excellent taste, with almost no trace elements of lead. In short, ideal for human consumption.

The group has continued to meet and develop several plans to develop the olive oil processing in Broken Hill. Some of these plans have a commercial angle but retain a central role for Community Inc. to maintain (and rent) a community-owned oil press for the use and benefit of all citizens. The core active group consists of five men, including local businessmen and a local handyman/artist, as well as the doctor. The group unveiled the olive oil at the community markets. From that, an additional sixty people have indicated an interest in the project and are on the group's mailing list. The group plans to incorporate as a cooperative.

Health Services Advocacy

Six people, mainly health professionals and their families, joined the health services advocacy solution group in February 2002, concerned with local standards of health care. Two of the group joined the Broken Hill Hospital Advisory Committee and, as part of that, held a public response survey at the August community markets. The group has chosen at this stage to work through the existing representative model set up by the health service. It will review the effectiveness and make a decision about future direction.

Professional Women

A small group of four women met at the fifth round table, held February 2002, and agreed to continue meeting on an informal basis each month. Three such meetings have been held, with a woman solicitor speaking at one meeting. It is unclear at this stage what direction the group will take.

Mulga Creek Walkway

In 1999, the Broken Hill city council community development officer and manager of recreation identified Mulga Creek as a potential location for a walkway to promote better health. At the first round table, the project was submitted and gained support, but participants considered other areas a priority. The project was put on the shelf. The matter was later raised by a local TAFE teacher, who agreed to assist develop a project plan. The project broadened over six months to include a wildlife corridor, water quality, land reclamation, Aboriginal bush tucker, guided walks, walking and cycling paths. The concept now involves some ten kilometres of path and 20,000 tree plantings.

The proposal did not generate sufficient interest to form a solution group. However, Bushcare (a local landcare group) has provided funding for the creation of a native plant nursery at the Centre for Community. The project will require the support and cooperation of the local council and negotiations are continuing.

Discussion

The description of these solution groups provides enough information to begin to apply the theoretical model of sustainability. In doing so we return to the research questions and attempt to identify the stakeholders, the knowledges, the leadership, and the role of government.

First, the round tables clearly attracted a great diversity of participants. They have included men and women of all ages, businesspeople and professionals, retired people, and working-class citizens. They include those born and bred in Broken Hill (the A groupers) but more often those who have recently arrived. There have been a number of working-class people and those on government pensions, as well as the wealthier and powerful. All have had a voice, though not necessarily the same attention. Many of the more marginalized (e.g., housing commission tenants) felt silenced by the process. There have been few if any Aboriginal people attending the round tables, and those involved admit that this remains a serious continuing divide in the community.

Conflict and tension is ongoing across several discernible boundaries in Broken Hill. First is the perceived interference of governments at state and commonwealth levels. These governments are seen to have taken the wealth of Broken Hill and then lost interest in its future. Nonetheless, government grants are available, but usually with strings attached. Government regulations, for example about appropriate land usage, lack understanding of the local conditions. However, government is seen as the major source of financial resources, and considerable energy is expended in trying to obtain those (diminishing) resources. The Commonwealth Department of Family and Community Services has provided consistent support for Community Inc. and has ensured that funding agreements be kept as broad and flexible as possible. This has not always been the case with other funding, as the case of Cool Communities indicates.

Community Inc. has had a turbulent history of involvement with local government. On the one hand, the organization was first formed in partnership with council, and the mayor is keen to be seen to share in the major events. Councillors regularly attend the round tables. Various projects, such as the Mulga Creek bush regeneration, will require the cooperation of council, as it is council property. The manager and president of Community Inc. provide a monthly face-to-face briefing for the mayor and general manager of council. Nonetheless, there is a sense of "us and them," of resentment on the part of Community Inc. that council wishes to charge rates for the centre facilities, and on the part of council that Community Inc. is usurping council's area of authority.

Within the community are several divides, between labour and capital (a hangover from the days when the mining unions held great power), between those who were born and bred in Broken Hill and those who are newly arrived, between black and white citizens, even between those who live in the south and those who live in the north of the central business district. There are also power struggles between competing men, each with their own vision and agenda. There is less divide on the basis of class, gender, age, religion, or political affiliation; while these divisions do occur, there are many bridging links between them that knit the community together in times of need.

Within Community Inc. there also are tensions, some of them the product of the larger tensions mentioned above. Sometimes it appears that Community Inc. is operating within a demilitarized zone of conflict and tensions. It is the significant achievement of Community Inc. that it was able to create an organization that bridged these divides through the formation of the centre and the round tables. However, while the round tables have been successful in bringing stakeholders together to discuss common issues, the resulting solution groups have been less successful. Problems and tensions have occurred in many, though not all, of the solution groups. The key problem concerns the decision-making process and the location of control associated with the solution groups. The round-table process was intended to generate self-initiated action by the community, drawing on the principles of participatory democracy. That is, each solution group is empowered to identify a potential course of action and take steps to address a particular problem. However, that leaves open the question of leadership, authority, and the implications for action by one party on the sphere of action of another. In some cases, those attending solution groups have failed to proceed with an ongoing action because there was no one to drive the process; each member took the attitude that "someone should do something." In those cases where clear leadership did emerge within the solution group, there sometimes developed a struggle of authority between the group and Community Inc. management. The problem remains one of coordinating the actions of individual groups to work within the cultural pitfalls and politics of Broken Hill so that the work of one does not damage the relationships of the whole. Newcomers do not have an understanding of these deeper politics, much of which remains opaque to the outsider. Much is left unspoken in order to keep the peace. The boundaries of authority remain ambiguous and contradictory and sometimes lead to a sense of disempowerment and disillusion by solution group members. There are no conflict management procedures in place. Such tensions could be largely resolved by a clearer set of protocols for all solution groups, which must include the requirement to communicate and negotiate between the interested parties. A culture of silence and innuendo in the face of conflict makes progress difficult.

Having said that, it is also clear that there is at times a remarkable sense of cohesion across the community and within Community Inc., a sense of pulling together to make events work despite the conflict and difficulties. There is a huge variety of people and skills and commitment to working together, and to hang in for the long haul.

To place the events at Broken Hill in a larger theoretical context, it could be argued that much of Community Inc.'s efforts involve developing bridging links across the various and multiple social divides of the city. In terms of the typology of community structures identified by Sharp (2001), Broken Hill represents a highly factionalized community. There have always been strong bonding links within fairly narrow social units. Extended family is strong, as are the ties of the old mining teams, various church groups, and so on. But if Broken Hill is going to reinvent itself, the bonding links are not enough, and are likely to be counterproductive. The challenge is to use the new coalitional structure of Community Inc. to transform the existing conflicts and tensions into a greater capacity for action (Chavis 2001). To access the available new energy and knowledges and resources, it is necessary to bridge the existing social units, to develop a broader bridging and linking social capital. It is significant that prior to 2001 there existed no umbrella or community field organization within Broken Hill. It has been the major achievement of Broken Hill Community Inc. to create this kind of bridging community field organization in order to generate a more coalitional structure for the town (Sharp 2001). One of the indices of this move is the multiple connection of each of the main players within Community Inc. All are key members in other organizations who would not necessarily come together in any other context. The newly formed ties are looser, and therefore more fragile. There is less shared history and understanding of the local culture. There is less trust. High commitment to attend the round tables does not necessarily equate with high trust. In the words of one informant, "They can't afford not to be at the round table"; commitment to participate is as likely to come from distrust of the other players as from trust. Trust grows from repeated and positive interaction over time, and from the respected input from professionals operating for the good of the community (Leonard and Onyx 2003).

Resources are both scarce and plentiful. Although there is never enough money, Community Inc. has been successful in obtaining over a million dollars in government grants. Community Inc. is already beginning to generate small amounts of returns from the community markets, and it intends to rent part of the premises for commercial use to generate ongoing revenue. However, more important than the financial resources is the huge input of skilled voluntary labour at all levels, estimated at AUD$800,000 worth for the development of the new centre alone. This includes management and administration of the centre, secretarial support, catering, building (including plumbing and electrical work), labouring, and the supply of donated materials. Almost all kinds of specialist technical advice are available at no cost, including detailed horticultural, environmental, and technical information. Government services provide considerable training and information, including at round-table workshops. Mentors provide access to valuable external knowledge. Broken Hill is famous for its artistic tradition, and visual, creative approaches are accepted as integral.

Leadership is sometimes lacking, sometimes overpowering. Probably as a consequence of Broken Hill's history of paternalistic control by mine bosses, unions, and the state, there is a residue of passivity by many of the A groupers, a fear of taking the initiative that is often labelled by others as apathy. However, there is also a tradition of the "strong," authoritarian leader who commands power and respect. This can lead to competitive and aggressive approaches to problem solving, and makes the more inclusive, collaborative style of leadership difficult to maintain. There is also a sense of independence, fiercely maintained by individuals and the community at large, which can be productive but makes collaboration more difficult. Nonetheless, there are examples of good collaborative action, some of them with a clearly designated leader, others with new forms of collaborative leadership evident. These positive examples provide a model that can be built on and encouraged.

Finally, we return to the initial statement of this chapter. If Community Inc. has demonstrated nothing else, it has demonstrated the need to integrate the social, the economic, and the ecological. The breadth of issues Community Inc. has undertaken attests to the concern for natural, economic, and social issues and the interconnection between these. The formation of Community Inc. itself was a significant response to the search for sustainability. The long-term sustainability of Broken Hill will emerge out of the struggles of human endeavour to collaborate, to think creatively, to bridge the factional concerns, to find effective ways of integrating the economic, social, and ecological imperatives.

References

Canadian Consortium for Sustainable Development Research (CCSDR). 1990. Background paper. <http://www.royalroads.net/ccsdr/index-hp.htm> (19 September 2002).

Chavis, D. 2001. "The Paradoxes and Promise of Community Coalitions." *American Journal of Community Psychology* 29(2): 309-20.

Dale, A. 2001. *At the Edge: Sustainable Development in the 21st Century.* Vancouver: UBC Press.

Fukuyama, F. 1995. *Trust: The Social Virtues and the Creation of Prosperity.* London: Penguin.

Herbert-Cheshire, L. 2000. "Contemporary Strategies for Rural Community Development in Australia: A Governmentality Perspective." *Journal of Rural Studies* 16(2): 203-15.

Leonard, R., and J. Onyx. 2003. "Networking through Loose and Strong Ties: An Australian Qualitative Study." *Voluntas* 14(2): 191-205.

Onyx, J., and P. Bullen. 2000. "The Different Faces of Social Capital in NSW Australia." In P. Dekker and E. Uslander, eds., *Social Capital and Participation in Everyday Life.* London: Routledge.

Putman, R. 2000. *Bowling Alone: The Collapse and Revival of American Community.* New York: Simon and Schuster.

Putman, R., R. Leonardi, and R. Nanetti. 1993. *Making Democracy Work: Civic Traditions in Modern Italy.* Princeton, NJ: Princeton University Press.

Robinson, J., and J. Tinker. 1997. "Reconciling Ecological, Economic and Social Imperatives: A New Conceptual Framework." In T. Schrecker, ed., *Surviving Globalism: Social and Environmental Dimensions.* London: Macmillan.

Sharp, J. 2001. "Locating the Community Field: A Study of Interorganizational Network Structure and Capacity for Community Action. *Rural Sociology* 66(3): 403-24.

Stone, W. 2001. "Measuring Social Capital." Research Paper 24, Australian Institute of Family Studies, Melbourne, Australia.

Wilkinson, K. 1991. *The Community in Rural America.* New York: Greenwood Press.

Woolcock, M. 1998. "Social Capital and Economic Development: Toward a Theoretical Synthesis and Policy Framework." *Theory and Society* 27(2): 151-208.

Woolcock, M. and D. Narayan. 2000. "Social Capital: Implications for Development Theory, Research and Policy." *World Bank Research Observer* 15(2): 225-50.

11
Social Capital Mobilization for Ecosystem Conservation
Jennie Sparkes

> The national parks of Canada are hereby dedicated to the people
> of Canada for their benefit, education and enjoyment, subject to
> this Act and the regulations, and the parks shall be maintained
> and made use of so as to leave them unimpaired for the enjoyment
> of future generations.
> – *Canada National Parks Act,* 2000, s. 4(1)

Parks Canada Agency maintains thirty-nine national parks and national
park reserves, located in every province and territory across Canada. National parks are established as representative samples of thirty-nine "natural" regions to which Canada has been divided. In most cases national parks
protect only small portions of the ecosystems in these larger regions and are
one of a multitude of regional land managers. Some regions are quite isolated, such as the Eastern High Arctic natural region, represent by
Quttinirpaaq National Park, while other regions, such as the West St.
Lawrence natural region, represented by Point Pelee National Park, are located in highly populated and industrial landscapes. In total, national parks
and national park reserves protect approximately 2.5 percent of the nation's
lands and fresh water ecosystems. One of the greatest challenges facing national park managers in the pursuit of maintaining or restoring ecosystem
integrity is the stressors from human activities. These stressors occur at
multiple scales, ranging from in-park stressors such as habitat impacts and
fragmentation from trails and roads, to community-generated waste and
industrial by-products, to large-scale stressors such as the persistent organic
pollutants (PCBs, dioxins, and DDT) transported globally before being absorbed into park ecosystems.

The *Canada National Parks Act* 2000, c. 32 8(2) identifies that the maintenance and restoration of ecological integrity within national parks is, as the
minister responsible for the Parks Canada Agency, the minister of Canadian
Heritage's first priority when considering all aspects of the park management.

The act defines ecological integrity to mean, in terms of a national park, a condition determined to be characteristic of its natural region and likely to persist, including abiotic components and the composition and abundance of native species and biological communities, rates of change, and supporting processes. To achieve this, national parks engage in a variety of ecosystem monitoring and restoration efforts as well as actively managing stressors resulting from the public's visitation to parks. Education, law enforcement, facility design, and visitor management is used to manage visitor behaviour. Outside park boundaries, where national parks hold no legislative authority, park managers build relationships with communities, organizations, and governments as a means of influencing and coordinating human activities toward behaviours that minimize stress on national parks and surrounding ecosystems.

The management of national parks is influenced by the dominant philosophies and world views that people bring to management. World views reflect systems of beliefs. Parks Canada, in managing for ecological integrity, reflects an ecological world view that accepts humans as part of nature and attempts to contribute to the sustainability of the larger ecological-social system to which the national park is a part. This ecological world view draws on ecosystem-based management to achieve the vision and objectives set out for park ecosystems. Parks Canada interprets ecosystem-based management to involve taking a holistic view of nature and ensuring land-use decisions consider the complex interactions and dynamics of park ecosystems. Its interpretation recognizes that park ecosystems have a finite capacity to withstand and recover from human stresses. Ecosystem-based management requires collaboration among all those whose activities influence the ecological integrity of the parks.

Societies and communities outside national park boundaries also structure their actions and investments based on world views that they hold. Understanding dominant world views held by communities builds a more complete picture of the scales at which park ecosystems are being stressed. This is important information for park managers engaged in ecosystem-based management and requires the involvement of all those who influence the integrity of the park. At times community world views align nicely with that of Parks Canada. At other times they clash. This suggests that park managers could benefit from understanding the beliefs in communities that validate and define those communities' world views and actions. Understanding community beliefs and world views could provide national park managers with insight into the assumptions and fears that hold certain behaviours in place. To gain this understanding, national park managers must examine equally the social and ecological dimensions of ecological integrity issues.

Steiner (2002) notes that social and ecological systems share some commonalities. Figure 11.1 paraphrases what Steiner believes to be the fundamental principles of human ecology. He notes that social systems, like ecosystems, are dynamic: they both have multiple ranges of scales/space; change episodically and are characterized by periods of slow change interrupted by abrupt events; contain multiple equilibria that define functionally different states such as political, cultural, community, and economic dynamics; and they have loose resilience when subjected to policies and management practices that attempt to homogenize the beliefs, norms, and institutions governing societies.

Maintaining or restoring ecological integrity within park ecosystem components is a critical, but only partial, contribution to protecting the national parks for future generations. Ecological integrity efforts will be ineffective in halting the destruction of biomass, physical structures, and nutrients if the world views and the relationships that communities have with their environment in the larger landscape are inconsistent with expectations of park managers. This highlights once again the importance of world view, and suggests the importance of encouraging collective community behaviours to reflect an ecological world view. It also highlights the importance of understanding the landscape of which a national park and representative ecosystem are a part. A landscape captures both the natural and cultural features that make that area unique and includes forests, buildings, roads, neighbourhoods, hills, and bodies of water.

Yaffee (1999), in his ecoregional approach to resource management, holds that abiotic and floristic components of a landscape define the boundaries of ecoregions. Within this ecoregional approach, "success comes through [the] maintenance or restoration of ecological functions associated with those landscape units" (ibid., 715). Yaffee emphasizes the integration of humans into ecosystems and the importance of "protecting natural processes in order to sustain human activities" (ibid., 716).

Supporting the observations of Yaffee and Steiner is the observation of Grumbine (1994), who believes that managing ecosystems is not only about ecological science but also largely about how people value nature and how people will learn to fit with nature. While science plays a role in making this connection, people connect to places through their senses. This suggests that the art of ecosystem management lies in mediating between the visible physical world that takes form around humans and the concealed mental interpretations of the physical world housed within humans. This creates a challenge for science-based organizations striving toward ecological integrity. For ecosystem management to be effective, it must draw on the understanding emerging through science to create knowing, while at the same time drawing on the "art of being" to recreate a sustainable harmony within the interactions and integrations between natural and cultural communities. "Art of being" relates to how humans choose to act toward nature and requires a different means of knowing than provided by traditional scientific methods. This dimension of ecosystem management involves human behaviours and the need to understand the evolution taking place within the concealed mental processes and factors that actualize behaviours toward nature.

Endter-Wada et al. (1998, 892) found that most applications of social considerations in ecosystem management were "included only as part of the decision making and political processes in initiating and implementing ecosystem management." Supporting Grumbine's observation, Endter-Wada et al. contend that humans play a greater role in ecosystem management than mere public involvement in planning processes, and argue that social analysis is also a critical element of understanding, monitoring, and influencing social behaviour. Four social components – public involvement processes, public involvement data, social analysis processes, and social analysis data – are necessary to create adequate social knowledge to address the human aspect of ecosystems. Because this dimension of ecosystem–based management is as much an art as it is a science, approaches other than traditional science are required in studying its attributes. Therefore, both the social and ecological dynamics at work within a system must be examined when managing for ecological integrity, as discussed by Steiner in Figure 11.1.

Machlis, Force, and Burch (1995) offer a human ecology perspective to help ecosystem managers understand the relationship between people and nature. Human ecology is described as the study of processes involving how people interact with each other and with their surroundings. Human ecology has emerged from what is termed "new ecology." New ecology is a reorientation of traditional ecology that recognizes

a shift from an equilibrium point of view where local populations and ecosystems are viewed as in balance with local resources and conditions, to a disequilibrium point of view where history matters and populations and ecosystems are continually being influenced by disturbances; and a shift from considering populations and ecosystems as relatively closed or autonomous systems independent of their surroundings, to considering both populations and ecosystems as "open" and strongly influenced by the input and output or "flux" of material and individuals across system borders. (Steiner 2002, 3)

Steiner (2002) argues that new ecology is rooted in the recognition that (1) humans engage in ecological relationships and (2) urban and suburban environments provide laboratories for ecological inquiry. This is based on the assumption that human interactions can be studied by using hierarchy as

Figure 11.1

Fundamental principles of human ecology

1. Systems thinking. Systems are organized and arranged through networks. For a system to exist there must be ordered, connecting channels of communications, the essence of the interaction process. An ecosystem is an interacting unit of material and energy flows. Human ecosystems create many of these interactions.

2. Language, culture, and technology. Language is used to pass knowledge from one generation to the next. Words and their meanings define common culture. Culture defines relationships. Technology enables humans to create a new form of environment and reshape what it means to be human.

3. Structure, function, and change. Function looks at how the parts of a system interrelate and result in connectivity. In human systems, energy flows are examined. Structures are the parts of the system. In nature, they include geological and biological processes; in human systems they include economic and sociocultural processes. Change is measured in terms of alteration to structure or function.

4. Edges, boundaries, and ecotones. These features exist within social systems as well ecosystems. Edges offer open spaces in otherwise built settings, such as greenbelts and parks in cities. Political boundaries may define an area of jurisdiction but not conform to ecosystem boundaries.

5. Interaction, integration, and institution. Interaction and integration occur in natural systems, but only people create institutions. Interactions are reciprocal actions on each other. Integration is a specific form of interaction that combines parts to create a whole. "Institutions regulate interactions between individuals and communities or society and between individuals or communities and their environment. Institutions regulate the flow of goods and materials through the system." (32)

6. Diversity. Diversity enables natural systems to be resilient and to adapt to change. Cultural diversity is more complex than diversity in nature. Yet natural and cultural diversity share patterns of distribution globally and enrich life. Within culture, pluralism is a theory where more than one principle or set of principles is accepted within a society, and through this act, pluralism acknowledges diversity.

7. Adaptation. Adaptation relates to adjustment to change and is a measure of the physical fitness of an organism in relation to the conditions of its environment. It also relates to a system's capacity to modify in response to disturbance. Humans are a highly adaptive species; this adaptation enables them to remain resilient when faced with change. Humans adapt both genetically and through learning.

8. Holism. Holism is a concept developed to explain that an entity could be both part and whole, and to integrate the concept of function as part of the larger whole.

Source: Paraphrased from Steiner (2002, 21-36), with permission.

an organizing device. Interactions occurring at one level, such as the family, are nested within a higher level, such as the community. Human ecology examines how relationships that occur in nature are mirrored in human systems through planning and management efforts.

The model that Machlis, Force, and Burch (1995) present is one model for depicting the interrelationships between social and ecological systems. It highlights the types of social data and analysis that may be useful in understanding how the flow of resources between humans and ecosystems are mediated by the structures and processes within the human social system. It recognizes that a set of critical resources is required to provide the human ecosystem with necessary supplies for survival, as illustrated in Figure 11.2.

Figure 11.2

Working model of a human ecosystem

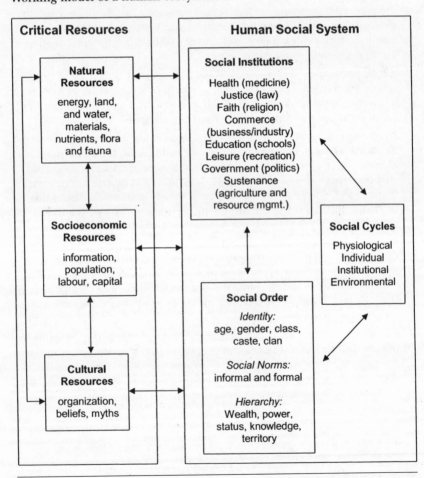

Source: Machlis, Burch, and Force (1995, 5) (reproduced with permission).

Three categories of critical resources are outlined: (1) natural resources, such as energy, fauna, wood, and water; (2) socioeconomic resources, such as labour and capital; and (3) cultural resources, such as beliefs and myths. These three categories of critical resources keep the human ecosystem functioning, the flow and distribution of these resources being regulated by the social system and the set of general social structures that guide much of human behaviour.

Depicted as separate from the critical resources is the human social system. Within the human social system are three components. The first is a set of social institutions that are collective solutions to universal social challenges or needs; the second is a series of social cycles that are temporal patterns for allocating human activity; and the third is social order, a set of cultural patterns for organizing interaction among people and groups. Social order consists of three key mechanisms for ordering behaviour: personal identities, such as age and gender; norms, such as rules for behaving; and hierarchies, such as those of wealth and power. Social order that is adhered to makes human behaviour predictable.

This complexity of flow between human social systems and critical resources provides valuable insight into how social systems mediate the flow of ecological, economic, and cultural resources. The human ecosystem model suggests that attributes of social systems determine which beliefs societies draw on, how social and economic resources are mobilized, and how natural resources are utilized or preserved.

Social-ecosystem models help park managers visualize and understand the complexity of relationships within and between ecological and human systems. They also assist in identifying the types of social system information that should be collected, analyzed, and monitored. Parks Canada, as a science-based organization, is focused on building knowledge through scientific methods and anchoring management actions within the science-generated knowledge. Any contributions related to building understanding about the social component of ecosystems must also be based on science-generated knowledge. This social component must provide insight to national park managers on (1) the flow of resources and energy between a community (human ecosystem) and an ecosystem, and (2) a community's capacity to organize toward collective actions that steward ecosystems. This second capacity is the focus of this chapter. A community's capacity to organize for collective and collaborative actions is captured within the concept of social capital. Social capital is a subsystem within the human ecosystem model that focuses specifically on human relationships with other humans. This research postulates that the characteristics of these human relationships (social capital) determine the dominant world views within human ecosystems that regulate the flow of resources and energy from ecosystems. Social capital is the supply of active connections between people, including the trust, mutual understanding, shared values, and behaviours that bind the members of human networks and communities and makes cooperative action possible (Putnam 1995). To understand how cooperative actions emerge in communities, one must examine at least four sources of social capital: trust, networks, beliefs, and norms.

Trust is "the expectations that arise within a community of regular, honest, and cooperative behaviour, based on commonly shared norms, by members of the community" (Fukuyama 1995, 26). Reciprocity-based relationships, such as in bonding and bridging social capital, are dependent on trust.

Trust forms networks. Networks are interconnected nodes of people who share the same communication codes, thereby making the sharing of information and ideas possible. They can expand without limits and can be influenced by social values, goals, priorities, policies, human health, technologies, and knowledge. A network's strength is the result of the density of connects within a network, connection to positions of influence, or its number of linkages (structural holes) to new forms of knowledge.

Beliefs are shared via networks. Common beliefs enable participants in networks to share their ideas and make sense of common experiences. Without goals based on shared beliefs, there is no reason for people to come together to form collaborative networks. Beliefs are reflected in world views, the stories communities share, and the actions people choose to pursue. Parks Canada's beliefs are defined and preserved within law, its policies, and its approaches to management.

Norms reflect beliefs that societies hold and at the same time represent the social demands for specific conditions to exist. A group's adherence to norms is the foundation of individuals coming together as a society. Coleman (2000) believes that the most important form of norms is the one that foregoes self-interest of the individual in the interest of the broader community. This suggests the importance of caring for and about others, and is captured by the term "stewardship." Stewardship can be focused on social or ecological outcomes. When considered on a landscape scale, stewardship could be viewed as a strategic norm for managers concerned with the sustainability of social and ecological systems within a region. Providing the conditions and opportunities for communities to cultivate beliefs and norms that contribute to the stewarding of a landscape requires a shift in the current social trend toward autonomy back toward valuing social and ecological interdependence.

How does a park manager provide conditions and opportunities for communities to cultivate beliefs and normative behaviours that contribute to this stewardship? Through action research, park managers can provide conditions and opportunities for communities to cultivate beliefs and norms while simultaneously researching the characteristics of the social capital and the flow of resources and energy within a community's human ecosystem. Action research, like ecosystem-based management and human ecology, has roots in the field of systems theory.

Like the adaptive management quality of ecosystem management, action research is based on the belief that scientific knowing is a product of continuous cycles of action and reflection. Solutions achieved through scientific knowing are only the best possible solution at that moment in time with the material and information at hand. Therefore, both ecosystem management and action research are pragmatic.

Action research engages in the study of social systems. It aims to solve problems that are pertinent to a community and that are defined within a specific context. It uses a democratic inquiry process to address problems that enable the researcher, such as a park manager, to collaborate with community members to seek and enact solutions to the problems the community has identified. Through engaging in a collaborative inquiry process, the park and community members become co-generators of knowledge on an issue. Action research is unlike traditional research where a question is framed, data are collected to address the question, and the results are recorded. Zeichner (2001, 271) cites the 1998 work of Newman:

> The research activity [in action research] begins in the middle of whatever it is you're doing – something happens that you did not expect ... and you begin wondering what is going on ... The hardest part of beginning an action research project is developing the discipline to keep a written account of what's happening, particularly when you have no idea of what you're looking for. For unlike traditional research, action research begins not with a research question but with the muddle of daily work, with the moments that stand out from the general flow.

A primary goal of action research is to create long-term sustainable learning capacities in communities. This commitment to working as equals creates a relationship between the researchers and the participants based on reciprocity. In the context of social capital, this reciprocity contributes to trust building and the formation of networks. It also moves government-community relationships from traditional linkage forms of social capital to more resilient, yet still fragile, bridging social capital. The reciprocity is based on a mutual sharing and generation of knowledge, which leads to the creation of actions to solve problems of importance to the community and the park. Through reflection on the actions they have taken, the participants interpret the results, thus creating a forum where both social learning and change can occur.

An important goal of action research is to generate knowledge that empowers communities to take control of their destinies. This includes understanding the sustainability of their day-to-day household and industrial actions in relation to the conservation of natural processes, landscape functions, and desired social and ecological conditions they wish to pass onto future generations. To facilitate empowerment that leads to change, learning must happen on three levels: instrumental, communicative, and transformational. Instrumental learning is akin to problem solving, while communicative learning relates to learning to understand and be understood by others. Transformative learning occurs when fundamental mental frameworks are questioned and revised, such as enabling a community to challenge its world views or beliefs about ecosystem stewardship. Transformative learning is dependent on the ability of people to reflect on what has been learned in the past and on openness to question whether the assumptions and premises associated with old paradigms of thinking are valid. Action research provides a place where participants can learn on all three of these levels. The role of national park managers in this process is of both researcher and facilitator. As researchers, they maintain detailed records on group dynamics and outcomes. As facilitators, their focus is on preserving the process and maintaining the rights of the participants to speak openly and to be heard.

There are several benefits of action research as a national park management tool:

1 The action research forum creates conditions for a community to build social capital for environmental issues of importance to that community. Through action research, a national park manager facilitates the creation of community-based stewardship ethics that contribute to the integrity of the park and surrounding ecosystems; assists in regulating the flow of resources and energy between human and ecological systems; and builds bridging social capital between itself and the community.

2 The action research forum provides a space for a park to engage Canadians in learning initiatives focused on empowering the community to positively contribute to regulating the flow of resources and energy between the community and its supporting ecosystem for the benefit of present and future generations.

3 Through engagement in the action research forum, the national park imports new skills and knowledge into a community, such as collaborative communications skills, leadership, problem solving, ecosystem information, and action research. This provides communities with capacities (human capital) that contribute to ongoing learning, adaptation, and resiliency within a community's human ecosystem.

4 The action research forum broadens a national park's traditional, often paternal, relationships with communities to relationships based on reciprocity, trust, and respect for the knowledge and capacities inherent in people to understand, adapt, and take responsibility for their futures. In doing so, a national park creates a new form of relationship with communities akin to bridging social capital, as opposed to traditional linkage social capital relations typical of government-community relations.

5 Action research designed to track networks in terms of social capital can result in a stronger understanding of the networks of resource and energy flows into the human ecosystem of a community. This knowledge can provide the national park manager with an understanding of the influence of broader political, social, and economic networks layered onto ecosystems. Economic exchanges are not an element of social capital because of their formal exchange of currency; however, gathering information on the trade networks can contribute to calculating the ecological footprint – the land and water area required to support a defined human population and material standards indefinitely (Wackernagel and Rees 1996, 158) – of a human ecosystem.

6 Action research provides an opportunity for a national park to track the evolution of beliefs, levels of trust, normative behaviours, and the structure of social networks (social capital) within a cross-section of a community. This study can "piggy-back" on existing park efforts to engage Canadians, such as educational programs, advisory boards, planning or regulatory development, and outreach efforts. Or, the use of action research and the study of social capital can be an independent project based on community-identified environmental issues. Regardless, the process provides feedback on the effectiveness of park-led education, learning, and public involvement processes.

Figure 11.3 is a hypothetical model depicting how a national park might use action research to create the conditions for environmental stewardship to be facilitated and social capital to be studied simultaneously in a community adjacent to a national park. The process is initiated by the community identifying an environmental issue of importance to it. The park recognizes this as an opportunity to work with the community to build understanding of the issue and enhance the integrity of the broader ecosystem supporting the park. The park manager offers to facilitate a working group of community members (an action research forum) to enable the community to examine the issue and create actions. The park manager also asks if, through the process of taking action to address, as in the case of Figure 11.3, the salmon spawning habitat problem, information could also be gather related to (1) the beliefs participants hold related to

Figure 11.3

Action research model for engaging a community in a stewardship initiative and tracking social capital evolution through the process

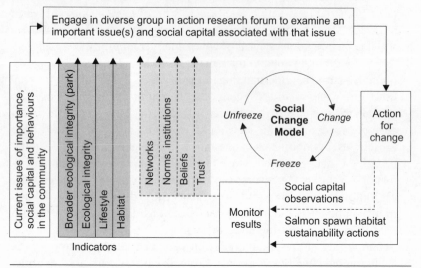

Source: Sparkes (2002).

their community and environment, (2) the levels of trust within the group, (3) the networks that are used or formed working together, and (4) the normative behaviours they see as barriers or opportunities, or which emerge. These elements of social capital influence, in part, the rate and type of flow of natural resources into the community and rate of waste assimilation or accumulation from the communities into ecosystems. Table 11.1 describes the process illustrated in Figure 11.3 in further detail.

Conclusions

Efforts to maintain or restore the ecological integrity of a national park will likely not be sustainable if the actions and world views outside the park boundaries contribute to ongoing stress on the park ecosystem. The beliefs and world views in communities that regulate the flow of resources into and waste from human systems must be understood to reduce stresses on national park ecosystems. This understanding requires social science and human ecology data, achieved through rigorous scientific research. Human ecology focuses on the relationship between social and ecological communities; social capital could be considered a subsystem within a human ecosystem that examines how human communities coordinate behaviour toward collective action. In doing so, social capital facilitates the creation

Table 11.1

Description of Figure 11.3

Element of Figure 11.3	Description
Current social capital and behaviour in community	Within this example, discussions in a community identify that the sustainability of salmon spawning habitat within the region (primarily outside park boundaries) is important to the community. The community feels that long-term economic benefits can be incurred by stewarding proper spawning habitat and that the residents will be able to maintain an enjoyed lifestyle by protecting the habitat. The national park has become aware of this issue through community meetings, conversations with key community members, the community newspaper, and being part of the informal dialogue among community citizens.
Engage diverse group in action research to examine an important issue and social capital associated with that issue within a community	The park (possibly with other partners such as the chamber of commerce or Fisheries and Oceans Canada) approaches key community members about facilitating a working group of community members (an action research forum) to enable the community to examine the issue of the sustainability of salmon spawning habitat within the region and create actions. Key community members are encouraged to draw on their networks to identify interested community members. Key community members may represent sport fishers, commercial operators, researchers, the local high school, and nongovernmental organizations.
	As part of this initial stage of engagement, the park and participants record the beliefs participants and/or the community holds related to salmon spawning habitat, community norms associated with the habitat, levels of trust within the group and/or the broader community toward working collaboratively to build solutions, and the networks in place and those required to address the issue. This provides baseline social capital information about the community participants.
Action for change (1) social capital observations	During the process of gathering knowledge about the issue, the participants may decide to break into smaller subgroups to take on different dimensions of the problem.

▶

◀ *Table 11.1*

Element of Figure 11.3	Description
(2) spawning habitat sustainability actions	Upon developing strategies, the participants are ready to take action. As a group, they decide when it is appropriate for the group or subgroups to report back to the larger group on the actions taken. The park may assist the participants, as requested, by providing access to new information or expert knowledge (either in-house or other known sources), or sharing and developing with the group new skills and processes. At intervals determined by the group (e.g., every six months), a new "snapshot" of the social capital within the group can be taken. Likely, observations about the relationship between the park and the community group will also surface. Observing improvements to salmon spawning habitat as well as the changes that occur within the group and their influence on the broader community provides a more holistic view of the learning and social change taking place (socially and ecologically) as a result of this problem-solving effort.
Monitor results: regional sustainability, ecological integrity, and social well-being indicators (1) networks, norms, institutions, beliefs, and trust (2) ecological stewardship, social stewardship	Part of any action plan is monitoring the results of the actions. Did the efforts improve the salmon spawning habitat and ultimately increase the quality and quantity of spawn? Did beliefs within the broader community change relative to working together to solve problems?; changing behaviours that contributed to the destruction of habitat?; valuing a national park in their neighbourhood? Were the economic and lifestyle interests of the community realized over time through these efforts? These questions can be answered only if monitoring programs are set up to track both social and ecological outcomes. Through monitoring the evolution of social capital among the participants, greater understanding is attained for the park manager about the human dimension of the ecosystems supporting the park, how social change occurs, and the effectiveness of behaviour-change efforts.

of dominant world views in communities and societies that in turn regulate the flow of resources and energy between social and natural systems.

Cultivating social capital within human ecosystems that fosters more sustainable relationships between humans and nature may be an emerging role for Parks Canada and other resource-management-focused agencies and government departments. Action research provides the rigor and structure for national park managers to monitor and measure a community's evolution toward stronger stewardships ethics. Examined in the context of understanding the flow of resources and energy associated with the human ecology within a landscape, social capital brings understanding to the dominant beliefs and norms that underpin humans' ecological relationships with their landscape.

Human ecology and social capital suggest that managing human stresses on park ecosystems is more than managing transient visitors to parks. They suggest that park management focused at maintaining or restoring ecological integrity should also analyze the structure and behaviour of the human communities nested within the landscape that accommodates a national park's ecosystems. This contemplates an additional role for national park managers, one that focuses on understanding the sustainability of community relationships to broader regional landscapes. It also suggests that national park managers forge new partnerships with agencies and government departments not traditionally associated with park management to create new knowledge of and to facilitate within communities learning opportunities for the social, economic, and ecological dimensions of regional sustainability. Using social capital indicator information correlated with ecological and economic indicators, park managers can track the sustainability of the human-nature relationship within a landscape that accommodates a park ecosystem. Tracking social capital as a dimension of national park management can also provide an indication of the effectiveness of park education efforts in enhancing the evolution of community world views and actions that contribute to the integrity of an ecosystem. Facilitating the building of stewardship-oriented social capital in communities can broaden a national park's educational efforts to become community learning opportunities.

Educational efforts focused at teaching citizens about ecosystems are rooted in the Cartesian separation of thought and action and are practised through one-way communication where the citizens are expected to imitate the thoughts of the teacher. An alternative approach is to engage communities in learning forums focused on building capacity in communities. Senge (1999) defines learning capacities as the skills and proficiencies that enable people to constantly enhance their ability to produce results important to them. Learning requires (1) the capability to orient both individually and collectively toward creating desired outcomes; (2) the ability to converse in ways that nurture reflection and inquiry and build networks of shared understanding; and (3) the capacity to see patterns of interdependencies underlying problems. Senge (1999) reminds us that people learn what they want to learn, and that that learning takes time.

Action research, a participatory means of creating understanding and change within social systems, is suggested as a new ecological integrity tool for national park managers. Through its rigorous process of taking action, recording, and reflecting, action research can engage national parks in a new form of relationship with Canadians.

References
Coleman, J. 2000. "Social Capital in the Creation of Human Capital." In E. Lesser, ed., *Knowledge and Social Capital: Foundations and Applications*, 17-41. Woburn, MA: Butterworth-Heinemann.

Endter-Wada, J.L., D. Blahna, R. Krannich, and M. Brunson. 1998. "A Framework for Understanding Social Science Contributions to Ecosystem Management." *Ecological Applications* 8(3): 891-904.

Fukuyama, F. 1995. *Trust: The Social Virtue and the Creation of Prosperity*. New York: The Free Press.

Grumbine, R.E. 1994. "What is Ecosystem Management?" *Conservation Biology* 8(1): 27-38.

Gunderson, C.S., and L.H. Holling. 2002. *Panarchy: Understanding Transformations in Human and Natural Systems*. Washington, DC: Island Press.

Machlis, G., J.E. Force, and W.R. Burch Jr. 1995. *The Human Ecosystem as an Organizing Concept in Ecosystem Management*. (Draft review) Moscow, ID: US National Park Service and University of Idaho.

Putnam, R. 1995. "Bowling Alone: America's Declining Social Capital." *Journal of Democracy* 6(1): 65-78.

Senge, P. 1999. *The Dance of Change*. New York: Doubleday, Currency.

Sparkes, J. 2002. "Social Capital as a Means of Maintaining and Restoring Ecological Integrity in National Park Ecosystems." MA thesis, Royal Roads University, Victoria, BC.

Steiner, F. 2002. *Human Ecology: Following Nature's Lead*. Washington, DC: Island Press.

Wackernagel, M., and W. Rees. 1996. *Our Ecological Footprint: Reducing Human Impact on the Earth*. Gabriola Island, BC: New Society.

Yaffee, S. 1999. "The Three faces of Ecosystem Management." *Conservation Biology* 13(4): 713-25.

Zeichner, K. 2001. "Educational Action Research." In D.J. Greenwood and M. Levin, eds., *Introduction to Action Research: Social Research for Social Change*. Thousand Oaks, CA: Sage.

12
Values, Social Acceptability, and Social Capital: The Canadian Nuclear Waste Disposal Case
Grant Sheng

Jenny Onyx, in the Introduction, states that the two themes addressed in this book are (1) collective action (or at least its potential) as a necessary ingredient for the building of social capital and realization of community sustainability, and (2) an exploration of what "goes wrong in the mobilization of collective action." In this regard, she distinguishes between two types of "disconnections" – those that prevent the reconciliation of the three imperatives (the ecological, the social, and the human), and those that occur between the local or micro-level and the global or macro-level of operation. This latter type is the main focus of this book and is manifest as, according to Onyx, "a recurring tension between the interests and needs of the small community and national agendas, between the discourse of the parochial and the discourse of big science." An excellent example of this is the siting of hazardous-material disposal facilities (e.g., chemical and nuclear waste disposal, incinerators, landfills). This chapter illustrates the second theme through a case study involving the process used to evaluate the Canadian High-Level Nuclear Waste Disposal Concept.

Experience over the last thirty years or so has clearly shown that the affected public wills no longer play a passive role in such endeavours. No number of information sessions and educational programs given by the proponent, nor town hall meetings and public hearings held under the auspices of government agencies or relevant authorities is sufficient to convince the public that the right choice is being made. People perceive information in such forums as flowing one-way: from proponent and/or government to the public, with the latter having little or no meaningful input into the process. Despite the opportunities offered by question-and-answer periods during information sessions or through written and oral presentations during public hearings, individuals do not clearly see how their views and values are taken into account in the decision-making process and eventually reflected in the outcome.

One major problem, if not the root cause, of the pervasive mutual discontent is the inadequacy of existing mechanisms in addressing individual and local community needs. Whereas information sessions and public hearings are set up primarily to provide and debate "facts," the input from individuals of the general public is almost always about interests and values intrinsically tied to their sense of moral right and wrong. Such feelings are often manifested through expressions of concern about health, safety, integrity of the local environment, and social issues related to the community. In a facts-dominated forum, however, the currency of weight is scientific information based on quantitative data, measurements, and expert testimonies. In the face of such a barrage of facts provided by government scientific staff, proponents' experts, hired consultants, and so on, individuals' expressions of concern, backed by nothing more than declaratory force, are often trumped or discounted. It is, therefore, not surprising that members of the general public feel that their participation in such processes is frustrating and not meaningful, with very little influence on the outcome.

The following case study addresses these issues and illustrates Onyx's point regarding the tension between the interests and needs of the small community versus the national agendas, and between the discourse of the parochial and the discourse of big science.

Background to the Canadian Nuclear Waste Disposal Concept

In 1978, the Canadian Nuclear Fuel Waste Management Program (CNFWMP) was established, with Atomic Energy of Canada Ltd. (AECL) as the lead agency to conduct scientific and technical research pertaining to the disposal of high-level nuclear waste (irradiated fuel from CANDU reactors). The international consensus of countries using nuclear power favours burying such waste in stable terrestrial geologic formations (NEA, IAEA 1991). The Canadian concept proposes disposal in an underground vault situated 500 metres to 1,000 metres deep in the granite rocks of the Canadian Shield. This research and development program was divided into three phases: (1) concept assessment, (2) site selection and, (3) facility construction. The first, concept assessment, involves research to determine whether, and to what extent, waste disposal in the granite rocks of the Canadian Shield can be achieved in terms of the stated objective of ensuring human safety and environmental protection. Formally initiated in 1981, this phase ended in 1998 after a national evaluation of AECL's CAN$500 million generic research and development program presented in the form of an environmental impact statement (EIS).

The second phase, site selection, would involve the actual process of screening, evaluating, and finally selecting a suitable site. Both the federal and

Ontario governments decided that actual site selection should not begin until the public had reviewed the disposal concept and the governments had deemed it acceptable (Canada/Ontario, 1978).

In 1988, the federal minister of Energy, Mines and Resources ordered a public review of the disposal concept under the federal Environmental Assessment and Review Process (EARP). In consultation with the provincial governments of the three nuclear-power-generating provinces (New Brunswick, Ontario, and Quebec) and nongovernmental organizations, the federal government developed the terms of reference for the review, including establishing an environmental assessment (EA) panel to hold national public hearings (Sheng, Ladanyi, and Shemilt 1993; Kuhn 1999). The mandate given to the panel included examination of the social and economic aspects of disposal, in addition to the original scientific and technical mandate given to AECL. The panel held scoping meetings in order to develop guidelines to assist AECL in preparing its EIS. After releasing draft guidelines, the panel issued the final guidelines in March 1992. AELC submitted its EIS in October 1994. The disposal concept, its evaluation process including public participation matters, particulars of the EIS documents, and some technical aspects of the R and D program are described in detail in Sheng, Ladanyi, and Shemilt (1993).

In March 1996, the panel held three phases of public hearings as part of the national process to evaluate the acceptability of the proposed disposal concept. The panel described the rationale of these public hearings as the following:

> Phase I focused on broad societal issues related to long-term management of nuclear fuel wastes in general ... Phase II focused on the safety of the AECL concept of geological disposal of nuclear fuel wastes from a scientific and engineering viewpoint. Community hearings during Phase III were the final opportunity in this process [i.e., the review of the disposal concept] for members of the public to voice their opinions on the safety and acceptability of the proposed concept. (CEAP 1998, 7)

The panel released its final report in 1998 and concluded that,

> from a technical perspective, safety of the AECL concept has been on balance adequately demonstrated for a conceptual stage of development, but from a social perspective, it has not ... As it stands, the AECL concept for deep geological disposal has not been demonstrated to have broad public support. The concept in its current form does not have the required level of acceptability to be adopted as Canada's approach for managing nuclear fuel wastes. (CEAP 1998)

The panel stated that much more work was needed on the social aspects of the disposal concept before the site selection process should proceed and suggested a four-phase plan for building and determining concept acceptability (CEAP 1998). The federal government concurred with the panel's recommendation that site selection not proceed without further work (Canada 1998), resulting in the CNFWMP being in abeyance for several years. On 15 November 2002, the federal government passed legislation, Bill C-27, the nuclear fuel waste act (Canada 2001), which initiates some of the steps recommended by the panel, including the establishment of a nuclear waste management organization.

The Problem Issue
In the panel's view, public acceptance was not achieved because non-technical aspects of the disposal concept, such as social, political, and ethical concerns, were not adequately addressed in the EIS. There is plenty of evidence to support this view. I point out below certain aspects in the EIS documentation, which I regard and which many others voiced during the hearings as failings regarding the proposed siting process:

1 The general framework for the siting strategy is imposed without the public having an opportunity to discuss the overall approach.
2 The initial siting process (i.e., site screening) starts with pre-defined candidate regions without public input.
3 Initial public involvement consists of informing inhabitants of a region of the plan to seek a site, followed by more two-way communication only with potential host communities. The focus here is really local rather than regional. Consequently, region-wide impacts are not addressed.
4 At the community level, the emphasis on the interaction is directed at negotiations to determine conditions required by potential host communities for their continued involvement in the process. Other affected communities and residents (e.g., those along potential transportation corridors, nearby First Nations) are excluded.
5 The participatory process as envisioned does not easily accommodate a collaborative process of multi-party dialogue wherein vastly different views and perspectives that form a wide range of stakeholders can be discussed and addressed. An example is the consideration and incorporation of the philosophy and views held by First Nations about land resources, and obligations to future generations.

Although the disposal concept may have been rejected on the basis of the substantives, such as those dealing with site selection matters outlined above, there is an equally likely possibility that the public's perception of the inadequacies of the evaluation process itself was a major contributing factor to the rejection. I submit that the concept evaluation process itself was flawed because it was not a framework designed appropriately to address the social acceptability by the public. As Murphy and Kuhn (1999, 2001) cogently argued, the process was fundamentally flawed because, in no small part, the mandate given to the EA panel at the outset explicitly excluded debate on the merits of nuclear power in Canada. For many, these discussion boundaries specifically prevented them from voicing their ethical concerns about the continued generation of nuclear waste. To address their concerns fully and adequately, they would have needed to discuss the necessity of nuclear power itself. Such concerns are associated with their fundamental values. Not surprisingly, a process that fails to address the core values people hold would be seen as inadequate and even illegitimate.

Thus, an important question arises: was the disposal concept rejected on the basis of inadequacies in the substantives, or on the basis of flaws in the evaluation process itself, or as is most likely the case, because the public perceived that both were flawed and inadequate? An unambiguous answer to this question is critical because it informs us where Canada should focus its future efforts. A detailed analysis of the issues associated with the substantives is beyond the scope of this chapter. Rather, I focus my discussion below on the important role of values in the public-hearing process.

The Need to Incorporate the Public's Values

The public hearing process employed to assess the public acceptability of the disposal concept was a facts-dominated forum. The framework in such a forum is designed to elicit pertinent information, verify the information presented, and identify and resolve areas of contention, with the ultimate goal of making a factual determination. Consequently, information based on quantitative data and expert testimony is regarded as the most compelling types of evidence in making such a determination. While facts-dominated forums are well suited to resolving disagreements about what happened or what will happen, these forums are not suitable to address all types of issues. In particular, I submit that facts-dominated forums are inadequate as the only type of mechanism to address normative questions, such as what should be done in a particular situation.

Analyses of the hearing proceedings led us to conclude that the nuclear fuel waste disposal issue in Canada is primarily a value-based conflict. I use the term "value-based conflict" to describe situations in which the disagreement of opinions arises primarily as a result of differences in people's core beliefs, as opposed to disagreements arising out of differences in interpretation of information or in perceptions of institutional competence (Renn, Webler, and Wiedemann 1995). Our characterization of this debate as a value-based conflict is supported by the fact that numerous groups that participated in the hearings and that were provided with the same information, and having the same beliefs in the various institutional competencies, arrived at contradictory evaluations of the disposal concept.

Employing a facts-dominated forum, as were the public hearings, to address a value-based conflict has negative repercussions for both members of the public and decision makers. For the former, a facts-dominated forum forces or, at the very least, exerts significant pressure on members of the public to "translate" their value-based concerns and interests into "statements of facts" in an attempt to be heard. In many cases, this translation results in members of the lay public expressing factually incorrect statements because of their lack of technical expertise. Compounding such mistakes in the public hearings on the disposal concept, verbal presentations and written submissions were often characterized by poor organization and delivery of material, unsubstantiated assertions of facts, passionate ramblings, and even outbursts of anger directed at panel members. The unfortunate outcome of these proceedings was that such testimonies and views presented by the public were often politely (and sometimes impolitely) dismissed or discounted. This is most unfortunate since the principle merit of a public participation process is to identify the interests and concerns held by the public.

This unfortunate situation arises because we confound the two very different goals of facts and technical-information gathering with identification of the sentiments of the public. The first goal informs us as to what is the right thing to do, while the second, just as importantly, informs us as to what is the socially acceptable thing to do. By discounting or dismissing the views of the lay public because the contributions are not scientific, not factually based, or otherwise do not conform to our preconceived notion of the relative value of different types of information, we undermine the very purpose of holding public hearings. The information provided by the public, no matter how disorganized, rambling, or factually off base, is information that speaks directly to the critical issue of whether something would be acceptable. Moreover, its expression is underpinned by the core values that people hold. Failing to take into account such information and ignoring the values at play is to guarantee failure. Since values lie at the heart of the nuclear fuel waste management debate, it is essential to address values directly through a value-base forum in assessing the acceptability of a proposed disposal plan.

The need to assess values in determining the acceptability of a proposal has been identified by Hansis (1995) in the context of another value-based conflict. Hansis suggested that values needed to be assessed in determining the acceptability of a proposed logging strategy in the Northwest Pacific region of the United States. He defined assessing acceptability as the process by which people determine how a proposed solution aligns with their values and how effectively the solution solves the problem as defined by members of the public. To determine the public acceptability of a proposal, these individual evaluations must be aggregated to reflect the evaluations of the group as a whole.

Adopting this definition, there are at least two important reasons to examine people's values in assessing the acceptability of the disposal concept. First, the extent to which the concept aligns with a particular individual's values cannot be assessed without comparing them. Second, a person's definition of the issues that nuclear fuel waste disposal poses depends on what values the individual sees at play. Thus, the extent to which the proposed concept represents a solution to safe disposal is ultimately related to an individual's values. More broadly, I contend that public participation processes used to determine the acceptability of a proposal by members of the public should ultimately involve an analysis of both individual and collective values. Elicitation of values is a prerequisite for an analysis of values. Consequently, such a process, whether it is called a public hearing or something else, should be structured for value elicitation and evaluation and not simply be a forum for the presentation and verification of facts.

To its credit, the EA panel recognized the need to examine values in assessing public acceptability. However, it also acknowledged that "an appropriate process for determining the acceptability of the AECL concept has not yet been developed" (CEAP 1998, 41). While there seems to be a small but growing awareness and recognition of the role of values in complex decision making (e.g., Sheng et al. 2001), there is lack of understanding as to how to incorporate values into decision-making processes generally and into acceptability assessments more specifically (Fortier, Collins, and Sheng 2001).

I describe below a framework with which to evaluate social acceptability, including enunciation of certain basic principles and a seven-phase value elicitation process.

Framework for Assessing Public Acceptability

The Principles of Effectiveness, Transparency, and Fairness
A framework for assessing public acceptability of the disposal concept must itself be socially acceptable. And it must be predicated, at least, on the principles of effectiveness, transparency, and fairness.

An effective process, by definition, is one in which it does what it purports to do. Although it seems an obvious assertion, its ramifications are quite far reaching when applied to a complex phenomenon. In the context of a value-based conflict, I define an effective process as one that successfully identifies all the values, their roles, and their interplay in the conflict. In our experience, current public participation processes examine the facts of an issue rather than the values or value systems that underpin those opinions and perspectives. Since it is unlikely that a facts-dominated forum will be effective in addressing value-based conflicts, it is important first to identify accurately the nature of the dispute and then formulate a process accordingly. The design and implementation of such an effective process requires mechanisms that can gauge and aggregate issues, concepts, and matters of importance to the public.

I define a transparent process as one in which all participants have unfettered access to all relevant information, all steps involved in the larger decision-making process are clearly stated, the role of each participant within the process is clearly articulated, and there is a means for participants to see how their participation contributed to the final decision. In addition, both the implementation of the process as well as its evolution must be open to public scrutiny. Since fairness cannot be effectively assessed without transparency, adherence to this principle is a precondition for the next.

For a process to be fair, it must be so both in fact and in perception. If the public does not perceive the process as being fair, they are unlikely to participate in a meaningful manner, and they will not consider the results of such a process legitimate. Since fairness is a subjective, context-specific evaluation, what one person regards as fair may not be what another person regards as fair. In our view, a process that successfully incorporates the principle of fairness within its framework is one where even though the parties may disagree with the final outcome of the decision, the majority would at least agree that the process gave due consideration to all views and perspectives presented. Furthermore, the value-elicitation process must be incorporated effectively into the larger decision-making process for the value-elicitation process to be perceived as fair.

An important consideration in assessing fairness is the application of power. The decision maker must not have, or be perceived to have, unbridled control over the process or its outcome. It also means that members of the public must be given a voice as to the manner in which they are participating in the process and, thus, contributing to the decision-making process.

Based on these principles of effectiveness, transparency, and fairness, I propose the following seven-phase value-elicitation process as a way to assess the public acceptability of Canada's nuclear fuel waste concept. Figure 12.1 illustrates this process.

Seven-Phase Value Elicitation Process

Phase I: Initial Information Dissemination
Before the assessment process begins, information pertaining to the disposal concept, as well as to the process itself, should be disseminated to

Figure 12.1

Seven-phase value elicitation process

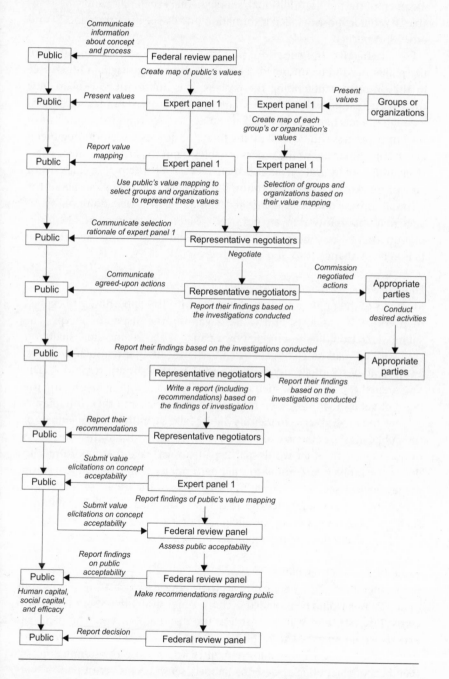

members of the public. This information should be provided as a background package of reasonable length in language that is understandable to members of the public. Additional, supplementary materials should be available to provide more detailed information on all aspects of the concept and process as needed.

For an effective and successful process to be implemented, members of the public need to be informed about both the process itself and their role in the process. In describing the process, it is important to explain how their participation will be incorporated into the decision-making process through the mechanisms of value elicitation, as well as how the outcome of the entire process will be used by the final decision maker. Informing members of the public about the process enables them to participate more effectively individually and encourages higher levels of participation collectively. One of the advantages of informing the broadest public possible about the disposal concept and assessment process is that it provides additional assurance that important values are not overlooked in the assessment. The information about the concept and process should be presented in a neutral manner to enhance trust and credibility.

Phase II: Value Elicitation and Mapping

Members of the public should be provided with the opportunity to express their concerns, interests, and values regarding the disposal concept. The submissions would be interpreted by a panel of experts in value elicitation (VE) with a broad range of expertise in relevant disciplines, such as ethics, anthropology, sociology, psychology, and alternative dispute resolution. The VE panel of experts would then create a collective mapping identifying the types of values involved, their roles, their frequency, and their interplay.

Since the process seeks to identify values held by individuals, members of the public must be able to express themselves freely without the constraints of boundaries. In other words, participants must have the opportunity to define the problem according to their perceptions of the nuclear fuel waste management issues. It is crucial that members of the public be allowed to self-delineate the boundaries of the issues as they perceive them. Without such freedom, the results of the elicitation process may be altered such that it forms an inaccurate mapping of the public's aggregate values.

Phase III: Value Representation

Before members of the public present their values, participating groups and organizations would be provided with the opportunity to present their concerns, interests, and values regarding the disposal concept. The panel of experts would analyze and record the values presented by each group and organization. The panel would then, after interpreting the submissions of members of the public as described above, select a number of parties that best represent the values of the public as expressed through the collective value mapping. Since representation encompasses the types of values, their roles, their frequencies, and their interplay, the criteria for the selection of "representative parties" would take all four of these factors into account. Regardless of the format to select the parties, a rationale for the choices would be made public so as to adhere to the principle of transparency.

Phase IV: Negotiations
The representative parties would determine what must be examined in order for members of the public to assess the disposal concept. More specifically, the goal is to agree on actions to be undertaken in order to examine how particular values may be impacted by the concept. The parties would set the boundaries of the negotiations. In accordance with the principles of effectiveness and fairness, the EA panel would select a neutral intermediary to facilitate these negotiations. In addition, the panel would set deadlines for the negotiations such that sufficient time is provided to achieve a meaningful agreement without countenancing excessive delays or filibustering.

Since each party represents a segment of the public's values, each party has legitimacy and decision-making authority to negotiate to the extent that they act in a manner consistent with the values they represent. Ultimately, the groups' and organizations' credibility is on the line for the actions taken in the negotiations, which would be publicized to further increase accountability, as well as keep members of the public informed. Thus, the individuals who participate in the negotiations must have decision-making authority for their particular group or organization.

Phase V: Undertaking Negotiated Actions
Once the representative parties come to an agreement on what needs to be done to assess the disposal concept, the parties would implement these actions. Since these actions are the product of negotiations with self-delineated boundaries, the agreed-upon undertakings could be almost anything. At least a portion of the undertakings is likely to be a form of joint fact finding. To facilitate an effective, transparent, and fair process, a rationale for the negotiated actions would accompany a description of what was undertaken and the results of its implementation, which would be made readily available to the public in an accessible form. Once all the agreed-upon results are collected, the parties would write an assessment regarding the findings of the undertakings. Parties would have the option of writing individual or collective assessments, which would be made readily available for public scrutiny, as well as being submitted to the EA panel. If a consensus or even a partial consensus is reached, it would exert a stronger influence on the panel's decision.

Phase VI: Public Participation through Value Elicitation
Having been provided with information about the potential impacts on particular values, subsequent and separate value elicitation hearings would be undertaken specifically to hear members of the public express their opinions and concerns. These public hearings would provide a forum for the lay public to assess the disposal concept, as well as the process that was undertaken to examine it. Public participation would, once again, emphasize value elicitation in order to avoid contorting a predominantly values-based debate into a facts-based presentation. The value-elicitation mechanisms would provide the information necessary to determine how the concept aligns with the values of members of the public and the extent to which the concept resolves the nuclear fuel waste management issue as defined by members of the public. The value-elicitation experts would submit a report on the concept based on their analysis of the public's values to the EA panel, as well as make this report available to the public.

Phase VII: Input by EA Panel to Decision Maker
Ultimately, the EA panel would submit its recommendation to the decision maker. The EA panel would have explicit material on the disposal concept and would describe in detail the rationale for its recommendation.

The influence of the recommendations is likely to be significantly greater because of the political power attached to the product of a more effective, transparent, and fair assessment process. In most cases, decision makers will examine more than one source of information in their deliberations and, ultimately, weigh different sources accordingly. To foster meaningful public participation in the decision-making process, it is important that the product of the value-elicitation process receive significant weight from the final decision maker. Furthermore, if the final decision maker concludes that the issue is not resolved, this detailed analysis would provide a starting point for modifying an existing proposal or designing a new solution.

Although the preceding discussion has focused on the design of an assessment process regarding the public acceptability of the concept, the underlying procedural concepts of this process are transferable to other public value-based forums. The procedural concepts in phase I to phase V create an elaborate fact-finding mechanism that informs how a proposed solution may impact interests of members of the public. The procedural concept in phase VI provides an example of a new value-based approach to public hearings. Likewise, the procedural concept in phase VII provides an example of how one might link a public participation process into the larger decision-making process. In summary, these procedural concepts provide a method for incorporating many people's values relating to a particular issue into the decision-making process, and for increasing transparency, as well as enabling members of the public to assess the fairness and effectiveness of a value elicitation process.

The implementation of such concepts is more likely to result in an acceptable process, both as perceived by members of the public and as one that more accurately reflects the values of the public. Although a socially acceptable process is a prerequisite for reaching an acceptable solution, I recognize that an acceptable process does not guarantee such a solution.

Human Capital, Social Capital, and the Efficacy Gap

Our analysis is based on the public hearing process forming part of a national evaluation of the acceptability of Canada's High-Level Nuclear Waste Disposal Concept. Although I identified several possible key factors as to why the concept did not garner broad public support (inadequacies within the concept itself; flaws in the evaluation process; failure to take into account explicitly people's values), there are undoubtedly equally valid explanations in a broader context. More specifically, the decline of trust in government institutions and a widening of efficacy gap associated with the notions of human capital and social capital can be put forth as deeper underlying reasons.

The efficacy gap refers to that gap between external efficacy – how responsive citizens believe the political system is to their demands – and internal efficacy – the subjective competence associated with the degree of influence an individual citizen feels he or she has on the political process (Nevitte 2000, 86). Kanji (1999) refers to this citizen competence as human capital – a cluster of attributes including greater knowledge, more awareness of and interest in the political landscape, and a more critical approach to acceptance of political information and leadership. Based on analysis of Canadian Election Study data gathered since 1965, Kanji shows that Canadians are increasingly likely to believe that the government doesn't care much about what "people like me" think and that elected officials soon lose touch with the people. This low confidence in government institutions and mistrust of politicians contrasts with people's sense of their own increased political competence, thus creating the efficacy gap, which has widened sharply since 1988 (Kanji 1999; Dogan 1997).

Putnam (1995b) holds that civic engagement is a prerequisite for building social capital, which, in turn, is an essential ingredient for effective functioning of governments. While the level of social capital is related to the strength of interpersonal trust, democratic governance is more related to people's trust in government and confidence in political institutions. Putnam's view of the civil society/social capital dynamic has empirical support from Young's (1999) analysis of individual-level data from the 1999 Alberta Civil Society Survey, in which she develops three types of engagement: civic, professional (involvement in union, professional, or business organizations), and political (membership in political parties or political action groups). Young's analysis shows that civic engagement is a strong predictor of personal trust – people who are active in the community are more likely to have high levels of interpersonal trust. An interesting finding is that although interpersonal trust is also correlated with trust in government and political institutions, civic engagement is not. Furthermore, her data show that political activism is positively related to distrust in government.

Roese (1999, 42) provides a possible explanation for these findings when he stresses the "value of healthy skepticism born of increasing individual cognitive sophistication." His view that the increasing skepticism toward government may be associated with the public's increased sophistication in political engagement is consistent with the efficacy gap hypothesis.

Structural Transformations and Value Shifts

Nevitte (2000) provides empirical evidence and compelling argument that this schism between Canadians and their government is due to value shifts of citizens and structural changes in society over the last forty to fifty years. Structural changes that paved the ground for value shifts include:

1 dramatic increases in wealth over the last fifty years due to economic expansion
2 a shift in economic expansion from the industrial sector in the post-war years to the present expansion in the tertiary sector; the vast majority of people in this "advanced industrial" economy do work very different from that of previous generations
3 dramatic expansion of access to post-secondary education, resulting in rapid expansion of the middle classes and greater occupational and geographic mobility
4 greater transformations in communications and information technologies, resulting in rapid decreases in cost for information access and rapid access of information by the global community at an unprecedented scale
5 ever-broadening availability of modern modes of transportation by the global community, resulting in virtually unlimited access to anywhere in the world.

Nevitte (2000) contends that the institutions of democratic governance, initially borne of the industrial era, now operate in a vastly different environment because of these dramatic structural transformations. These transformations that are rapidly reshaping our society and economy must also be having an impact on the political dynamics of how citizens are relating to the state. One manifestation of such impact is that citizen's values, their skills, and expectations they have of governments underwent changes together with these structural shifts. Nevitte cites Inglehart (1997) to support how value change is linked with the emergence of late advanced industrialism. Economic security created by advanced industrial society inevitably changes the goal orientation of citizens – from a primary concern about economic and materialistic matters to one in which self-expression, freedom, and the quality of life become increasingly the focus. Other authors support this view. For instance, Bell (1973) characterizes the value shift associated with the transition to advanced industrialism as the increased salience of individual autonomy. Ignazi (1992) sees the transition as a shift away from solidarity towards self-affirmation. Still others associate it with the emergence of individualization (Ester, Halman, and de Moor 1993) or focus on the rise of self-expression (Inglehart 1997).

A widely accepted definition of social capital is one provided by Putnam et al. (1993, 167): "Those features of social organization, such as trust, norms, and networks[,] that can improve the efficiency of society by facilitating coordinated actions." Other analysts have also emphasized the centrality of the two factors of trust and social networks (e.g., Portes 1998; Fukuyama 1995; Misztal 1996). Thus, if the foregoing analysis were accepted, it could be said that the failure of the CNFWMP to garner broad public support can be attributed to the lack of one of the essential ingredients of social capital – namely trust.

Social Networks

What of the other essential ingredient – social networks? Here we have an interesting dichotomy. By and large, the general public was not even aware of the existence of the CNFWMP until announcement of national public hearings to evaluate the program. In sharp contrast, there was acute awareness and even coordination among industry stakeholder organizations, such as those represented by the Canadian Nuclear Association, and professional and learned societies such as the Royal Society of Canada, Academy of Engineering, Canadian Biological Federation, Geological Association of Canada, Chemical Institute of Canada, Canadian Association of Physicists, and Canadian Information Processing Society. Many of these organizations were involved since, or soon after, the inception of the CNFWMP. Of particular note, the scientific and engineering organizations named above were represented through membership on TAC, the Technical Advisory Committee (Sheng, Ladanyi, and Shemilt 1993), which reviewed and advised on the program on a continual basis from 1979 to 1997. TAC, its members, and the organizations they were affiliated with did much to facilitate coordinated actions to raise awareness and ensure rigorous review of the program. TAC even published public annual reports providing results of its reviews, partly in order to engage the public (e.g., TAC 1995). However, the impact of these activities was, by and large, limited to the scientific and technical communities nationally and internationally.

It is fair to say that no corresponding social network ever developed at the public, community, or grassroots level. Some such groups did emerge, but mostly just before or during the public hearings and, not surprisingly, were constituted specifically to oppose the disposal concept. This was in sharp contrast to the industry stakeholder groups, professional organizations, and learned societies, many of which worked with each other on an ongoing basis, with the vast majority supporting the disposal concept.

Conclusions

This chapter provides an explanation, cast in a social capital framework, with which to understand the outcome from Canada's nuclear waste disposal evaluation process. It is sobering to note that the CNFWMP, a twenty-year R and D program costing over CAN$500 million, and one of the largest technical endeavours ever undertaken in Canada, was rejected not on the basis of technological merit but ostensibly on the basis that it did not have broad public support. Although this chapter makes a distinction as to whether the reason was because of the disposal concept itself, or the process used to evaluate it, or most likely both, the point is that social acceptability was the critical issue. It is difficult not to at least entertain the strong possibility that citizens' values played a crucial role in the outcome. Just as other government projects and institutions are the targets for citizens' discontent in the current social landscape of value shifts, the CNFWMP, by its intrinsically controversial nature, stood as the shining example of all that is perceived as big technology and big government. The CNFWMP lacked two essential ingredients of social capital: trust and social networks.

Since values lie at the heart of the nuclear fuel waste management issue, I contend that it is essential to address values directly in a value-based forum in assessing the acceptability of any future proposed solution, especially in relation to the siting of a disposal facility. The proposed seven-phase value elicitation mechanism and its formal incorporation into a hearing process as part of an EA process can be seen as a way of gaining public trust and serve as a catalyst for developing social networks.

The interesting question is, had a social network formed involving communities and the general public, would the disposal concept have gained social acceptance? Even more importantly, would even the achievement of both public trust and social network formation be enough to confer social acceptance of future proposals? Given the extreme controversial nature of the subject matter, this is a most difficult question to answer. However, had such a network existed, the nature of discourse and debate would certainly have been on a more focused and informed level. This would have been a much more productive outcome for at least two reasons. First, the values held by the citizenry would have been made explicit, and clearly articulated, rather than having to be inferred, as was the case. Second, rather than simply being critical of the disposal concept, a social network might have fostered a climate of constructive criticism in which the general citizenry contributed productively to addressing, clarifying, and distinguishing between real and perceived problems and inadequacies.

As for the future, it is essential that people's values be explicitly taken into account through a formalized process. This should constitute an integral part of a comprehensive social capital building process within the general citizenry. Although there is no guarantee that this would produce the desired outcome, at least all involved would feel that they have been heard and that the process is fair.

Acknowledgments

I wish to acknowledge the important contributions of two former students, Michael Fortier and Allison Collins, in the development of this chapter. The seven-step value elicitation process is based on M. Fortier's master's thesis done under my supervision (2001). Some other material in the chapter stem from three conference proceedings coauthored with them. I thank Ann Dale and Isabel Cordua-von Specht for their encouragement and guidance throughout the preparation of this chapter. I also express deep appreciation for the support of the Office of Research at Royal Roads University while on sabbatical leave from York University, and especially to its director, Mary Bernard, and her staff, Colleen Hoppins and Sonja Persaud. This work was supported under a NSERC Standard Research Grant to the author.

References

Bell, Daniel. 1973. *The Coming of Post-Industrial Society,* 148-49. New York: Basic Books.

Canada. 1998. *Government of Canada Response to the Report of the Nuclear Fuel Waste Management and Disposal Concept Environmental Assessment Panel.* Ottawa: Natural Resources Canada.

–. Ministry of Natural Resources. 2001. *Bill C-27, An Act Respecting the Long-Term Management of Nuclear Fuel Waste.* 1st Sess., 37th Parl.

Canada/Ontario. 1978. *Joint Agreement by the Minister of Energy, Mines, and Resources Canada and the Ontario Minister of Energy.* Ottawa: Supply and Services Canada.

Canadian Environmental Assessment Panel (CEAP). 1998. *Nuclear Fuel Waste Management and Disposal Concept: Report of the Nuclear Fuel Waste Management and Disposal Concept Environmental Assessment Panel.* Ottawa: Canadian Environmental Assessment Agency.

Dogan, Mattei. 1997. "Erosion of Confidence in Advanced Democracies." *Studies in Comparative International Development* 32(3): 3-29.

Ester, Peter, L. Halman, and R. de Moor. 1993. "Value Shift in Western Societies." In P. Ester, L. Halman, and R. de Moor, eds., *The Individualizing Society: Value Change in Europe and North America.* Tilburg, The Netherlands: Tilburg University Press.

Fortier, M. 2001. "Evaluating Social Acceptability Frameworks that Assess Canada's Nuclear Fuel Waste Disposal Concept." MA thesis, Faculty of Environmental Studies, York University.

Fortier, M., A. Collins, and G. Sheng. 2001. "Integrating Efficiency, Transparency and Fairness into a Value Elicitation Process." Paper presented at the 2nd VALDOR (Values in Decisions on Risk) Symposium Addressing Transparency in Risk Assessment and Decision Making, 10-14 June, Stockholm.

Fukuyama, F. 1995. *Trust: The Social Virtues and the Creation of Prosperity.* London: Penguin.

Hansis, Richard. 1995. "The Social Acceptability of Clear Cutting in the Pacific Northwest." *Human Organization* 54(1): 95-101.

Ignazi, Pierro. 1992. "The Silent Counter-Revolution: Hypotheses on the Emergence of Extreme Right-Wing Parties in Europe." *European Journal of Political Research* 22: 3-34.

Inglehart, Ronald. 1997. *Modernization and Postmodernization: Cultural, Economic and Political Change in 43 Societies.* Princeton, NJ: Princeton University Press.

Kanji, Mebs. 1999. "Information, Cognitive Mobilization, and Representative Governance." Paper presented at the National Trends Conference, November, Ottawa.

Kuhn, R.G. 1999. "Public Participation in the Hearings on the Canadian Nuclear Fuel Waste Disposal Concept." In J. Sinclair, ed., *Canadian Environmental Assessment in Transition,* 19-49. Waterloo, ON: University of Waterloo Press.

Misztal, B.A. 1996. *Trust in Modern Society.* Cambridge, UK: Polity Press.

Murphy, B.L., and R.G. Kuhn. 1999. "Limitation of the EIA Process for the Assessment of Nuclear Fuel Waste Disposal in Canada." VALDOR (Values in Decisions on Risk); A Symposium in the RISCOM Programme Addressing Transparency in Risk Assessment and Decision Making, p. 279-86. Stockholm, Sweden, 13-17 June.

–. 2001. "Setting the Terms of Reference in Environmental Assessments: Canadian Nuclear Waste Management." *Canadian Public Policy* 27(3): 249-66.

Nuclear Energy Agency, International Atomic Energy Agency. 1991. *Disposal of Radioactive Wastes. Can Long-Term Safety Be Evaluated? A Collective Opinion of the Radioactive Waste Management Committee Advisory Committee, International Atomic Energy Agency.* Paris: OECD Nuclear Energy Agency.

Nevitte, N. 2000. "Value Change and Reorientations in Citizen-State Relationships." *Canadian Public Policy* 26 (Supplement 2): 80-94.

Portes, Alejandro. 1998. "Social Capital: Its Origins and Applications in Modern Sociology." *Annual Review of Sociology* 22: 1-24.

Putnam, R. 1995a. "Bowling Alone: America's Declining Social Capital." *Journal of Democracy* 6(1): 65-78.

–. 1995b. "Tuning In, Tuning Out: The Strange Disappearance of Social Capital in America." *PS: Political Science and Politics* 28: 664-83.

Putnam, R., R. Leonardi, and R. Nanetti. 1993. *Making Democracy Work: Civic Traditions in Modern Italy.* Princeton, NJ: Princeton University Press.

Renn, O., T. Webler, and P. Wiedemann. 1995. "The Pursuit of Fair and Competent Citizen Participation." In O. Renn, T. Webler, and P. Wiedemann, eds., *Fairness and Competence in Citizen Participation: Evaluating Models for Environmental Discourse.* Dordrecht, The Netherlands: Kluwer Academic Publishers.

Roese, Neil. 1999. "Canadians Shrinking Trust in Government: Causes and Consequences." Paper presented at the National Trends Conference, 15-7 November, Ottawa.

Sheng, G., B. Ladanyi, and L.W. Shemilt. 1993. "Canada's High-Level Nuclear Waste Disposal Concept: The Evaluation Process and a Review of Some Aspects of the Research Work." *Energy Studies Review* 5(3): 165-79.

Sheng, G., K. Yam, J. Sorrell, and A. Hassas. 2001. "Enabling Participatory Decision Making through Web-Based GIS." Paper presented at the International High-Level Radioactive Waste Management Conference, 29 April-3 May, Las Vegas.

Technical Advisory Committee (TAC). 1995. *14th Annual Report of the Technical Advisory Committee on the Nuclear Fuel Waste Management Program.* Report TAC-14. Hamilton, ON: McMaster University.

Young, Lisa. 1999. "Civic Engagement, Trust and Democracy: Evidence from Alberta." Paper presented at the National Trends Conference, 15-17 November, Ottawa.

13
The Challenges of Traditional Models of Governance in the Creation of Social Capital
Tony Boydell

This chapter discusses how traditional command and control models of governance typically fail to support or sustain innovative practices in sustainable community design. One such practice is the design of public space to influence human behaviour, which creates the necessary preconditions through which elements of social capital can emerge. The case of the Bamberton Sustainable Community Design Process is set in the context of governments desiring to control the outcomes yet lacking the institutional capacity to understand both the vision and the means required to achieve it. A shift from the traditional models of governance is necessary to create a broad framework of policy and standards within which local communities are empowered to make decisions.

The Traditional Governance Model

Webster's dictionary defines governance as "the act or process of governing, specifically authoritative direction and control." Despite mounting evidence that this model is increasingly inappropriate in the contemporary community development context, why is it that governments still seem to be firmly wedded to the principles of command and control?

The answer to this question may be found, at least in part, at the root of the sustainability challenge for governments today, a challenge created by three, interrelated elements: structure, public interest, and accountability.

At both federal and provincial levels, planning in one government agency often takes place in splendid isolation from other related agencies. This is a function of the stovepipe structures of governments, presenting significant challenges in the development and implementation of truly integrated programs across social, economic, and environmental envelopes. Agencies are most often held accountable for program- and project-specific outputs (did the road get built?) rather than more holistic outcome criteria (did the road add to the quality of life of the community?). Even the interagency committees that are supposed to achieve integration of program objectives typically engage in a form of outcome negotiation. For the most part, this simply leads to compromised solutions, since it is much more difficult to measure, and develop accountability measures about, the holistic outcome. It is therefore not surprising that, for the most part, agencies prefer to avoid the challenge.

At the local government level, stovepipes also exist, commonly as a set of functional responsibilities, but at this simplified scale that reflects dependency on less than adequate resources. There are often imbalances in the power structures as a function of budget allocation. An engineering department, for example, with its wide array of infrastructure-related responsibilities, will often hold the balance of power in determining the outcomes of cross-sectoral initiatives. As a result, engineering perspectives and priorities will influence an outcome despite the need for a holistic solution.

Governments have traditionally regarded themselves as keepers of the public interest, although in many cases, the interests that are being served are seemingly those of the government rather than the public. This paradigm is beginning to disappear. Individuals, stakeholders, and community groups now expect to have a much more strategic role in the business of government. Progressive governments are responding to this challenge by setting out a broad public policy agenda and then unleashing the power of the private sector and community groups to achieve the policy objectives. In British Columbia in the 1990s, for example, the provincial government applied its consensus-based decision-making philosophy to many of its program initiatives. While this fell well short of functioning within a broadly defined public policy framework, it did open up the business of government to a wide range of stakeholders.

The third element of challenge lies in the degree to which different levels of government hold themselves accountable to the public they serve. Recognition of accountability is, to a large degree, a function of exposure. In other words, the more the decision maker is exposed to those affected by the decision, the more likely it is that their interests will be served. Decision makers in a multi-layered federal bureaucracy are more likely to be insulated from those affected by their decisions than are their counterparts in local government, whose only degree of insulation is the office door. Thus, it is the front line public employees who understand only too well the meaning of accountability as the point of contact with their constituents.

In the senior governments, this absence of an appropriate accountability structure translates into interminable bureaucratic processes, inflexibility, and inability to respond effectively to changing needs and circumstances. At the local government level, it is likely to result in imposed, arbitrary political solutions. In neither case are the needs of the public likely to be met.

The Design of Public Space

In the 1930s and again in the 1950s, a paradigm of architectural design flourished, principally in Europe, which became known as architectural determinism. It embodied the notion that the social behaviour of building users could be influenced, even determined, by the physical environment in which the behaviour occurred. Thus, the paradigm included the notion that architects could direct social behaviour patterns through their work. Determinism was exemplified by the Congrès Internationaux d'Architecture Moderne.

In the 1970s, the focus of attention shifted to quality of life in the urban environment. Appleyard and Lintell (1972), in their study on the environmental quality of city streets, noted in their conclusions that "heavy traffic is associated with much less social interaction and street activity. Conversely, a street with little traffic, and many families, promotes a rich social climate and a strong sense of community." Yancey (1971), writing about the Pruitt-Igoe Housing Project in St. Louis, Missouri, showed that a community based on informal social networks was greatly influenced by physical design.

The "new urbanist" movement of architects and planners has built on the experiences and mistakes of post-war urban planning to focus more on the design of space and livable environments, rather than individual buildings. Andres Duany, through his speech on "the merits of neo-traditionalism" in Boston in 1992, is widely considered to have been the founder of this movement. His basic premise was that in the face of continued deteriorating quality of life in urban America, the result of misguided urban planning, the only solution was the re-creation of the American small town. Many of the problems were attributed to the segregation of functions such that residential housing was physically separated from places of work, which in turn were separated from shopping, schools, recreation facilities, and other services. The net effect of this was to create a dependency on, and proliferation of, the automobile and the sterile infrastructure necessary to support it. It gave rise to the great suburban shopping malls, the "asteroid belts of architectural garbage" as Kunstler (2001) calls them, and the concomitant decline of the inner city core.

The fundamental unit of urban design became the neighbourhood, and the process became known as traditional neighbourhood design (TND). Much emphasis was placed on the design of the public realm, for the most part represented by the street, since its design, in the context of the built environment, became the principal determinant of quality of life. Although Duany was talking about principles of urban design, the underlying message was about the creation of community through the development of opportunities to build social capital:

Planners ... seem to think that a sense of place can be created by a combination of decorative landscaping, exciting architecture, varied pavement textures, elegant street lights, and colorful banners. We think that achieving a sense of place is ... better thought of in terms of space. The designer's chief task is the making of space that draws people out from their private realms to stroll and loiter with their neighbors: public space. (Duany 1992)

The Bamberton Project

Bamberton was designed as a sustainable community, to be built over a period of fifteen to twenty years, ultimately attaining a population of between 10,000 and 12,000 residents. It was located some thirty kilometres north of Victoria, British Columbia, on a partly forested, part former cement plant site of 1,650 acres (668 hectares), overlooking a fiord-like arm of the sea known as Saanich Inlet. It was the vision of David Butterfield, a new urbanist developer, who acquired the necessary land with the financial backing of four major union pension funds.

In all ways the antithesis of the post-war North American model of suburban sprawl, the community design incorporated a mix of housing types that were built close to narrow streets, on small lots. The mixed-use concept resulted in the creation of a series of neighbourhoods, each offering a blend of residential and commercial sites, as well as employment opportunities. The neighbourhoods were located as satellite communities to the town centre, and insistence on a human-scale approach influenced the location of all amenities within comfortable walking distance, limited the footprint and height of buildings, and created opportunities to forego the use of the automobile within the community.

As the design took shape through the contributions of leading innovators in their fields from all over North America, so it began to become clear that government – local, provincial, and federal – appeared to lack both the institutional capacity and the understanding necessary to support the process. Indeed, one might argue that government was primarily interested in ensuring that the appropriate controls were in place through law, regulation, and doing things by the book.

Nevertheless, the project was receiving considerable national and international attention. It was chosen as one of two launch projects at the Globe international conference in Vancouver in March 1992, and the design team appeared at both the third World Urban Forum in Curitiba, Brazil, and at the Earth Summit in Rio de Janeiro later that year. The concept won awards from The Body Shop, the Prince Charles Society for Social Innovation, and the American Institute of Architects.

Locally, it was a different story. Ineptitude and apathy on the part of the provincial government, and lack of capacity in the local government, all contributed to effectively stalling the necessary approvals. Despite some three hundred hours of local community consultations with a wide variety of interest groups, a small but well organized and highly vocal opposition was able to manipulate the media, spread misinformation about the project, and create a general sense of apprehension and uncertainty in the minds of government and community alike.

The Vision, the Process (April 1992)

The planning process began in 1991 by taking a vision to the local community and asking what they would wish to see if Bamberton were to be built. People said they wanted to preserve the Saanich Inlet, maintain as much natural vegetation as possible, create a livable community, and create a local economy. From these suggestions and ideas that were the reflection of community values, principles were developed to guide the way in which this sustainable community would be planned.

These principles, the development of which was the second step in the sustainable community planning process (see Figure 13.1), determined the entire evolution of community design in the framework supplied by the basic building blocks of sustainability: ecological limitations, social equity, and economic viability.

Each building block in the model contains examples of elements of sustainable community design, but they are by no means exhaustive. The blocks

Figure 13.1

Sustainable community planning process

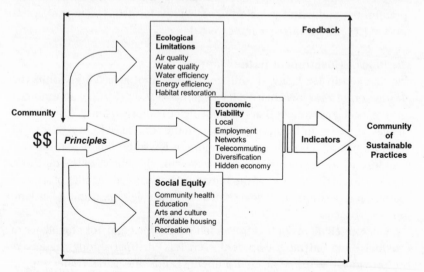

Source: A.N. Boydell (1994). Based on original concept for the Sustainable Communities Theme Paper, BC Round Table on the Environment and the Economy, 1991.

overlap to show that both they and their many elements are highly inter-related. Their positioning underscores the importance attached to using social equity and ecological limitations to shape the framework within which economic activity may occur.

Every task associated with each of the community development processes had to be devised and carried out according to the principles and frame-work created by the building blocks.

So how did the three building blocks of sustainability apply to the out-comes of the community planning process? The ecological limitations (rules based on acceptable environmental quality criteria) were to be enforced through the zoning bylaw, the registered building scheme (through the use of restrictive covenants), and the licenses and permits issued by provincial government regulatory agencies.

The opportunities to maximize the quality of life (social equity) were to be found in the registered building scheme (e.g., friendly, pedestrian-oriented streets, opportunities to shop, meet people, or recreate within a few minutes of home, affordable housing), and in the official community plan with the provision of parks and other green spaces, schools, public meeting places, fire protection, health care, and other essential services.

The goal of creating a viable (diversified) local economy gave rise to a comprehensive planning and advertising process to attract home-based businesses, telecommuting, and cottage and service industries, as well as to establish an environmental technologies park. The process of designing and building a sustainable community does not assume self-sufficiency as an end goal. For the community to be sustaining, it must interact with other communities and with the region in which it is located. The flow of goods and services is both internal and external.

The Role of Government in the Planning Process

The Bamberton lands are an unincorporated rural area lying within the jurisdiction of the Cowichan Valley Regional District (CVRD), an umbrella form of local government that typically includes municipalities (towns) and villages, as well as unincorporated areas. In the context of local government decision making, municipalities are more or less autonomous entities, villages less so, and unincorporated areas are entirely subject to the decisions of the regional district and of the provincial government. Under provincial municipal legislation, local government has the sole responsibility for land use.

Numerous elements of the project fell within the regulatory mandates of provincial and federal government agencies. Principal among these were the provincial Ministry of Environment, Lands and Parks (water supply, solid and liquid waste management, storm water, contaminant remediation, biodiversity) and the provincial Ministry of Transportation and Highways (road standards, traffic impacts, road maintenance, subdivision approvals).

Bamberton Code and Principles

The Bamberton Sustainable Community Project created a so-called Bamberton Code (South Island Development Corporation 1992) from which flowed a series of design issues and principles that guided the community design process. The Bamberton Code consists of four commitments:

- that Bamberton represent a way of living that seeks to serve the needs of the twenty-first century
- that Bamberton represent a new possibility for the way people co-exist with nature, upholding the ideal of responsible stewardship and seeking to be ecologically sustainable in the use of natural resources such as water, soil, habitat, energy, and raw materials
- that Bamberton represent a rediscovery of the traditional virtues of community, being conducive to social interaction, care and mutual support; encouraging of responsibility in the pursuit of shared goals; and supportive of cultural and artistic richness
- that Bamberton represent a new possibility for the building of a self-reliant community economy, emphasizing enterprise and initiative; the contribution of labour, mutual economic support, innovation, research, and development; personal, social, and global responsibility; and long-term ecological sustainability.

The principles, of which there are 328, are grouped into ninety issue areas, and then further grouped into eleven categories of sustainable community design, for ease of reference: community planning, character and culture, social planning, environment, economy, transportation and travel, town site, housing, utilities and amenities, visual impact, and leisure and tourism.

Each category is characterized by a number of issue areas, such as "social streets," "families and children," and "belonging," with each issue area containing a number of design principles. For example, within the social planning category are eleven issue areas and forty-seven principles. Under the issue area of "families and children" are listed eight principles, one of which reads: "Design streets and houses to encourage face-to-face contact, and to build up personal friendships and relationships."

Elements of Social Capital and Community Design

Social capital refers to the processes between people that establish networks, norms, and social trust, and that facilitate coordination and cooperation for mutual benefit. Onyx and Bullen (2000), in their study of five communities in New South Wales, identified five elements of social capital: networks, reciprocity, trust, shared norms, and social agency. While each of these elements can be viewed as expressions of relationships between individuals or groups within a community, the strength of these relationships appears to be a significant determinant in how social capital evolves, and out of what need or objective. Recent literature on this subject has characterized this strength as representing either bonding (strong ties, deep trust) or bridging (weak ties, thin trust) social capital.

In terms of community design, there are elements of social capital that may be facilitated through deliberate design, and those that will emerge spontaneously. It can be argued that the emergence of strong or weak relationships will occur not in an absolute order of progression from one to the other but, rather, as an expression of tendency toward bridging social capital as the foundation on which the critical bonding social capital can be built. It can be further argued that this progression is both iterative and cyclical as the community responds individually and collectively to internal and external needs.

Design Principles for Social Capital

At Bamberton, as elsewhere (Ferrell, Camblorand, and Goodman 1998; PPS 2000; Wilson-Doenges 2001), the emphasis was on design criteria applied not only to the public realm but also to the relationship between public and private domains, the so-called transition spaces that are the functional extensions of domestic spaces that connect private dwellings with public spaces. The approach was based on three interrelated assumptions:

1 that the built environment (including its spaces) can directly shape human behaviour and practice
2 that the design of this environment will create opportunities but may also apply constraints to behaviour
3 that when presented with the design, an individual is free to adopt a pattern of behaviour that is congruent with his or her value system, though there is a significant probability that the exhibited behaviour will be that intended by the design.

Design Mechanisms for Social Capital

Triangulation is the process by which some external stimulus provides a linkage between people and prompts strangers to talk to other strangers as if they knew each other (Whyte 1980). In a public space, the choice and arrangement of different elements in relation to each other can put the triangulation process in motion (or not). For example, if a bench, a wastebasket, and a telephone are placed with no connection to each other, each may receive limited use, but when they are arranged together with other amenities, such as a coffee cart, they will naturally bring people together (PPS 1998).

Creating a space that offers a sense of place is not simply, therefore, a matter of design. It requires the introduction of a variety of physical elements that will attract users by offering them comfort, safety, and convenience. Seating, landscaping, interesting pedestrian circulation patterns, public art, public games such as chess or checkers – all contribute to a comfortable image and a sense of community.

In recent years, attention has also focused on the importance of transitional space, both in its definition through the use of fences and facades, and its use through the reintroduction of design elements such as the front porch (Wilson-Doenges 2001). The concept of the front porch is a critical element in TND, as it creates a bridge between the private and public realm. It offers the opportunity of participation in the public space while maintaining a clear sense of privacy. Wilson-Doenges, in her empirical study of porches and porch use, noted a number of push and pull forces that have resulted in their general demise. Air conditioning, television, and large private backyards all had the effect of pulling people into their homes. Increasing traffic volumes, fear of crime, and dislike of insects pushed people from their front porches. She concludes that, while there is no quick fix to reducing indoor lifestyles, a number of TND elements, such as garages at the rear of the house, back alleys, and the reduction of traffic, may well encourage a front porch revival.

Application of the Bamberton Principles to Social Capital

As noted above, the Bamberton principles were grouped into eleven categories of sustainable community design. Not all the categories are relevant to the following discussion on the application of the principles to social capital. This is not intended to be an exhaustive review of all the principles but an illustration of some that were key to the design and how they were applied in practice. The example used is the social planning category. Within this category, a number of issue areas are described through a brief discussion, leading to a consideration of the principles and how they were applied to the creation of opportunities for the emergence of social capital.

Social Planning

The overall objective of social planning was to foster a sense of community at Bamberton. To achieve this objective, eleven issue areas were identified, of which a number are relevant to the theme of this chapter:

1 Face-to-face. Studies have shown that an increase in the number of a community's face-to-face interactions improves the quality of life and

reduces crime. Bamberton will create and promote ways to encourage the number of face-to-face meetings.

Principles:

(a) Design the width and structure of roads to encourage pedestrian use.
(b) Construct public buildings and meeting areas to provide a community focus for neighbourhoods and community activities.
(c) Design seating areas where small groups can sit together.
(d) Site houses relative to the street and to each other with human interaction in mind.

2 Belonging. Belonging to a community contributes to people's well-being and satisfaction. This feeling occurs when healthy relationships based on shared values, desires, and sense of purpose have been established.

Principles:

(a) Design an identity for the Bamberton community as a whole.
(b) Encourage the formation of neighbourhood groups and associations.
(c) Promote a degree of neighbourhood self-management through programs such as block parents and daycare centres.

3 Social streets. Streets in a workable community are more than just channels for funnelling traffic. They are multi-dimensional spaces operating as public places. Community streets can be used for lingering, casual strolling, chatting with neighbours, walking the dog, teaching kids to ride bikes safely, and walking to the local store or pub. Community streets can function as large, unroofed public rooms.

Principles:

(a) Allow buildings right up to property line so that porches and entries are a conversational distance away.
(b) Provide public spaces and benches along the street.
(c) Design low-speed roadways that are safe for everyone.

4 Remembered image. Certain communities (e.g., Florence, Venice, Paris) possess qualities that resonate in the minds of most people. People delight in these qualities and remember them fondly. There are special elements in each of these places that contribute to the creation of a remembered image. For residents, it helps to establish a feeling of belonging to something worthwhile – something well planned and sensitive to people's needs, fostering a sense of community.

Principles:

(a) Create distinctive and understandable forms that are familiar to people.

(b) Create a range of public services, amenities, and buildings to develop a sense of community self-containment.

(c) Pursue a vision of community by demonstrating its goals to protect and enhance the environment, and to provide a sense of shared values among its residents.

(d) Offer ample opportunity through civic organizations and the design of space for people to meet in formal and informal settings.

Government Control

"Command and control" was very much in evidence in the Bamberton project, as government agencies sought to exercise their regulatory responsibilities and, in so doing, ultimately deny opportunities for innovative design through the application of the Bamberton principles.

As noted above, the opportunities for social capital to emerge were to be created through the design of transitional and public space. The concept of social streets, the siting of houses to encourage face-to-face interactions, the use of multi-functional buildings, such as a community school to allow groups to meet – all were counteracted by inflexible provincial government rules. Local government dictated the size of building lots, density, setbacks from streets, and parking for every commercial building, regardless of access.

The following example illustrates the difficulty governments typically have in dealing with innovation. As noted above, approval to implement the key principles are a collective responsibility of both provincial and local governments, with the larger share attributed to the provincial Ministry of Transportation and Highways. This government agency is responsible, among other things, for approving road design through the enforcement of road standards. These standards are based largely on considerations of public safety, and include road width, design speed, road materials, sight stopping distances, turn radii, and use.

From the Bamberton perspective, as noted in the list above, streets were to be more than merely channels for funnelling traffic; they were thought of as multi-dimensional spaces operating as public places. Designing these social streets employed a number of key principles:

- streets need to be narrow rather than wide
- streets within the community are pedestrian-oriented but multi-functional – shared use
- road design must discourage vehicular speed
- low vehicular speed limits must be posted
- most buildings should be located close to the property line so that porches and entries are a conversational distance away

- garages are to be located at the rear of lots and accessed by alleys
- public spaces and benches must be provided along the street.

These key principles are interdependent and create the synergies necessary to contribute to the formation of social capital. Thus, if the street is wide, or given over to automobiles, or fronted with garages, opportunities for social design are mostly foregone.

Most of the government standards were related to design speed, with the lowest speed being 50 km/h, and no design criteria had been developed for lower speeds. Similarly, road width was prescribed by regulation, with the narrowest permissible width being about twice what was designed for the internal streets of Bamberton. Finally, the ministry regulations required the physical separation of road users, so that pedestrians were separated from bicycles, which in turn had to be separated from automobiles – all in the interest of public safety. Although numerous meetings were held to try to vary these standards, government bureaucrats were bound by their own inflexible regulations, and the design issues remained unresolved.

New Forms of Governance

In July 1992, the British Columbia Round Table on Environment and Economy held a workshop to which were invited representatives from twenty communities across the province; community and industry associations and groups; experts in various fields; and provincial government agencies. Cross-sectoral working groups addressed four themes:

- qualities of a sustainable community
- barriers affecting sustainability
- objectives for a sustainable community
- processes or actions required to achieve the objectives.

Despite the broad-ranging scope of the themes, the focus of the dialogue was largely on governance models and the inability of the existing system to accommodate the needs and aspirations of local communities. This comment from a working group is typical: "[We must] recognize the need for different criteria to operate at different levels of government. This applies from the neighbourhood or community level right through to the provincial level. Thus, a generic formula for governance is not appropriate. Certain strategies will work very effectively at the local level and less so at the provincial level, and vice versa. We have to become sensitive to that fact." It was clear to everyone that there were many barriers to local community empowerment, particularly inflexible provincial government rules and regulations and the government's need for control. An emerging consensus served notice to provincial, regional, and local governments to support and facilitate community empowerment. The province would determine the overall policy framework but would have to be sufficiently flexible to accommodate regional and local differences. Decision making at regional and local levels would be open, participatory, and contribute to individual empowerment. Changes to the contemporary governance model would be required, however, in order to create a new method of allocating wealth to local communities based on a more equitable distribution of tax revenues.

In the intervening ten years, what has been accomplished? Local governments in British Columbia have been scrambling to accommodate further devolution of responsibility from the provincial government in the face of declining net revenues. The British Columbia Round Table on Environment and Economy and the Bamberton project were both terminated in 1995. However, changes are proposed that, if followed through, would satisfy many of the recommendations of the 1992 workshop. The provincial government has proposed a community charter that would see new legislation giving broad powers to local government to carry out its mandates within a framework of consistent, province-wide standards. In essence, it would remove much of the provincial government's authority to regulate local government, particularly in terms of development. Government has also acknowledged the problem of lack of resources but is currently seeking input on how best to address the issue. It is debatable as to whether or not the community charter will lead directly to empowerment of community groups, since its discretionary powers are vested in the hands of local politicians. Perhaps what is needed is a legislated requirement to commit to the types of "deliberative processes" (Killerby 2001) that have been initiated in New Zealand. These processes, which emphasize the importance of face-to-face discussion and debate among citizens as a feature of decision making are designed to ensure active and meaningful involvement of communities in the decisions affecting them.

The realization of a broad framework of principles and standards that would overcome the three previously noted institutional barriers is dependent on satisfying three key requirements:

- commitment, by governments, to a new model of governance
- the ability, and willingness, of governments to develop the necessary mechanisms to create the framework
- a resource generation model that would permit local communities to function effectively within the framework.

If we accept the notion that governance embraces the elements and principles underlying "good government," such as accountability, transparency, participation, and the rule of law, then good governance must include predictable, open, and enlightened policy making; a bureaucracy acting in furtherance of the public good; the rule of law; transparent processes; and an empowered civil society participating in public affairs.

Creating a broad framework of principles and standards will require a high degree of horizontal integration across provincial government agencies at a policy level. Currently no such mechanism exists other than through an as yet dormant cabinet committee. Thus, one agency is developing the broad framework for the community charter while another is attempting to create a similar framework for sustainable resource management. In a resource-based economy such as that of British Columbia, there is a strong argument for the integration not only of these two frameworks but also of others that still need to be developed in health care, education, and myriad social services.

Mechanisms of horizontal integration are not new to British Columbia. Through the 1970s there existed the Environment and Land Use Committee Secretariat, an agency dedicated to both planning and problem solving in matters involving land use and the environment. Its demise in the early 1980s was officially attributed to redundancy of function, although in reality it was a casualty of changing political philosophy. In the late 1980s, the province created the Cabinet Committee on Sustainable Development. Chaired by the ministers of Environment and Economic Development, but with no secretariat to support it, it existed largely to approve programs at the political level and could provide no direction for sustainable development. Even at the delivery end, models such as community resource boards have been proposed in the past, but the implied level of local autonomy was more than the government of the day was prepared to accept.

Resource generation or wealth creation at the community level is largely dependent on the local tax base, and while there is, at least in theory, discretionary income, many communities are struggling to keep up with maintaining their infrastructures. Grants may be available, but they are generally allocated to specific projects. Some additional taxation powers are probably required, but there has been no appetite, to date, to really address this problem.

It is clear, therefore, that commitment is required at all levels of government. If senior governments are prepared to adopt a facilitation role by establishing the ground rules of a broad framework of policy and standards, they must also be prepared to develop a performance measurement process through the use of indicators that would, for example, require local governments or communities to demonstrate accountability. In this way, they would be able to get out of the "doing" business and into performance-based governance models. Local government and communities must play their parts by developing decision-making processes that are open, participatory, and inclusive.

Conclusions

I've argued in this chapter that a fundamental overhaul of traditional models of governance is required so that communities can acquire a greater degree of autonomy in decision making and the resources to get the job done. Governments, both at provincial and local levels, have traditionally viewed their roles as protectors of the public interest by providing leadership through regulatory control. Commitment to good governance must be supported by a resource-generation model that would permit local communities to function effectively. "Doing it by the book" and stovepipe structures of accountability need to be replaced by flexible standards and cross-sectoral approaches that would facilitate and empower communities in the creation of social capital.

References

Appleyard, Donald, and Mark Lintell. 1972. "The Environmental Quality of City Streets: The Residents' Viewpoint." *Journal of the American Institute of Planners* 38(3): 84-101.

Boydell, A.N. 1994. Bamberton: Building for Sustainability. Paper presented at the Project Management Institute International Conference, 16 February, Vancouver.

Duany, Andres, and Elizabeth Plater-Zyberk. 1992. "The Second Coming of the American Small Town." *Wilson Quarterly*, Winter.

Ferrell, G., M. Camblorand, and D. Goodman. 1998. "Design Principles for Neighborhoods and Towns." *TND Homes.com.* <http://www.tndhomes.com/phd01.html> (27 August 2002).

Killerby, Paul. 2001. "Social Capital, Participation and Sustainable Development: Recent Examples of Inclusive Consultation in New Zealand." Paper presented at the International Community Development Conference, April, Rotorua.

Kunstler, Howard J. 2001. "Breaking the Habit of Suburbia." Keynote at the 5th annual TND Breakfast, Atlanta.

Onyx, J., and P. Bullen. 2000. "Measuring Social Capital in Five Communities." *Journal of Applied Behavioral Science* 36(1): 23-42.

Project for Public Spaces (PPS). 2000. *How to Turn a Place Around: A Handbook for Creating Successful Public Spaces.* New York: PPS.

South Island Development Corporation (SIDC). 1992. *The Town of Bamberton Review Process, Volume 3: Issues and Principles.* Victoria, BC: SIDC.

Whyte, William H. 1980. *The Social Life of Small Urban Spaces.* New York: Project for Public Spaces.

Wilson-Doenges, G. 2001. "Push and Pull Forces Away from the Front Porch." *Environment and Behavior* 33(2): 264-78.

Yancey, William L. 1971. "Architecture, Interaction, and Social Control: The Case of a Large-Scale Public Housing Project." *Environment and Behavior* 3(1): 3-21.

Part 4
Assessing Progress

14
Exciting the Collective Imagination
James Tansey

There was a time that the concept of sustainable development held a radical appeal; it was a rallying point for those who were becoming disillusioned with the traditional development paradigm. The critique ventured that modern industrial societies systematically exceeded the limits of environmental systems, created poverty and inequity, and delivered a shallow and unfulfilling sense of well-being, measured primarily through economic growth. The second year of the second millennium could have marked an important milestone for sustainable development. It was the year of the tenth anniversary of the UN Conference on Environment and Development, an unprecedented international meeting to address concerns about the growing impact of industrial societies on the planet's ecosystems. Instead, 2002 was a terrible disappointment. The Johannesburg conference, which many had hoped might revitalize the sustainable development agenda, proved highly disappointing. The Canadian government signed the Kyoto Accord on Climate Change, but only once concessions were granted that reduced the already meagre targets for emissions reductions to levels that would be politically palatable. More ominously, the Western world was being goaded into military action by a US leader who seemed committed to a crusade that most people accept has at least something to do with access to oil in the Middle East. In a time of defensive politics and military action, there is little room in the agenda of the United Nations for issues raised by sustainable development.

There may be more reason for optimism in the more down-to-earth realm of national politics. Indeed, the argument of this chapter is that the most appropriate scale for addressing sustainable development is regional or, ideally, bioregional. This argument adds more than a silver lining to a dark cloud. It is difficult enough in the domestic realm to gain the attention necessary to initiate policy formation on the diverse issues under the umbrella of sustainable development – issues ranging from energy production to agricultural policy. International accords remain largely toothless beasts, since policy is still developed, implemented, and policed by sovereign domestic institutions. We expect too much of these international regimes, and it certainly is not clear that the global nature of sustainability issues means that global consensus is required before progress can be made. The first section below provides a brief overview of sustainable development. The second section describes an initiative, focused on the Georgia Basin region of Western Canada, that uses computer-based scenario models as discussion tools to engage members of the public in a process of defining what constitutes a desirable future for the region they inhabit. I argue that in order to revitalize the concept of sustainability, we must recognize that there is no template or preordained model of the kind of structural shifts that society must undertake. Sustainable development is not an outcome that can be identified in advance but a process by which citizens negotiate what kind of world they would like to inhabit and what trade-offs they would be willing to accept. A sustainable future requires a significant revitalization of the democratic process – in simple terms, a massive investment in the creation and maintenance of social capital – in order to succeed. This investment will open up a new political space that is essential to the shift to a more sustainable society. In the final section, I suggest what shifts in governance would be necessary for these kinds of tools to have greatest impact.

Sustainable Development

Sustainable development is a slippery and ambiguous concept. There is a "definition industry" in the academic world that has expanded at a rapid pace, and there were more than eighty definitions and interpretations of the core concept by 1994.

The formalization of sustainable development as an organizational focus for a wide array of governmental, nongovernmental, and business institutions resulted in the loss of the primary emphasis on the quality of the Earth's ecosystems. Indeed, some would argue that the concept is a contradiction in terms, precisely because conventional development is the cause of the declining quality of global ecosystems. In his critique of sustainable development, Wolfgang Sachs (1993) argues that the original radical concept of sustainability was colonized and usurped by the mainstream institutions. Others argue that the concept is now used in so many contexts that it has become meaningless (Viederman 1994). Regardless of what one thinks of the concept, sustainable development is here to stay. It exerts an influence in the policy realm, and a wide range of policy initiatives have sought to incorporate sustainability principles. In the words of two researchers: "sustainability, coupled to the notion of 'development,' has become a rhetorical talisman for our common present" (O'Mahoney and Skillington 1996, 42).

Interdependence and Limits

The most consistent argument in the literature is that sustainable development recognizes that socioeconomic systems are embedded in environmental systems. At the simplest level, socioeconomic systems extract resources from environmental systems and transfer waste back into them, although clearly most examples one might think of are significantly more complex. While traditional development pathways tend to either downplay or ignore the impact of society on the environment, sustainable development recognizes that socioeconomic and natural systems are interdependent and co-evolve through time. Much of the literature has emphasized that both environmental and social systems have limits, beyond which they will collapse or change in a non-linear and negative fashion. Using the systems metaphor, a more complex general framework has been developed that identifies three systems – the ecological, the economic, and the social – each of which is characterized in general terms by four features (Robinson and Tinker 1997):

- they are composed of complex subsystems and are becoming increasingly globalized
- the systems can be conceived of as self-organizing, though the extent to which scientific enterprise is able to reveal these mechanisms of self-organization is often limited
- they change in response to "stress," with consequences that may be both positive and negative to human society
- they may have limits, beyond which they may "collapse."

It is from these assumptions that the definition of sustainable development presented in the beginning of this book is derived. This definition underpins the remainder of this chapter. To borrow a phrase from international relations, the systems exist in a state of complex interdependence. Human society has developed such that we have the capacity to significantly modify natural systems at all scales – from the micro to the global – but at the same time, we remain highly dependent on these systems for their life-support functions. At the core of sustainable development is a sense that some balanced and considered compromise is required: a reconciliation of the imperatives of complex systems. The original emphasis in the literature was on absolute limits, in particular, to the carrying capacity of environmental systems. There are two weaknesses with the emphasis on absolute limits. The first is that "limits" implies rigid and unchanging ecological systems. Holling (1986) and others have pointed out that one of the factors that enable ecosystems to endure over time is their capacity to absorb shocks and restore equilibrium. Thus, the more dynamic concept of resilience has emerged in recent years to reflect the fact that systems can respond to acute insults, even where this involves some short-term functional change.[1] Second, the emphasis on limits implies a level of scientific knowledge of systems that is rarely present. In most instances, our knowledge of environmental systems is characterized by great uncertainties. While in most cases, we become aware of environmental limits only after they have been breached, this does not mean that science has become useless. In the approach described below, it is assumed that science can be used to define a possibility space where the general impacts of development on ecosystems can be represented but where mechanical prediction of the future remains a Holy Grail. At the heart of sustainable development is a tension between biogeophysical limits to natural systems and the commitment that human values, expressed through open dialogue, ought to shape and influence the redirection of society toward desirable futures. The space opened up by this tension is a world that is always imperfectly understood as one that can be shaped and influenced by human choices.

The remainder of this chapter outlines one practical attempt to develop tools that create a possibility space, informed by current scientific knowledge that can be shaped and formed through public dialogue into regional scenarios. The approach emerged out of the field of integrated assessment, traditionally populated by scientists seeking to expand their understanding of critical policy issues by working across disciplinary boundaries in the natural sciences. The project below is the most ambitious attempt to engage the public in the use of the science-driven tools.

Integrated Assessment

There are a number of excellent reviews of the current state of the art in integrated assessment; the goal of this section is to distil some of the key challenges identified in recent years (Rotmans and Dowlatabadi 1998; Tansey et al. 2002). The defining goals of integrated assessment (IA) are to develop interdisciplinary approaches to policy-relevant questions. Traditionally, IA practitioners have sought to develop large-scale models of environmental systems in order to explore the neglected but often fascinating spaces between predominantly patriotic and self-referential disciplines, but in recent years, a number of models have been developed at the regional or bioregional scales. The two key forces that appear to be shaping IA are the increase in the rigour and sophistication of models, and the development of mechanisms for greater public participation in the application of models to contemporary policy questions. Clearly these forces have the potential to be antithetical, since the former implies greater technical complexity, while the latter implies greater accessibility. The project described below has certainly been more influenced by the latter force than the former. This is consistent with a trend in a number of other fields, including environmental assessment and risk management. While traditionally these fields have been dominated by scientific approaches to the management of social problems,

it has increasingly been recognized that these have had only limited success. Habermas was among the first to describe the tendency in modern
societies for the technical rationality of the expert to become more important in areas of everyday life that have traditionally been understood through
a more egalitarian communicative rationality. Habermas's critical theory
built on the ideas of Adorno and Marcuse, who argued that an increasingly
technocratic society was alienating and dehumanizing. Awareness of the
need for a more sustainable society has been driven by the technical rationality of scientists concerned about the impacts of human systems on the
natural environment, but, if Habermas and others are to be believed, socially
sustainable solutions need to be driven by human values and choices. A
revitalization of the democratic process – the significant injection of social
capital that I describe above – is essential to achieve a socially sustainable
future.

A number of researchers have mapped out the standards to which participatory integrated assessment (PIA) might aspire. Ravetz (1999, 20) envis-
ages an integrated environmental assessment "operating at local or regional
levels, where computer applications are based on geographical information
systems and virtual reality simulations of key environmental features. Then
the very real problems of uncertain futures and conflicting values can be
managed through an essentially societal process, in which the 'hardware' is
a tool for guiding discussions." Note that Ravetz sees the discussion on values as primary and the hardware as a secondary tool, useful for framing and
informing discussion. Similarly, based on the experience of the European
Ulysses project, van der Sluijs identifies a list of characteristics for the use of
IAMs in citizen dialogue:

- strong interest at the regional level
- the potential to evaluate user-defined policy options
- realistic and credible inputs and results
- easy to follow, detailed, and flexible user manual
- understandable model presentation
- interactive and attractive user interface
- explicit and intelligible presentation of uncertainties
- the need for adequate model moderation. (van der Sluijs 1997, 143)

Building better models is a necessary but not sufficient condition for the
advancement of the PIA agenda. Both Ravetz and van der Sluijs recognize
the need to develop more open and dynamic fora that can accommodate
the diversity of values likely to be expressed in a public forum. Ultimately, it
is clear that the "key to good practice in this current age is to appreciate
that the problems of uncertainty and value-loading cannot be solved within
the confines of computer systems" (Ravetz 1999, 20). The initiative described

in the remainder of this chapter has sought to advance participatory IA in some of the directions described above.

Georgia Basin Futures Project

Georgia Basin Futures Project (GBFP) builds on an earlier initiative that resulted in the development of Lower Fraser Basin Quest (LFB-Quest), an interactive modelling tool. The latest incarnation of the model is Georgia Basin Quest (GB-Quest). The Georgia Basin is the watershed that drains into the Strait of Georgia, the body of water separating the southwest corner of British Columbia from Vancouver Island. Around 80 percent of the population of the province of British Columbia resides within the Georgia Basin, and the cities of Vancouver and Victoria, as well as the famous Whistler ski resort, fall within its boundary.

The model was inspired by the tremendous popularity of the computer game SimCity. The developers of LFB-Quest recognized that users embrace the opportunity to design and manage an imaginary city. They reasoned that if even a small part of that energy could be channelled into public consultation using a game-like model of a real region, the quality of the dialogue about the future of that region could be improved significantly. Broadly, the design criteria for the model were to

- assume a bioregional approach to modelling that assures greater detail and relevance than has traditionally been possible in the field
- operationalize a backcasting approach to scenario development through a computer-based model
- utilize a design approach to modelling
- develop an interactive relationship both with the regional stakeholders who supported the development of the model and with potential users

A more technical elaboration of these design criteria is available in Tansey et al. (2002).

One can distinguish three distinct levels to GB-Quest. The underlying sectoral submodels – the first layer – were developed using a variety of techniques. In general terms, GB-Quest was developed using an executive summary approach to modelling. Traditional research has resulted in complex models of particular social or environmental systems to improve scientific understanding of air pollution, forestry, and transportation, to name just a few. These models are typically developed within the boundaries of a single discipline, with the result that, while they may achieve great complexity, they remain naive of the functioning of other linked human and environmental systems. The executive summary approach depends on some level of simplification of these complex disciplinary models and focuses instead on critical points of linkage across the human and environmental systems of which the region is composed. The goal is to develop a simpler, but more sophisticated, model of the region. These linked models create a possibility space, within which forty-year scenarios can be developed for the region.

The second layer is the visible portion of the model: the interface. The design criteria above established two critical objectives for the interface development process. The first was to create an interface that was not only usable by non-scientists but was actually engaging and fun to use. Second, the choices presented on the interface had to be relevant to the model's target audience. To ensure that the interface presented choices that resonated with the way people have experienced these critical issues in their everyday lives, a broad issue identification process was undertaken. Data were gathered from multiple sources, using a range of methodologies:

1 Official community plans were prepared by each municipality in the region under the requirements of the British Columbia *Growth Strategies Act*. The plans were analyzed on a sectoral basis to identify the key issues, their relative significance, and the manner in which these values were expressed.
2 A series of five sectoral workshops was held in late 2000 for forestry, agriculture, neighbourhoods, food systems, and transportation. Sectoral experts were invited from academia, the nongovernmental sector, and relevant government departments. The explicit goal of the workshops was to identify a limited number of development archetypes for each sector; that is, structurally distinct branching points that were plausible and relevant to the bioregion. For instance, in the food systems workshop, a series of underlying dimensions were identified, as shown in Table 14.1.

In the final stages of the workshop, participants were asked to identify the two most significant dimensions. The two dimensions intersect to produce four distinct archetypes, and the participants were asked to populate the archetypes with examples. The full range of archetypes developed through this process are presented in a separate paper, but the example above illustrates the advantages of including stakeholder input in the design process.

Table 14.1

Developing archetypes for integrated assessment design

Appropriate scale	↔	Factory food
Balance/range of option	↔	Corporate control
Food shed	↔	Global food system
Slow food	↔	Fast food
Maximum mimicking of natural system	↔	Maximum use of inputs and substitution

Finally, LFB-Quest was used as a pilot model to inform the development of GB-Quest. Feedback garnered from multiple presentations and workshops that utilized LFB-Quest was incorporated into the interface design process.

The process of developing a scenario within GB-Quest is broken into a number of distinct stages. In the first stage, users must make a number of contextual decisions that set the parameters of the model. Since the Georgia Basin region is embedded in a global economy, users must make a decision about the relationship between the region and the rest of the globe. Four alternatives embodying distinct branching points are presented. For instance, users can choose to build the scenario in a world of global policy reform in the direction of greater sustainability. Conversely, they can choose a global scenario known as Fortress World, which is much more pessimistic about the future of international relations. Second, users are asked to identify priorities within the model. This set of choices does not affect the underlying models but does select particular indicators for emphasis in the final scenario. Third, users are asked to make choices related to the treatment of uncertainty within the model. These choices have a direct impact on the rate of technological change, social adaptation, and ecological resilience within the model.

The second stage of GB-Quest is for users to make policy choices. The model is designed so that users can choose at what level they make choices and the level of detail required for their decision. At the highest level, users can make preset choices about urban development, resources, and economy. The next level down offers more detail in each of these areas. For instance, within urban development, users can make choices about urban growth, lifestyles, neighbourhoods, and transportation. Really keen users are able to drill down one layer further, for instance, to make explicit choices about development focus, natural land protection, urban density, and flood plain development within the urban growth section. Users do not need to make choices in every section of the model, as there is a default setting for each choice. This means that users can focus on the areas of the model of greatest interest to them.

The final stage to the model is to view the results generated by the scenario development process. Results are presented initially in the form of a report or newspaper, with hyperlinks to more detail. Detailed information is available in the form of maps and graphs relevant to each sector, and users can customize the manner in which results are presented. Since the model is complex, a section of the interface shows which initial decisions influenced the results being viewed. The broad goal is that individual users or groups of users play iteratively and learn about the consequences of their decisions on the region in the coming forty years. Through iterative play, users will have to make trade-offs in order to develop a scenario they like. For instance, a scenario involving high population growth with low to medium density will result in urban sprawl that incurs on areas of natural and agricultural land. This may be a trade-off users are willing to accept, while declining air quality due to greater private transportation may be deemed unacceptable. Thus, the purpose of the model is to help reveal what trade-offs people are willing to accept and what commitments or choices remain relatively immutable. This process will reveal the landscape of social barriers to adaptation within the Georgia Basin region.

The final and most important layer to the GB-Quest approach is the range of processes in which the model is embedded for the purposes of public participation. In the past, IA models have been used as the focal point for a rather static dialogue between experts and small representative groups from the public domain. A typology has been developed that identifies the range of methodologies that could be used, depending on the goals of the research (Tansey and VanWynsberghe forthcoming). Broadly, the typology distinguishes between methodologies that are extractive, interactive, and transformative. Extractive methodologies are guided by the traditional social scientific approach to research. Users play the role of research subjects and are considered a source of data that will be used in a traditional social scientific analysis. The most common approach in the IA literature is to use small focus groups from the general population (Kasemir et al. 2000). Interactive approaches see the process of interaction as more of a dialogue between the social scientist and the users of the model. There is a two-way flow of information, and users are able to make a substantive contribution to the scenario building exercise. The famous Mackenzie Basin Impact Study is one excellent example of this approach. Local stakeholders were engaged in an interactive context and contributed substantively to the products of the research process (Cohen 1995). Transformative approaches are drawn from feminist action research and also from the broader participatory education literature. The purpose is not to simply deepen understanding of a group of participants' social circumstances but to alter them. The emphasis is on empowerment and the meaningful transformation of social conditions.

The design of the processes in which the model is to be embedded is a non-trivial exercise.[2] To put it another way, it is not easy to create new social capital. Suspicion of expert models runs deep in the public domain, and the model interface, while designed to be salient, still requires some degree of technical competence. In short, users must pass through a significant learning curve before they are competent in the use of the model. A basic understanding of the use of traditional computer software and a reasonable command of the English language are both prerequisites for the use of GB-Quest. While a manual similar to the one developed for LFB-Quest has been developed, it is possible that only the minority of users will engage with GB-Quest on their own in an unsupported environment. Indeed, the goal of the project is explicitly to engage stakeholders ranging from ordinary citizens to government scientists in a series of conversations about the future of the region. The formal model is simply a means to an end; it represents a possibility space that indicates where some of the biogeophysical limits of the region lie. The interface is designed to resonate with the clusters of values that inform the choices users can make on a range of everyday issues, from neighbourhood style to transportation choice. Nonetheless, it is recognized that it would be technically impossible to design a model that was sufficiently flexible to accommodate the vast range of values users might express. Rather than insist that a diverse world conform to the narrower choices that are hard-wired into the model, we argue that the model is a discussion tool that allows users to explore the crude implications of distinct value choices as they are multiplied across time and space in the bioregion.

Novel Contribution to Sustainable Development

This commitment differs from other approaches to the exploration of sustainability through scenario and backcasting models. Users of GB-Quest are able to create both positive and negative scenarios of the future. The key difference is that the public is no longer seen as passive recipients of the loose predictions of scientists but, rather, can become actively involved in the process of creating scenarios.

GBFP has resulted in the development of a unique approach to sustainable development that recognizes that, while the concept can be defined in broad rhetorical terms as the "three-legged stool," in terms of the three imperatives, the devil lies in the detail. In other words, the specific geographic and cultural context matters a great deal to the relative sustainability of a policy or a behavioural change. In addition, interpersonal and inter-institutional dialogue has a significant role to play in making sense of the issues, in identifying acceptable trade-offs between different value choices, and in arriving at a consensual and therefore legitimate decision. The meaning of sustainable development is manifest in the qualitative debate within social groups regarding the form of the future considered desirable. The role of GB-Quest is to crudely test some of the implications of the translation of individual or group values into long-term bioregional scenario. In this sense, GB-Quest opens up a new political space between the values of citizens within the bioregion and the known biogeophysical limits represented in the model.

Sustainable development is treated as exogenous to the model but endogenous to the debate on what constitutes a desirable future for the Georgia Basin bioregion. In a sense, the goal is to provide the population at large with access to the kinds of tools that have been restricted to the specialist academic domain of future studies. One possible criticism of this explicit democratization of what has been a science-driven field is that environmental limits remain, regardless of what people think represents a desirable future. Development pathways that fail to recognize these limits will sustain the problems that have led to widespread environmental degradation over the last century. I would argue in response that it is essential to recognize that social limits are just as important as scientifically determined environmental limits. Politicians and policy makers are highly responsive and sensitive to the concerns of their electorates and are unlikely to pursue policies that will endanger their chances of re-election. The process of defining desirable futures through the kinds of scenario-building exercises supported by GB-Quest will reveal these social limits. At the very least, this form of large-scale community engagement will raise public understanding of the complex issues surrounding sustainability and ideally will help create more informed constituencies for change in the direction of greater sustainability.

The diagnosis of the causes of sustainable development and the assessment of cures require the technical rationality of scientists, but the process of selecting the most desirable cures requires negotiation within a reinvigorated democratic realm. Without a serious investment in social capital, sustainable development will falter as another technocratic solution to social problems. The title of this chapter expresses the goal of GBFP quite accurately: to excite the collective imagination of the population of the region, both to identify what constitutes clusters of desirable futures and, more optimistically, to create a broad and informed constituency for change.

Conclusions

GB-Quest differs significantly from its earlier incarnations, and the project is in the early stages of a series of public engagement exercises to test the framework outlined above. At this stage, two broad classes of dilemma have emerged regarding this framework. First, despite all the best efforts of the project team to insist that the tool be designed to enable users to project plausible scenarios within a realistic possibility space, many users instinctively treat the results as formal predictions. Moreover, it is not uncommon that members of the project team find themselves in heated discussions with policy makers and government scientists about whether the algorithms beneath the model produce a reliable result for a specific geographic locale represented with GB-Quest. They are often not satisfied that the model simply shows an accurate direction and magnitude of change, and demand a level of specificity and reliability beyond the scope of the model (and beyond the scope of any similar model).

Second, while the model presents results on a bioregional scale and allows users to zoom into the municipal scale to view results, none of the agencies involved in the project plans or governs at a synchronous scale. To put it another way, nobody thinks like a bioregion. The problem is that while a clear agenda for the region might become more obvious through some large-scale scenario-building exercise, institutions of governance in the region may be not be able to deliver without significant reform.

Third, even on the seemingly enlightened west coast of Canada, the home of participatory planning, there is still a tendency on the part of decision makers and politicians to want to control the nature and extent of public discourse on the region's long-term future. Ultimately, the public engagement exercises described above will fail if they remain curiosities of social science research projects. To be successful, they must be incorporated authentically and honestly into the everyday processes of governing the regions we inhabit. Politicians and decision makers must be willing to open up new political spaces and to provide sufficient support so that public consultation is treated on a par with other forms of civic duty, such as jury service.

Notes

1 For a comprehensive review of resilience see W.N. Adger (2000).
2 For a detailed review see van Asselt and Rijkens-Klomp (2002).

References

Adger, W.N. 2000. "Social and Ecological Resilience: Are They Related?" *Progress in Human Geography* 24(3): 347-64.

Cohen, S. 1995. "An Interdisciplinary Assessment of Climate Change on Northern Ecosystems: The Mackenzie Basin Impact Study (MBIS)." In D.L. Peterson and D.R. Johnson, eds., *Human Ecology and Climate Change: People and Resources in the Far North*, 301-16. Bristol, CT: Taylor and Francis.

Kasemir, Bernd, Urs Dahinden, Asa Gerger Swartling, Ralf Schule, David Tabara, and Carlo C. Jaeger. 2000. "Citizens' Perspectives on Climate Change and Energy Use." *Global Environmental Change* 10(3): 169-84.

Lafferty, W.M., and O. Langhelle, eds. 1999. *Towards Sustainable Development: On the Goals of Development – and the Conditions of Sustainability*. Hampshire, UK: Macmillan; New York: St. Martin's.

Meadows, D.H., J. Richardson, J. Randers, and W. Behrens III. 1972. *The Limits to Growth*. New York: Universe.

Mebratu, D. 1998. "Sustainability and Sustainable Development: Historical and Conceptual Review." *Environmental Impact Assessment Review* 18: 493-520.

Milton, K. 1996. *Environmentalism and Cultural Theory*. London: Routledge.

Moffat, I. 1995. *Sustainable Development: Principles, Analysis and Policies*. New York: Parthenon.

O'Mahoney, P., and T. Skillington. 1996. "Sustainable Development as an Organizing Principle for Discursive Democracy." *Sustainable Development* 4: 42-51.

Ravetz, J.R. 1999. "Developing Principles of Good Practice in Integrated Environmental Assessment." *International Journal of Environment and Pollution* 11(3): 243-65.

Robinson, J., and J. Tinker. 1997. "Reconciling Ecological, Economic, and Social Imperatives: A New Conceptual Framework." In T. Schrecker, ed., *Surviving Globalism: Social and Environmental Dimensions*, 71-94. London: Macmillan; New York: St. Martin's.

Rotmans, J., and H. Dowlatabadi. 1998. "Integrated Assessment Modeling." In S. Rayner and Elizabeth Malone, eds., *Human Choice and Climate Change*, 292-377. Columbus: Battelle.

Sachs, W.E. 1993. *Global Ecology*. London: Zed Books.

Tansey, J., J. Carmichael, and J. Robinson. 2002. "The Future Is Not What It Used to Be." *Global Environmental Change* 12(2): 97-104.

Tansey, J., and R. VanWynsberghe. Forthcoming. "Integrated Assessment as an Organisational Focus for Sustainability Research." *Futures*.

van Asselt, M.B.A., and N. Rijkens-Klomp. 2002. "A Look in the Mirror: Reflection on Participation in Integrated Assessment from a Methodological Perspective." *Global Environmental Change* 12: 167-84.

van der Sluijs, J. 1997. *Anchoring Amid Uncertainty: On the Management of Uncertainties in Risk Assessment from Anthropogenic Climate Change.* The Netherlands: University of Utrecht Press.

Viederman, S. 1994. "Five Capitals and Three Pillars of Sustainability." Working paper from the Jessie Smith Noyes Foundation.

Conclusion: Reflections
Ann Dale

> Some people on this Earth occupy only the space of a tree, but when
> they leave, they leave the space of a forest. Daniel James Frazer was
> such a being. We are all trying to learn to live at the edge of a
> forest, and sometimes at the edge, the greatest changes lay.

Throughout human history, we have continuously lived through boom and
bust cycles of exploitation (McNeill 1992). Yet we seem incapable of recognizing that we may be simply substituting one species for another upon
depletion, with a trend line moving consistently downward. It would appear that our inability to implement sustainable community development
is a fundamental failure to learn from our past. And if unsustainable development is a failure to learn, then it is primarily a social problem, and we
may have become the master architects of our own destiny. This is the critical link between social capital and sustainable community development;
they are both necessary and sufficient conditions for each other's realization, and the mobilization of one is dependent on the mobilization of the
other. They are interdependent. As Memmott and Meltzer point out in their
chapter, this interdependence is integral to Indigenous communities, as their
concept of social capital is not easily separable from natural capital; the two
are mutually interdependent in an epistemological sense.

Yet the social dimension is often discounted by an economic system that
values the quantifiable over the qualitative, the large-scale over the small-
scale, the formal over the informal, and hard systems over soft systems. It is
much easier to quantify economic measures and far more complex to quantify social measures. This does not mean that we should not continue to
develop quantitative measures of social capital and sustainable community
development; we should, however, realize that not everything in human
life can be measured and that often it is the immeasurable that contributes
the most value and agency to humankind. Moody and Cordua-von Specht
emphasize in their chapter how loss of culture in communities connects

integrally with loss of traditional knowledge and the weakening of bonds of family and kinship ties, leading to a deadly combination of social dislocation, poor economic conditions, and substance abuse. Hill reinforces the criticality of the explicit inclusion of the personal: it is "building of personal capital [that] establishes the foundation on which social and natural capital can be built and maintained." Thus, social dimensions such as trust, autonomy, respect, and relatedness may be just as important for community development as economic factors, and indeed, it is their disconnection that leads to consistent patterns of spiralling down in some communities.

Most authors in this book argue that it is this fundamental disconnection of the economic from the social and of both from the ecological that has led to our current modern crisis of unsustainable development. Moreover, Hill argues that sustainable development is limited and enabled by the level of sustainability and capital at the personal level – that this is the essential limiting factor. The two dominant features of all living systems – maintenance and development – are critical to all communities. As Wilson points out, we must recognize the activities of humans as a connected species and a component of a web of ecological interactions that are critical to all life on Earth.

But this Holy Grail of sustainable development may prove elusive if we cannot learn from our past, live in the present, and stop discounting the future of our children for the sake of our present needs. Paradoxically, we are more connected globally economically than ever before and appear to be living in a time of even greater interconnection ecologically, as evidenced by climate change and many other critical environmental issues now facing humanity. Disease in one country is now almost instantaneously transmitted worldwide because of international travel. Where one generation once considered Europe the trek of adventure, younger people now consider the world, and in particular, the East, their adventure. We are more tightly coupled through access to improved modes of transportation, television, and information communications technologies, yet paradoxically we appear to be more loosely coupled socially, fragmented within and between communities, and with greater cultural and religious conflicts between communities than ever before. Why are the seeming forces of dark so much more easily transmitted than the forces of light? Are we the architects of our own doom when we don't celebrate the wonderful innovations and creations we are capable of, because for so many institutional reasons we lack the ability to diffuse our knowledge and implement the light?

Black and Hughes's research shows that the strongest predictor for unsustainable community development is a perceived lack of vision for future community directions; next in importance are population loss and declines in local business, and the only other significant predictors are the extent to which the respondent knows close neighbours well enough to be aware of their personal concerns. Barraket also emphasizes the importance of the role of local actors in achieving effective responses to community challenges across the three imperatives. However, she critiques the exclusive focus of social capital on the individual and collective agency, and argues we must not discount the impacts of external structures and institutions on communities of place. All communities are embedded in larger political, economic, and social systems that influence local development.

More tightly coupled ecological systems and globally interconnected economic systems are occurring at the same time as increasing social and spatial disconnections, as many of the authors discuss in this book. For example, both Canada and Australia are facing regional marginalization associated with uneven development, and "rural renewal" is now at the forefront of policy discourses in both governments. However, once again, the large-scale agenda may be dominating at the expense of the smaller scale, given the predominance of the urban agenda in Canada. What is needed for sustainable community development is a reconciliation between urban and rural communities – there is a relationship, as both are subject to optimal scales and corresponding limits to development. The missing link is again a dynamic balance between rural and urban communities, recognizing that just as there are limits to development, there are equally important social limits to human settlements.

Just as we are socially disconnected from natural systems, we are temporally disconnected, in electoral cycles that favour short-term incremental solutions, to problems that are increasingly longer term and that transcend current geopolitical boundaries. In terms of scale, there are elemental disconnections between levels of government, nationally and locally, and between their scales of activities. There are fundamental disconnections between what local communities value and think is important to their futures and what federal systems of government fund. Often, the latter value the large-scale mega-projects over the smaller scale projects initiated by local communities. Larger projects that are easier to measure by current ways of doing business are valued at the expense of smaller-scale projects that may or may not lead to increased capacity through innovation and unproven methods. As Hill and Sheng both argue, we need to make explicit the clarification of values and their centrality in our day-to-day discourse, decision making, and actions. When the values of the formal, large-scale, and easy-to-measure are combined, they provide powerful incentives for maintaining the old ways of doing business, even if it means shutting down whole communities wholly dependent on a single resource economy.

More importantly, there are key disconnections between communities and even between people within communities. As Memmott and Seltzer point out in their chapter, the disconnection between the formal traditional governance of white society and the informal governance of Indigenous peoples has had tremendous ramifications on the latter. Aboriginal communities are often very integrated and equally connected to kinship and a deeply rooted sense of place. In the global village, capital and human resources are increasingly disconnected from place. Disconnection and dislocation become a vicious cycle as capital and resources become hyper-mobilized in the global village marketplace, as well as disconnected from a sense of place (community). Mobility without connection may prove to be as valueless as connection without mobility.

Black and Hughes examine Trungley Hall, where the move to agribusiness has changed the fundamental nature of that community. Capital now outflows from the local economy, and many farms are no longer owned by families from the community but from afar and managed on that owner's behalf; this has contributed to a breakdown in trust. Trust is important to institutional functioning, as confidence in institutions is a form of trust. Black and Hughes identify three realms – informal, generalized, and institutional – in which there is confidence in the operation of various expert systems and institutions.

These disconnections and breakdowns in trust may also underlie the democratic deficit now of increasing concern in industrialized countries. Indeed, Putnam, Leonardi, and Nanetti (1993) hold that civic engagement is a prerequisite for building social capital, which in turn, is an essential ingredient for effective functioning of governments. Governments clearly need to examine their role in "external efficacy – how responsive citizens believe the political system is to their demands [;] and internal efficacy – the subjective competence associated with the degree of influence an individual citizen feels he/she has over the political process" (Nevitte et al. 2000, 86).

Barraket discusses another kind of disconnect: disparities between rich and poor, socioeconomic advantage and disadvantage, access and non-access to opportunities in the new information economy, and, most critically, between rural and metropolitan centres. Our differing values, our fundamental disconnect from the natural world, within and between communities, between levels in human organizations, between sectors and countries, is everywhere profoundly affecting our ability to live sustainably in communities. As Tansey points out, sustainable development is not an outcome that can be identified in advance but is a process by which citizens negotiate what kind of society they would like to inhabit and what trade-offs they are willing to accept. Just as this is dependent on revitalization of the democratic process and shifts in governance, it will need unprecedented levels of collaboration and dialogue to transcend and build new institutions that can reconnect and build on emergent new connections that transcend current geopolitical boundaries, and ultimately change them.

If human societies are truly disconnected on multiple levels from the things that matter to human life, are there lessons we can draw on from natural systems for reconnecting? Simplified a great deal, natural systems depend on networks, nested systems, cycles, flows, development, dynamic balance, limits, and diversity (adapted from Capra 1996).

The behaviour of every living member of the ecosystem depends on the behaviour of many others, that is, on networks. The success of the community depends on the success of its individual members, while the success of each member depends on the community as a whole. Domestic security is now a global phenomenon. Ecological systems are nested hierarchies. All members of an ecological community are interconnected in a vast and interconnected network of relationships (nested systems). Similarly, human security (intellectually and culturally) flows from being embedded in larger social systems (Stevenson 2002).

Benn and Onyx in their chapter discuss the need for networked relationships and interorganizational domains. Networks of engagement also facilitate the flow of communication and provide information about the trustworthiness of people and organizations (Bridger and Luloff 2001). Trust is essential to building relationships, as many authors in this book argue. Ecological systems derive their essential properties and, indeed, their very existence from their relationship to other things. What is the glue that holds communities and people together? The underlying theme through all discourses on the topic of social capital is one of relationships, and as I discuss in my chapter, one of the most important relationships North American communities may have to relearn is their relationship with ecological systems and other species.

The flexibility of ecological systems is a consequence of multiple feedback loops that tend to bring the system back into balance whenever there is a deviation from the norm because of changing environmental conditions (dynamic balance). Communities everywhere have to begin to ask themselves, are they out of balance in their own numbers; their scale of industrial activities; the footprints they are imposing on other communities; their access to resources most critical to life – water, air, land, and food; and, finally, how much they value other species and the space they are leaving for their critical habitats? Tansey in his chapter discusses about how science can be used to define a "possibility space" where the general impacts on ecosystems can be understood, although predictions of the future remain a Holy Grail. All these questions are deeply normative; Sheng points out in his chapter the difficulties of reconciling deeply held societal values with scientific facts, and the inadequacy of existing mechanisms in addressing individual and local community needs, particularly regarding nuclear waste disposal.

It may be that the greatest lessons for sustainable communities lie in ecosystem properties of cycles, flows, and diversity. Nature is cyclical: the ecosystem's feedback loops are the pathways along which nutrients are continually recycled; what is waste for one species is food for another. Ecological systems are largely closed systems in terms of the flow of matter, while being open in terms of the flow of energy. The role of diversity is closely connected with the system's network structure. When a particular species is destroyed by a severe disturbance so that a link of the network is broken, a diverse community will be able to survive and reorganize itself because other links in the network can at least partially fulfill the function of the destroyed species. In a globally connected world, single-resource-economy communities, sometimes in place prior to resource extraction and other times deliberately created around a particular extraction, have tragically learned the consequences of a lack of diversity in economic imperatives and the subsequent crashes this will bring. As well, those communities dependent on a single ecological resource for their economies are equally vulnerable. In ecological systems, the complexity of the network is a consequence of its biodiversity and, thus, a diverse ecological community is a resilient community.

All ecological fluctuations take place between tolerance limits. There is always the danger that the whole system will collapse when a fluctuation goes beyond these limits and the system can no longer compensate for it. If one tries to maximize any single variable instead of optimizing it, it will invariably lead to the destruction of the system as a whole. This would appear to be the most difficult lesson for human societies: that the same limits that apply to natural systems apply to human communities of place, time, and scale. For some reason, we associate limits with the forces of dark rather than the forces of light, when in fact this knowledge might just be the elusive Holy Grail. Accepting limits may decouple progress from growth and reconcile sustainable with development. In developing ecological systems, different beings change differently and, in the process, each organism forms its own individual pathway of structural changes. Since these structural changes are acts of cognition, development is often associated with learning.

When do the greatest moments of development through learning occur? As mentioned in the quote that opened this chapter, they often occur "at the edge." In ecological systems, the places of greatest richness are often at the edges of two systems meeting; for example, the sea meeting a river, or the ocean meeting the land. And paradoxically, although all beings, including humans, place a high value on living in these areas, they are often the most abused and environmentally degraded. These are places of great beauty but also in great danger, where some of the greatest transformations take place as the two systems continue to meet over time. There are many periods in an individual's life when transformation may occur: on the edges of transitions – for instance, from adolescent to adulthood; through giving birth; or losing someone dearly loved. Often this transformation occurs when you are reaching outside yourself to try to understand something that doesn't come naturally to you, or when you are learning something inconsistent with your closely held beliefs and values. Equally, communities have transition points (often experienced as crises) that they can optimize for their future development if they embrace the learning to be gained from networks, nested systems, cycles, flows, development, dynamic balance, limits, and diversity from ecological systems. And the most important lesson of all may lie in realizing personal limits, in realizing that we all have the forces of light and darkness, and in realizing that we need to live in dynamic balance with our environment and one another, for in the end, "communities are social life support systems where people engage with each other, relate to the places and spaces around them and create meaning together" (Stevenson 2002, 738).

References

Bridger, J., and A. Luloff. 2001. "Building the Sustainable Community: Is Social Capital the Answer?" *Sociological Inquiry* 71(4): 458-72.

Capra, F. 1996. *The Web of Life.* New York: Doubleday.

McNeill, W.H. 1992. *The Global Condition: Conquerors, Catastrophes, and Community.* Princeton, NJ: Princeton University Press.

Nevitte, N., with A. Blais, E. Gidengil, and R. Nadeau. 2000. *Unsteady State: The 1997 Canadian Federal Election.* Toronto and London: Oxford University Press.

Putnam, R., R. Leonardi, and R. Nanetti. 1993. *Making Democracy Work: Civic Traditions in Modern Italy.* Princeton, NJ: Princeton University Press.

Stevenson, T. 2002. "Communities of Tomorrow." *Futures* 34(8): 735-44.

Contributors

Jo Barraket is a Lecturer in Public Policy in the Department of Political Science at the University of Melbourne.

Suzanne Benn is a biochemist and social scientist. She is a Senior Lecturer in the Corporate Sustainability Project in the Faculty of Business at University of Technology, Sydney, and an active member in the Landcare movement in Australia.

Alan Black is Emeritus Professor of Sociology, Edith Cowan University, Perth, Western Australia, where he was the foundation Director of the ECU Centre for Social Research.

Tony Boydell is Dean of the Science, Technology and Environment Division of Royal Roads University.

Isabel Cordua-von Specht is a senior researcher at Royal Roads University.

Ann Dale is a Professor with the Science, Technology and Environment Division of Royal Roads University, and holds a Canada Research Chair in Sustainable Community Development. She is a Trudeau Fellow and Chair of the Canadian Consortium for Sustainable Development Research.

Stuart B. Hill is Foundation Chair of Social Ecology at the University of Western Sydney, and currently serves on the editorial board of four refereed journals.

Philip Hughes is a Research Fellow in the Centre for Social Research at Edith Cowan University, and the Senior Research Officer of the Christian Research Association.

Sue Kilpatrick is director of the Centre for Research and Learning in Regional Australia at the University of Tasmania. She researches and publishes in learning by adults (especially in rural areas), social capital, and vocational education and training.

Anna Meltzer is an anthropologist employed in the Central Land Council at Alice Springs, Central Australia, where she maintains records of traditional land-owning Aboriginal groups in the Tanami Desert region.

Paul Memmott is an anthropologist and architect, and an Associate Professor and Director of the Aboriginal Environments Research Centre in the School of Geography, Planning and Architecture, University of Queensland.

Lesley Moody is an environmental health officer with Health Canada, First Nations Inuit Health Branch.

Jenny Onyx is a professor and Director of the Centre for Australian Community Organizations and Management (CACOM) at the University of Technology, Sydney. She is founding Editor of Third Sector Review and on the Board of the International Society for Third-Sector Research.

Lynelle Osburn is a Lecturer in Social Work in the School of Humanities and Social Sciences, Charles Sturt University, Wagga Wagga, New South Wales, Australia. She is also a member of the Centre for Rural Social Research.

Grant Sheng is a faculty member at York University, Faculty of Environmental Studies, and the Faculty of Science and Engineering (the Department of Earth and Space Sciences). Dr. Sheng is also an Adjunct Professor at Royal Roads University and co-director of York's Geomatics Research Laboratory.

Richard A. Skinner is President and Vice Chancellor of Royal Roads University and a Fellow of the World Academy of Arts and Science.

Jennie Sparkes is a marine regulatory specialist with the Social Science Research Unit of the Western Canada Service Centre, Parks Canada.

James Tansey is currently a Senior Research Associate at the Maurice Young Centre for Applied Ethics and the Institute for Resources, Environment and Sustainability.

Frank Vanclay is professorial fellow of rural sociology in the Tasmanian Institute of Agricultural Research. He is the 2000-2004 president of the International Rural Sociology Association.

Vivienne Wilson is a professor of ecology and environmental science, and is also Director of the Master of Arts/Master of Science in Environment and Management at Royal Roads University in Victoria, BC. She is on the Board of Directors of the Society for Restoration Ecology (BC), the Air and Waste Management Association (Vancouver Island Chapter), and on subcommittees of the Education for Sustainability Western Network.

Index

Printed in Canada by Friesens
Set in Stone by Artegraphica Design Ltd.
Copy editor: Judy Phillips
Proofreader: Jason Congdon
Indexer: Glenda Browne